Real Life, Real Love

Real Life, Real Love

Life Lessons on Joy, Pain & the Magic That Holds It All Together

RaaShaun "DJ Envy" & Gia Casey

Abrams Image, New York

Editor: Samantha Weiner
Designer: Jack Frischer
Design Manager: Diane Shaw
Managing Editor: Lisa Silverman
Production Manager: Rachael Marks

Library of Congress Control Number: 2021946829

ISBN: 978–1-4197–5278–0
eISBN: 978–1-64700–219–0

Text copyright © 2022 Gia and RaaShaun Casey
Photographs courtesy of the Casey Archives
Jacket © 2022 Abrams

Printed and bound in the United States
10 9 8 7 6 5 4 3 2 1

Abrams Image books are available at special discounts when purchased in quantity for premiums
and promotions as well as fundraising or educational use. Special editions can also be created to
specification. For details, contact specialsales@abramsbooks.com or the address below.

Abrams Image® is a registered trademark of Harry N. Abrams, Inc.

ABRAMS The Art of Books
195 Broadway, New York, NY 10007
abramsbooks.com

We dedicate this book to our parents, Edward and Janet Casey
and Antonio and Norma Grante, who have always supported
and stood by us on this long journey.

Envy's Dedication

Gia, this book is dedicated to you. I hope you know that my life is already and has always been dedicated to you. This book—like many things in my life—is another reflection of our togetherness. It would be corny for me to say that you complete me, but it's the truth. You are the sound in my headphones; the needle to my records and the bass in my speakers. You make this world of mine go round. Without you, my music is offbeat, and my mic doesn't sound nice. Not to mention, my meals are a lot better when you cook them.

Through the ups and downs, you have always been there for me. You are beautiful inside and out. Without you, I would be empty. You are my best friend, my confidante, and my passion. You are always there to comfort me, support me, and hold me when you know I need it. You are my soft place to land and my safe place to be myself. You push me to levels I never knew I could reach, and for that I am forever grateful. It is because of your support that I continue to reach higher grounds, and with you by my side, I know our lives will only get better. You never complain or ask for anything, so in turn, I want to give you the world.

To me, you are the clearest reflection of God. Your patience, grace, and selflessness make me so proud to call you my own. I know that there is no such thing as perfect, but you are the closest thing to perfection I have ever experienced. You are my angel who I know God selected especially for me. I love you for many reasons but mainly for your commitment to me and our family and for being an extraordinary wife and mother. You inspire me every day.

This ride has been breathtakingly beautiful, and with every passing moment, you continue to take my breath away. I pray that God gives us a lifetime together here on earth and for an eternity after that. Thank you for my family, thank you for sticking by me, thank you for teaching me unconditional love and believing in my potential as a husband, father, and provider. Mostly, thank you for being exactly who you are, because to me, love doesn't exist without you and I would have never known the true beauty of life without you in mine.

Gia's Dedication

Mommy, you were a force. You were and will always be my example of strength and independence. You were my living representation of beauty, humility, and kindness—my colorful picture of everything that a woman should be. You poured into me nearly everything that I am and everything that I will ever amount to.

You are my sense of comfort. You are my sense of home. In this life, I always felt as though it never mattered what went wrong or how badly I was tested, because I always had my mommy.

It felt as though you were my personal suit of armor—protecting me from the world.

You were my "backup" plan, my "back-out" plan, my "I'll always have your back" plan, my "I'll never turn my back on you" plan, and now, my "We'll be back together one day" plan.

You were unwavering. Since I was a little girl, you assured me that I could come to you *with* anything and *for* everything, and you would not judge me for any wrong turns that I would take or any bad decisions that I would make. You were my fixer. And you let me know that if I ever got myself into anything, you would be right there to get me out. You had the ability to take a bad situation and use it as an opportunity to teach me a valuable lesson and uplift me. You were my source of empowerment. You provided me with the playbook of how raise a daughter, and, with gratitude, I am able to refer to it daily as I raise my own daughters. To me, you seemed to know everything—as though you had all the answers. I came to you for guidance, advice, and support—consistently, as did many others. And you never, ever disappointed. You were my closest friend, the one with whom I shared everything.

You told me that, despite all the complications and disappointments of the world, I could always stand on my own. You taught me steadfastness. You taught me resilience. You taught me that my thoughts and my words matter. You taught me that I was important.

You were my sidekick. I always wanted to have you near me. And if I'm being honest, while growing up, I always felt badly for my peers because they didn't have you as a mother. In my eyes, they were missing out. You and Daddy were my greatest gifts. I enjoyed my childhood. I enjoyed my life. And I spent it with you by my side, cheering me on, grooming me to understand that I can accomplish anything and teaching me to cultivate a life from all the choices that were at my feet.

I remember sliding into the bed at night while you were watching *The Young and the Restless* on our VCR. I would lie next to you and you would cuddle me with your left arm. I remember the comfort that I felt with the touch of your hand. There was something special about that touch. It made me feel warm and safe. Without words, it made me feel loved and close to you. I remember thinking this was your special power, and I wondered if I would have the ability to make my children feel the same way, if I was blessed enough to become a mother one day.

Even as a grown woman, married and with those children of my own, I would slide into bed next to you, wanting to feel that same comfort. It amazes me that, even as your memory and mind were failing, your heart never forgot how to share that touch with me.

You always referred to me as spunky and fun, as were you. As two kindred spirits, we laughed and explored together. We traveled to different parts of the world to experience varying perspectives on life. We enjoyed absorbing the cultures and diving into what each destination had to offer. It didn't always go as expected, but at least we did it hand in hand.

Once, when we were in Hawaii, I encouraged you to go zip-lining through the treetops at the heights of Haleakala. You were, at first, resistant; on the way, terrified; and once you got there and looked down, noncooperative. But eventually, you agreed to give it a try. After the first course and at a speed of about thirty-five miles per hour, you cried and told me off for making you do it.

Then, when we were in Saint Martin, I encouraged you to participate in a mock America's Cup sailboat race—and you did. The sea was rough and the boat swayed vigorously, frightening everyone aboard. You were drenched and swore that it was going to capsize. You cried and, yet again, told me off for making you do it.

On another occasion, we visited Antigua, and like me, you couldn't swim, but I encouraged you to Jet Ski anyway. You fell into the water as you climbed onto the Jet Ski from the boat. You thought you were drowning, believed you were going to lose your life in the Caribbean Sea that day, cried, and, yet again, told me off for making you do it. This time, you actually went and sat on a big rock on the beach by yourself and didn't speak to me for about an hour while you collected yourself.

While I look back at all these occasions with a laugh, more importantly, they share one thing in common besides the tears and cussing: Each time, you signed up for the next adventure and thanked me for pushing you out of your comfort zone so that you can truly experience an even fuller life—because, as you put it, life is for living! It is because of you and Daddy that I teach my children to never lose sight of the joys in life created by collecting experiences. You were curious and willing, even when you were uncertain. I marveled at your ability to look back, laugh, and retell those stories as fun and exciting memories of time spent with your daughter.

I thank God that I had the opportunity to share those times with you.

You were humble and forgiving. You taught me that people are not perfect and at times, they will falter. That we must have an open heart. You would say to me, "If you have an opportunity to help someone, you should." And you led by example. You routinely gave anything you had, including your home, to anyone who was down on their luck and in need. Often enough, I would walk out of my room, see a stranger in the kitchen, and say to myself, "Oh, so who's living with us now?" It was as though your measure of yourself was determined by the degree to which you could help someone else. Through those examples, I learned compassion, generosity, and selflessness. They say that our parents are our first teachers. Well, Mommy, you taught me well.

The work of a mother is immeasurable because the trickle-down effects of her influence, and the generations that those drops transcend, are boundless.

I will speak about you daily. I will never let your grandchildren forget your greatness, and that it is because of that greatness they will be raised with greatness.

I honor you for the child of God that you were, the human that you were, but most important to me, the mother that you were. My angel now has wings.

I love you, Mommy.

—IN MEMORY OF NORMA SOWDEN GRANTE
SEPTEMBER 7, 1941–MAY 4, 2021

Contents

This Thing Called Life . . . a Note from Gia and Envy

When we were first approached with the idea of writing a book, we were excited. We knew that it would be an opportunity to expand the conversations we have on our podcast, *The Casey Crew*, and to talk more deeply about our relationship and family life. We were thrilled about the idea of a book tour, knowing that it would give us the chance to get out there in the paint and hear about how the book has resonated with you and your partner or spouse. We couldn't wait to share our journeys in marriage and family and hear about yours as well. But, more than anything, we were overjoyed to celebrate our twentieth wedding anniversary in 2021, as it recognized the inception of our relationship, its hardships, and most importantly, its triumphs. Then COVID happened. Everything shut down, and the world was at a standstill. While this gave us more time to ensure the book was exactly what we wanted it to be, the reality that everything had to be pushed back a year stung quite a bit.

So many of us have been in survival mode since March 2020 that we really haven't taken a moment to grieve our own losses, no matter how insignificant they may seem in the grand scheme of things. Maybe 2020 and 2021 were the years you were finally going to launch that business or take your dream trip. Maybe you were looking to shift careers, but the pandemic caused so much upheaval in the market that the transition was too dangerous and didn't make sense anymore. It's okay to be honest about the fact some things didn't work out, even if you've moved ahead with a new plan. So we abandoned our hopes to celebrate our twentieth with the release of a book that would document our love, and adjusted to sharing it with you the way we wanted, just a year later.

Like everyone else, we adapted to the new normal of working from home and virtual school. We weren't the only ones who watched our oldest graduate from high school and spend her first year of college quarantined in a pandemic. And just like you, we felt as though if we had to do another Zoom work call, we would spontaneously combust! In an instant, life became so different for all of us. None of us were able to leave home for work or school to create the time away from each other that we'd all grown accustomed to—time that, for many of us, is necessary to decompress, maintain peace of mind, and sustain sanity. Unfortunately, instances of domestic violence, child abuse, substance abuse, and mental health challenges were on the rise during the pandemic, giving concrete proof that everyone hasn't processed the lockdown and social distancing in a way that was beneficial to themselves or society. At the time this book is going to press, more than 700,000 Americans have died of COVID-19 and the Delta variant is spreading rapidly throughout the world and across the country, threatening another lockdown. These are scary times, indeed. In these moments, we have to hold on to faith and family.

So many have said that time in the house has brought you closer together, instituting family game nights and opportunities to rediscover your connections and love on each other. Some of you, like us, even found yourselves increasing the population with "quarantine babies." When we found out we were pregnant, we were absolutely ecstatic! We had wanted another baby for a very long time and encountered many struggles along the way. The road to baby number six has been a tough one, and this pregnancy is a true answered prayer. Some must think we're crazy. Our oldest is nineteen, and we're about to start over again. But this is exactly what we've always wanted—to raise a large, beautiful family surrounded by all of the love we have to give. In the midst of a terrible time, God has blessed us, and we are incredibly grateful.

We're not the only ones who experienced happiness in the middle of a pandemic. If you look back, we're sure you can recall moments of deep joy and gratitude. That's really how the world works. Even when we lose, we don't lose everything. There's still something left in our lives that gives us hope for better days and provides us with the strength to hold on until those better days come. For many, a global pandemic pushed them to truly evaluate what they want in their lives and pursue it with everything they have. And when they look back on this time in their personal and collective histories, they'll remember that. They'll look at their accomplishments with pride and their families with delight. All was not lost.

Even as we celebrated the new addition to our family, our worlds were rocked when Gia's mother, Norma Grante, passed away unexpectedly after a long battle with dementia. This happened shortly before our anniversary and Mother's Day. Two decades before, we selected Mother's Day as our wedding day to pay tribute to and honor our beautiful mothers. For this reason, twenty years later, it was very important for us to lay her to rest on Mother's Day, to do the same. Life is a full circle, and God's blessings can be mysterious and abundant. On our wedding day, Gia was three months pregnant with our first baby and honoring her mother in her life. Now, here we are, exactly twenty years later, three months pregnant with our last and honoring Gia's mother in her death. We feel as though this baby is a very special gift from both her and God. Losing a parent is unimaginable. There are no words to fully express the pain and sorrow that we feel. Mommy was everything to us, and we miss her more than words can ever express.

So many of us have lost people during this pandemic. Whether we lost them to COVID-19 or other illnesses, racial unrest, or gun violence, there has been a collective grief felt around the world. To ignore that is to be dishonest. We've all felt it, and it hurt. Still, we've had to find a way to keep on living, because life is filled with beautiful moments, excruciating ones, and all the moments in between. And we don't get to choose which ones we experience or at what moments in time. We have to consume them all. The only thing we can hope to control is how we navigate our way through them and eventually get to the place where we are meant to be.

Life looks a lot different for us than when we first set out to write this book. We have always been committed to telling the truth about everything in our lives, and this occasion is no different. We are excited about the new life we're bringing into the world, and we're brokenhearted that our beautiful baby will never meet her grandmother. This is us. The joys, the pains, the magic. As you read this book, we hope you'll remember that we're just like you. Every day, we are trying to dig our heels deeper into our purpose and loving each other and our family along the way.

Introduction: We Wanted This

We have been together more than half of our lives. When we met, we were two teenagers who had absolutely no idea what love really was, but we knew that there was magic between the two of us. The spark was undeniable and the connection was real. It's been what's kept us together for twenty-seven years.

GIA: RaaShaun was a sixteen-year-old aspiring DJ who would wait outside our high school in his bright blue Con Edison van (which he bought because it was cheap and the electric company replaced its company vehicle every five years), watching me run track. We'd actually met a week before at his birthday dinner and spent a significant amount of time together during the celebration at Dallas BBQ in NYC. The group and I had a falling-out, though, because, without my being aware, RaaShaun had a crush on me and I'd spent time that night allowing other boys to chat me up and give me their numbers. The group thought that I was insensitive to RaaShaun's feelings and got on a different subway car than me. After about five minutes, RaaShaun found me on the train and expressed how he felt about me and apologized for his sensitivity and for taking it too far. Shortly after that, school started, and he began showing up at my track practices. He'd approach me every day after practice, until one day he boldly gave me his number. Before this, even though he liked me, we hung in group settings and hadn't yet exchanged home phone numbers. After he gave me his, RaaShaun would go home and wait for my call daily, but that call never came. Unbeknownst to RaaShaun, I was seeing Jonathan, a diver on a rival school's swim team, who happened to have my attention at the time.

RaaShaun grew tired of sitting around waiting for my call and finally asked me for my number instead. He was persistent. He called and called until finally—I picked up. After one conversation, I knew there was something there, but I was the new girl in school and wanted to keep my options open. If another guy came along whom I could have been more interested in, I didn't want to limit myself. I continued my relationship with Jonathan, until one day, it all came to a head. RaaShaun found out that I was "talking" (that's what we called it at the time) to Jonathan and was furious! RaaShaun called me and had Jonathan on the line, demanding that I pick between them, right then and there. I fell in love with his assertiveness and the fact that he knew what he wanted and went after it full throttle. No pride, no worry of embarrassment or rejection, just his eye on the prize—me. After this display of manliness, the decision was clear. We've been together ever since.

Two weeks into our relationship, RaaShaun wrote me a letter in which he detailed his plans for our future. I still have it. In it, he shared that he saw us married and with children. People don't believe me when I say this, but without a doubt, RaaShaun *knew* we were going to be together forever. Before I was sure about us, he was certain. We were going to have an amazing life.

Those early years were filled with many ups and downs. I was only fifteen years old when I met the love of my life, but as we watched everyone around us falling in and out of love every other week, we knew that we had something special. Still, we will never romanticize those growing pains. Because we were so young when we met, whatever friendship circles we had grew to involve each other all the time. Our families became intertwined, as did our entire lives. We were so in love that when we went off to college, we chose universities that were only fifteen minutes away from each other. We spent every single day of our college years together—before class, after class, and sometimes, instead of class. We couldn't stay away from each other. Along with that came the inevitable. Arguments and disagreements became routine. If one took place while driving, RaaShaun had a habit of making me pull over, then getting out and walking in the middle of the highway if he saw fit. He would continue this until I would get out of the car and plead with him to get back inside so we could go home. Those were some wild times.

Whether we fully knew it at the time or not, we were building a life together. But it was a life where we were *too* dependent upon one another, and we lacked the maturity and perspective needed to support that level of closeness.

There weren't a lot of compromises on his part. He was very obsessive, possessive, and controlling. He sought to keep me away from not only other men, but friends as well. At times, I felt like Rapunzel trapped in the tower. Looking back, I believe that our dynamic was set up this way because we were each other's first love and he was the only man I'd ever been with both seriously and intimately. He truly believed that if I was exposed to other relationships and opportunities, curiosity would get the best of me and I would then realize that what I had with him wasn't the best that I could do. Nothing could have been further from the way that I actually felt. I adored RaaShaun, but there was no convincing him of that or easing his burden. His insecurity was a constant cloud raining on our relationship; that didn't change when we graduated from college, and it plagued us throughout the early stages of our marriage.

When we first graduated from college, RaaShaun's parents were on him about getting a real job. While he was frustrated and saw it as them not believing in his dreams, I completely understood their point of view. When parents send you to college, they expect you to mature and enter the "real world" upon graduation. He had a degree in business management and marketing; they expected him to use it. Deejaying, to them, was a successful hobby that got him through school, but it wouldn't be sustainable for a grown man who wanted a family. But even as I completely saw where his parents were coming from, I fully supported RaaShaun, because I loved him and believed that he could move mountains.

If I'm being honest, I couldn't foresee RaaShaun's career developing into what it has become, simply because I watched him grow daily and only defined his success by the measure of his happiness. I am a firm believer that if you do what you love, you will be successful. But there is no true definition of success. It can only be determined by the individual who is chasing it. Even with all of our ups and downs, I was too busy enjoying our love story as the page turned every day. Where his career would end up was never a thought in my mind. I always believed that we would be successful by our own standards. My main concern was to be his rock, supporting him and his dreams in a world full of naysayers, and to make sure that he felt safe and comfortable pursuing them.

There was no way that, during our first years of marriage, I would have been able to conceive that DJ Envy would be known worldwide—that his career would transcend decades and would go on to create all of the opportunities that it did for himself and others.

Right as RaaShaun's career began to take flight, we got married—and I was pregnant with our first child. He insisted that I stop working, stating that it would be best for the pregnancy and for raising our baby as well as other babies to come. I had always envisioned being a working mother with a thriving career as an attorney. In college, I majored in communications with my sights on law school. But RaaShaun's insecurity fueled his desire for me to stay home instead. He didn't want me experiencing the world and those who occupied it. If I worked, it would result in a broadening of my experiences and views. He was threatened by that. He said he couldn't concentrate on his career if he was consumed with worry about what I was doing and who I was meeting while working.

And this applied to my personal life as well. While out shopping and spending time with friends, he would spontaneously pop in on me in order to make sure that I was doing what I said I was doing with who I said I was doing it with. There were times when I had no idea how he knew where I was. He was like a spy. He would then use jokes to cover the serious nature of his action by saying things like, "Just know, I'm always watching . . ." And he always was.

He claimed that he was always on pins and needles waiting for me to leave him. He did not believe that he deserved me and felt as though if he kept me sheltered with blinders on, I would never have the opportunity to see what I was missing. This was, in part, how he demonstrated his control.

But I always saw another picture, and RaaShaun has been so open and transparent about growing out of his jealousy and the controlling ways that were present in the early years of our relationship. What people don't know is that I never succumbed to his demands. RaaShaun could never tell me what to do; I was my own woman. I made the decision to stop working because I saw validity in his desire for me to do so. He didn't make me. He couldn't make me. I wasn't the first woman to prioritize her family over her career, and I certainly won't be the last. For many, it's difficult to make the transition, and for some, it's impossible. For me, I was committed to our family, and it was a sacrifice I was willing to make for my husband's well-being and for the children that I intended to raise.

At the same time, I also understood that more lenience from me was going to be required to make our life together work as he pursued his career. I have always loved my husband, and I have always loved the life that we were creating together. However, I didn't always like how I felt undervalued and unappreciated at times. I didn't like feeling as though my identity as Gia was becoming totally consumed by my role as wife and mother. I knew too many women who felt suffocated and grew to resent their families because of it. I never wanted to let that happen and knew that I had to be the one to make a change. I couldn't just accept that RaaShaun's life, along with his career, was more significant than my own. After all, that was part of the problem I had in the first place—the possibility of losing my identity in the shadow of his. If I wanted parts of my life back, I would have to take them myself. And, for the most part, it was a shift in my mindset. I had to ensure that I always prioritized my needs and interests as much as I valued RaaShaun's.

ENVY: Now, to be fair—I was young. I was still a kid when I met Gia, and she had older, much more esteemed men trying to holler at her. As I was establishing my career in an industry as uncertain as music, it was easy for me to believe that my wife would overlook me and my potential and look to someone who could provide more stability and structure. I was insecure and controlling because I was constantly terrified of losing Gia.

Just as I was Gia's first love, she was also mine. It's hard coming of age with your best friend and the love of your life. When I considered what I thought was needed for us to thrive as a unit, I now realize that I didn't always take her feelings into account.

I tell people all the time that if it weren't for Gia and her mother, I probably wouldn't be in music today. I love my parents and I know they love me, but their push for me to get a "real job" felt as if they didn't fully understand who I was and what it was that I really wanted to do with my life. Gia did. People don't realize that, in the early years, it was Gia holding us down. She had the success-ful career and high-paying job. It was me hopping out of her Cadillac Escalade to ask the corner store owner if I could sell my mixtapes there. She was the one driving me into the city to meet with record executives. She believed in me when no one else did, and without her support, I don't know where I would be.

As men, we're taught that our primary responsibility is to provide and protect. I knew that every decision I made was an effort to create more stability. No matter how far I had to go or how long I had to be away, I was doing what men are supposed to do by taking care of home. Having that kind of work ethic and commitment is important. However, I made the mistake of believing that my dreams and desires were synonymous with those of my wife. I didn't know it at the time, but I was inadvertently distancing Gia and compromising my marriage as a whole. Many of us know women who seemed like they were okay with something because they never said anything about it. They did what they were expected to do, and if they weren't happy about it, nobody knew because they were taught to play their position, be grateful, and protect the image of their marriage. That wasn't the woman I married. Far from it, in fact. Gia had no problem telling me what she liked and what she didn't like about anything. She made it very clear when something was bothering her. And she didn't hold back when she wanted me to realize that her life mattered just as much as mine.

As a husband, it devastates me to hear that she felt stifled and imposed upon. She gave up her career and personal goals for me, while all along, spending so much time supporting me in mine. I was so wrapped up in my world and so immature that I didn't recognize the sacrifice. I think back on all the ways Gia held me down. I couldn't have done any of this without her. To know that while I was away or working hard to pursue my dreams, she felt unappre-ciated? Hurts. Because in fact, I did appreciate her. Unfortunately, I wasn't always able to convey that effectively. Sometimes, as men, we can become so single-minded that we take our partners for granted and don't sit back and think about the compromises that we need to make to ensure that our relationships are stable. Our wives and partners shouldn't have to come to us, at their wits' end, upset because we're not taking time to invest in them the same ways they've invested in us.

* * *

Why are we telling you all of this? Because it matters, to be honest. As beautiful and amazing as our life together is, it has not always been this way. We made a lot of mistakes. Jealousy, insecurity, and manipulation were part of our relationship. There were a lot of times when we should have gone to see a counselor, pastor, or therapist to work through our issues, but we didn't. And, in the beginning, God wasn't ever a central part of what we were building. Even though we can look back on the years we've been together with deep gratitude that we've made it, we can also be honest that there were many hurdles that we had to jump over.

That's why our podcast matters so much to us. Couples from all over the world listen in to hear us discuss love, relationships, and family from our perspective. And they ask questions because they're interested in what we have to say. We're always clear that we're not professionals, and our approach won't

"There are no shortcuts." —ENVY

work for everyone. But even then, we're willing to share what we know, what we think, what worked for us and what didn't in hopes that other couples can relate, benefit, and succeed.

And that is what has led us to this book. It is an opportunity to take the conversations we've had on the podcast, in our DMs, and at busy New York intersections and expand them with tangible resources and exercises. We believe in love. We believe in marriage. We believe in family. And we believe all of those things can be healthy and thrive *if* we're willing to do the work. There are no shortcuts. You'll hear us say this all the time. It takes a commitment to being the best you can be for yourself, your spouse or your partner, and your children.

There is something absolutely undeniable about our family. We've never seen or experienced anything like this. There's a certain energy that exists around us. We call it our magic. There's so much love, joy, and gratitude surrounding us at all times. Every time either one of us walks into the house, our youngest three come barreling toward us with hugs and kisses, as though we've just come home from war. Throughout the day, they continually tell us we're the best mommy and daddy in the world and they love being a part of our family. The joy is always evident on their little faces. Our two oldest tell us they love us every day, several times a day, and show it in part by spending several hours a day sitting at the end of our bed "telling us everything," as they would put it. We enjoy each other as a family. We laugh. We joke. We are affectionate; some may consider us overly affectionate and ask themselves, "How many kisses does one person need in a day?" But that is the Casey way and how we've raised all our children—in abundant and tangible love. What they see between us and how we engage with each other and those around us have become the model for what they want to emulate. As parents, you plant the seeds and watch them grow.

This magic—the essence of our family—isn't unique to us. You have it too. It's in how you interact with each other. It's in the way you look at and love each other. Every family has magic. It's up to us to recognize it and nurture its growth. That's really what this book is about: realizing the magic that holds your relationship and family together. So many changes happen in the world and within our relationships. There are so many distractions. So much can pull us apart and cause us to forget why we love each other. Some relationships end. For those who experience that, we offer support and empathy as they journey through. But there are some relationships that make it through the storm and come back from the brink of losing it all stronger than before. We've been blessed to be one of those couples, and while we're not big on giving advice, we hope that our story will encourage you to know what's possible. We have been through much misfortune but came out more fortunate than we could have ever imagined. We've beat all the odds and have a remarkable story to tell.

For many, *Real Life, Real Love* will offer new language and concepts for nurturing the magic of your relationship and family. As you read this book, journey with us through our story and possibly implement the strategies and suggestions we offer along the way. We hope you'll give yourself the grace to be okay with where you are now. Sometimes, we can get upset that we didn't learn certain lessons or make appropriate changes sooner, but we can't dwell on that. All we can do is move forward, trying to be better. Reading this book and being open to what you'll find here is a great first step.

We believe that the magic of a relationship and a family begin with what we call "the roots and the fruit." You know the image of a family tree? When creating one, you start with the first generation you can remember as the base, or roots, of that tree, and each section of the family branches off of that (literally) as the fruit. We see relationships the same way . . . When we plant the seeds of a tree and nurture them, we have the ability to watch them develop roots, grow, and produce fruit. Remember, the roots ground the tree. They give the tree strength and support, and they enable the tree to weather the worst of storms. The roots comprise everything that we have invested in them, and the fruit is a direct representation of the nurturing that the roots have (or have not) received. If your relationship is rooted in dishonesty, distrust, disconnection, and disrespect, then contention, insecurity, loneliness, and strife will be the poisonous fruit that will tear you apart and leave you hungry. But if your relationship is rooted in commitment, honesty, abiding love, and sincere grace, then healthy communication, happiness, understanding, and true joy will be the plentiful fruit that will hold you together and feed you for a lifetime. Another thing about this life truth: Whether we are consuming poisonous fruit or plentiful fruit, we are feeding our children from the same tree, so either beware or rejoice.

We can be honest and say that for years our roots weren't as strong as they needed to be. We weren't grounding our relationship in everything it needed to thrive. And when the storm came and our tree was battle tested, we were presented with a choice: either we tend to the roots so the tree can grow stronger, or we allow the entire thing to wither and die. When we looked back at all those years together and what we'd created, we believed the tree was worth saving. We're blessed to say that it is now stronger than ever.

Maybe you're reading this as a single person hopeful to find yourself in a loving relationship, or a dater trying to learn more about yourself and how to successfully join your own personal needs with the needs of a potential partner. Maybe you've found yourself in the throes of a serious relationship and are trying to ascertain whether it has what it takes to stand the test of time. Or maybe you've already gone through that phase, decided that it did, and are about to embark on the beautiful journey of marriage. Maybe you're a few years in, with your first child already here or on the way, and you want to ensure that everything remains solid. On the other hand, maybe the storm has come and you're trying to figure out whether the roots can be saved. Or maybe you are trying to figure out if you, yourself, are relationship material or not. No matter where you are on your relationship journey, this book is for you. Consider this an opportunity for a much-needed *checkup* (to assess the health of your relationship, whether your relationship is with yourself or a partner) and *check-in* (to talk with your spouse or partner about the roots you've been establishing and the issues that need to be addressed).

In addition to our own story of dating, marriage, and parenting, we've also included some questions you can ask yourself and your loved one to get to the heart of the matter. You'll find exercises you can do together and our answers to some of our most-asked podcast questions. Like us, you will laugh, you will cry, you will cuss and get frustrated. But if you stay committed to the care of the roots of your relationship, we can assure you that you will enjoy ripe, delicious fruit. With God, conviction in yourself, and faith in your partner, you can have the healthy, lasting relationship you want. It's possible and it's available to you. Let's get to work so you can enjoy it!

PART ONE:

Personal Life and Identity

W e've been together for a long time, and there isn't much, if anything, we don't know about each other. But as much as we love being around each other, it's also been important for us to grow and develop as individuals. These essays are all about those first years, when we were learning and growing together—and they're also about the mistakes we made as we fumbled our way through some of that growth. No relationship can survive without two people who are always working on themselves to be better. We didn't always get it right, but we were always committed to trying.

1. Finding Life's Common Denominator

We can romanticize relationships all we want, but at the end of the day, it's two people bringing together all of their experiences in the hopes of building something magical. Learning each other is *also* a continuous journey of self-discovery. It's why so many people say they didn't truly know their spouse or partner until they married or moved in together. Being friends as long as we were had its advantages in that department. We'd been together since high school and through college. By the time we got married, we had already been together for seven years and knew it all—from each other's hygiene regimens to just how much time we needed to ourselves in the morning before we were fully functioning and ready to deal with each other. When we started dating, we fell in love so quickly—and it was intense. But because we were young, we were really able to form our friendship first. We became each other's best friend. Whether it was just the two of us or we were hanging with our group, we did everything together. We're not suggesting that every relationship that begins in friendship can turn into a love story. Some people can just be great friends and that's it! From the beginning, though, we knew. We were in love.

Still, we were two people coming in with our own definitions of love. In the early years, the relationship may have been too much about whose definition would prevail at any given moment. In time, we learned that being in a successful relationship was actually about rewriting this definition together.

All the questions we are asked, whether on the podcast or on a street in Manhattan, boil down to couples wanting to know how to make their relationships work. Ask this of anyone and you'll get the same answer: "Communicate! Communicate! Communicate!" And that's true. The basis of any healthy relationship is communication, and there's a right way and a wrong way to do it. You'll never hear us disparage proper communication. In fact, there's an essay in the next chapter, on "right fighting," that digs even deeper into what we believe is effective communication. But more than being an effective communicator in a relationship, we believe you have to know who you are in the relationship.

Knowing who you are goes beyond the gender roles we think define us. It's so much more than being the breadwinner or the primary caretaker of the children. To know who you are in a unit, you have to understand who you are as an individual. For some, the first inclination is to think of your profession or occupation. Who you are may manifest itself in your job, but we are so much more than what we do for a living. Truly knowing who you are means discovering your life's "common denominator." When you think back on the span of your life, it's that theme that is the most present and consistent. It's what informs the perspective you can offer in any given situation, and it's also what informs the lessons drawn from your experiences. It's usually also what tends to get you in trouble when it's left unchecked. Your life's common denominator is the growth you've achieved over the years and how far you still have to go to be your best self. It's the lens through which you see the world.

Often, when we're explaining our position or perspective on an issue or when we're acting in a way that totally confuses our partner, it's because we're understanding the situation through the context of our life's common denominator and they didn't know it. Truth be told, we probably didn't know it either, because we rarely take the time to sit and process our life experiences. We sat down together and looked at who we are in this relationship; we took some time on our own to explore our life's common denominators. When we did this, it made so much sense looking back on our lives together and apart. We'd like to share what we learned with you.

Gia: Strength

Everyone who knows me knows that I am steady. People know they can count on me, and that matters. In hard times, you need an anchor, and I am equipped to be that for the people I love. I have conditioned myself to carry the burdens that may be too heavy for those close to me. I want to be their soft place to land and their safe place to retreat. I want them to know that no matter what they've gotten themselves into, I will be there to help get them out—unconditionally and without judgment. Everyone needs that person in their lives—someone who will never turn their back on you, no matter what. My parents were those people for me. They taught me how to love and be solid. They taught me to be unwavering and strong. Born out of that strength is a resilience. No matter what, I'm going to be okay. A failed plan doesn't shake me. If it doesn't work, I've either already thought through the next plan or am constructing one as we speak. Either way, I'm going to be okay, and thus *we'll* be okay.

My mother was my idol. Growing up, I watched her be a pillar for our family and her friends. She modeled for me what it meant to be dependable and reliable, and I knew that, within my own family, I would be the same. My oldest son, Logan, started calling me "The Fixer" because that's who I am to my kids. That's who my mother was to me. In our own ways, so many of us are continuing the legacies we saw lived before us when we were children.

Strength is inherently positive, but at times, it can cause issues. Because I'm always putting everyone else first, my feelings are oftentimes overlooked. When I present myself as the rock of my family, I'm inadvertently encouraging the notion that they don't have to worry or be concerned with my well-being. It reminds me of the saying "The squeaky wheel gets the grease." You're only going to give attention to what looks like it needs attention. It's the difference between people who only take their car in when there's a problem and those who schedule routine maintenance. When we're perceived as strong and having it all together, there is an inclination for those we love not to check in on us. In my life, I have learned that the myth of a strong woman can understandably be reinforced through our selfless actions. And I say "myth" because we all know that society likes to portray "strong women" as unaffected by painful and hurtful experiences, and that's simply not true.

My whole life I've been someone who is always thinking about the future and what lies ahead. For me, the end goal is paramount, and being thorough and thoughtful about how we get there matters. Sometimes, when being so focused on the end goal, we can forget that the journey is what's most important. It is on the journey when you are loved and cared for. Through self-evaluation, I've learned that it's important to say what I need. And, more than anything, I firmly believe that you teach people how to treat you in all facets of life.

Strength doesn't make me a doormat. Over time, I've had to learn what it means to be there for people while also vocalizing what I need. With

"What so many of us find is that, when we create the boundaries around what we need to be well, the people who love us willingly support that." —GIA

RaaShaun, I'm able to express what I need and also readily accept when he meets those needs. With the kids, if Mommy needs a moment, then Mommy's going to take one. And you know what? The world doesn't end when I do. What so many of us find is that, when we create the boundaries around what we need to be well, the people who love us willingly support that. It enables me to show up as a better me and be that constant source of love without feeling as if I'm not being heard, considered, or appreciated. Taking the first steps to honor that part of us only ensures the people we love will honor it too.

Envy: Heart

I've always been the more romantic one in the relationship. I believe in being touchy-feely. There's nothing wrong with a little PDA! Whatever Gia's into, I let her know it's important to me. For instance, there's a particular handbag that she loves. In addition to buying it for her, whenever I see someone carrying it, I sneak and take a pic and send it to her. And when it's late at night and I'm dog-tired from the day but she wants to watch one of those reality shows simply because we haven't had enough time alone together, I'm all in. What matters to her will always matter to me.

Heart and ambition, for me, go hand in hand. I came along at a time when being a professional DJ was laughable. People thought it was a great hobby, but you didn't dare think about making it a living. Everyone believed I should focus on something more serious, especially when I went off to Hampton University. When my friends and classmates were getting dressed in suits for internships and Career Day, I was in jeans and T-shirts headed to another party. It took heart to make my dream happen when the rest of the world wanted me to wake up.

Being invested in your passion isn't necessarily a bad thing, but it is possible to become too passionate and let your emotions override common sense. This has gotten many of us into trouble. And being so focused on my success has often made me less present. Unintentionally, you can create tunnel vision and become so laser-focused on that particular goal that you're not giving attention to the other things in life that matter. I'm often told (and I tell myself) to put the phone down. Learning how to become more responsible with my emotions and ambition has become one of the most amazing and eye-opening journeys of my life.

* * *

We can't change each other. We actually don't want to, and neither should you and your partner. A rule of thumb is asking yourself: If your partner never changes, can you build a life with them? You should never go into a relationship expecting a person to change. That's a risk and gamble none of us should be willing to take. People only change on their own accord, for their own reasons, and in their own timing. We should want to be the best for ourselves first and for each other second. Strength and heart, when reinforced with healthy boundaries and respect, are beautiful in a relationship. Our common denominators help us understand how we are showing up in the world and for ourselves. Those attributes also create the benefit of the doubt that we can and need to give each other. There are times when we have to take a step back and remember that, even though we're in this together, we still see life much differently at times. It also evens the playing field between us. No one is more important than the other, and no one is dispensable. Our relationship needs both of us equally.

If you're reading this book alone or with your partner, we encourage you to discover your life's common denominators. You can do it by asking yourself a few questions.

> *What personal qualities have carried you through the tough times? What negative characteristics, inabilities, or personal traumas have created the tough times?*
>
> *What do people admire most about you?*
>
> *What, in your opinion, consistently differentiates you from others?*
>
> *What personal characteristics have had you "circling the drain" and repeating unproductive cycles, rendering you unable to learn the lessons necessary to progress?*
>
> *What keeps showing up for you over and over again as an issue holding you back in life and needing to be addressed?*

Remember your life's common denominator has positive and negative attributes. But it's negative only in the sense that, when you don't keep it in check with everything else you know to be true about yourself, it can create obstacles. But even those challenges work to show how full and complete our lives truly are.

There is no cheat code to making relationships work. You have to work at them every day. But, just as much as you're working on the relationship, you have to work on yourself. We've seen and heard about so many couples who become so consumed by the relationship that they don't remember who they are. You don't have to lose yourself in a relationship. Any relationship that requires you to do that isn't the one for you. We've grown a lot, but we're still those two kids who were friends and lovers first. The core of who we are, as individuals, hasn't changed even as we've evolved. Relationships that allow you to truly be yourself are what we all need. Figuring out who we are, though—that will always be the first step.

In addition to knowing your life's common denominator, it's important that you identify and hold fast to the beliefs, activities, and hobbies that make you who you are. Those shouldn't all go away once you decide to be with someone else. A healthy relationship should enhance you, not diminish you. Now, if your favorite pastimes are inherently disrespectful to your partner and will only work to destroy the relationship, a serious conversation and meeting of the minds is warranted. But we all have things that make us come alive that we should be free to engage in without our partner hovering over our shoulder. In the beginning, we did everything together because we were friends. Even though we had our own friends, our circle was ultimately the same. To this day, we're still constantly around each other in ways that would annoy most couples. But you know what? It works for us. We built our love and family on friendship, and even after all these years together, we never tire of being around each other—rather, we prioritize it.

Every relationship is different and comes with its own set of needs. If you're someone who values monthly standing self-care dates with the girls or a man

> "Too many people think their relationships will fall apart if they tell the truth, when the reality is that the relationship is hanging on by a thread because truth-telling is not a habitual practice." —ENVY

cave where the movies are loud and there are no disruptions, say that. Too many people think their relationships will fall apart if they tell the truth, when the reality is that the relationship is hanging on by a thread because truth-telling is not a habitual practice. It's as simple as a conversation in the beginning stages of dating or whenever you finish this chapter. Giving our partners room to speak their individual desires and giving them space to go after those desires is what we're supposed to do. All of us had goals for our lives before we fell in love and decided to give a relationship a try. Finding love and creating a family may have been one of those goals. But it wasn't the only one. And, truthfully, some of our goals do shift once we join our life with someone else's. But not all of them. We should be able to pursue our dreams because we deserve a life where we get to see our dreams come true. We also deserve someone to champion us along the way. And the added benefit to that is the reality that the relationship is greatly strengthened when everyone

"Relationships become a place where we're able to learn more about ourselves through the process of journeying with someone else." —**ENVY**

is thriving. As partners, nothing should make us happier and more inspired than watching our loved ones' visions come to fruition.

* * *

Relationships become a place where we're able to learn more about ourselves through the process of journeying with someone else. They were never meant to become the totality of our lives and existence. We cheat ourselves out of so

"Healthy relationships have healthy people in them." —**ENVY**

much when we forget that. Think of just how rich your relationship could be if you took more time to tend to the parts of you that need the work. We haven't weathered all the storms because we stayed up under each other for almost thirty years. We learned very quickly that forever is a long time, and if we were going to last, we each needed to maintain pieces of ourselves that were not up for negotiation—pieces that belong solely to us. Healthy relationships have healthy people in them. Above being in love and with someone else, we all have to be committed to being in love with ourselves first. That can be a journey in and of itself.

---

2.   100 Stitches (Gia)

I was fifteen years old and a junior at St. Francis Preparatory School in Flushing, Queens. I was the youngest in my year because I had skipped a grade in elementary school. It was the day before Thanksgiving, and we were lucky to have an early dismissal from school to start off our holiday. RaaShaun and I had only been together for two and a half months at the time. On any other day, we would have been together, as we were inseparable. It was our routine to spend time together after school every day before he brought me home. But on this particular day, he had agreed to cover a work shift for a friend. Always thinking of me, he had made arrangements for another friend to bring me home in his place. However, that friend was an athlete and had a scheduled practice after dismissal. I did not want to wait until his practice was over to begin my early vacation, so I decided to take public transportation instead. Had I only decided to wait, my life would have had a drastically different outcome.

All we wanted was McDonald's. So when my best friend, Dahlia Haynes, and I left school to get our usual Number 1, there was no reason to believe anything out of the ordinary would happen. But as soon as I walked in, something felt off, very off. No sooner than I was able to take my money out of my bookbag did I hear "piss-colored bitch," "Casper," and a slew of other racial epithets hurled at me. I was no stranger to hearing insults based on my complexion directed toward me in the past, but I didn't know this girl, had never seen her before, and hadn't done anything to offend her. I hadn't even noticed the presence of her and the group of kids that she was sitting with until I heard their voices. In other words, they were complete strangers. We were both kids. At first sight, with the exception of our complexions and my Catholic school uniform, there was nothing different about us. And yet, in her eyes, those two factors created a world of difference. We were growing up at a time when skin color and privilege made enemies out of people who, under any other circumstances, could have been the best of friends. At another point in time, attending the same school or living in the same neighborhood could have produced a different result. Who knows what we could have been. But on that day and at this point in time, she hated me.

As the taunting persisted, I did my best to ignore it. Her insults grew louder and more forceful, but I never matched her energy. That wasn't who I was. McDonald's security responded by kicking us *all* out of the restaurant. Patrons inside the restaurant were outraged that I was thrown out along with the girls that had verbally attacked me. However, I had no choice but to leave. Once we were outside, the verbal attacks persisted and escalated to threats. The police were called; they instructed us to go our separate ways. Once we saw the girls walk in the opposite direction, we breathed a sigh of relief. Whatever that was, it was over. That was, until we saw them again shortly after. Little did we know, once the police were gone, they had doubled back to find us.

It was my plan to take a dollar van (the closest thing to Uber before there was an Uber) home and Dahlia's to take the subway, but she decided to wait with me to see me off safely. Thankfully, she did, because before we knew it, they were coming up the street. And without a police presence or the McDonald's crowd, they were free to carry out a plan that we had no idea was in place. This group of five girls and two guys surrounded Dahlia and me, with all of the ringleader's energy directed toward me. "This light-skinned bitch thinks she's all that. We're going to take care of that for her." I hadn't done anything to her, I didn't even know her name, and yet, I had become her enemy. But I wasn't weak, and I didn't believe in cowering to bullies. The threats continued, and a large crowd of spectators gathered. During the interaction, a worrisome and unfamiliar feeling came over me. I later came to learn that it was my intuition, letting me know that this wasn't going to end well.

I saw the ringleader suspiciously reach into her pocket and pull something out. It was a razor blade. Quickly, she attacked Dahlia by pulling her hair from behind. She then raised her hand in a motion to cut her. I immediately grabbed the girl and threw her to the floor. She nicked the back of Dahlia's hand with the blade as she fell. In an instant, the entire group of five girls was on top of me. I found myself at the bottom of a pile, being viciously jumped. I was repeatedly punched and kicked, and had my head stomped into the pavement. The ringleader haphazardly swung her razor at me, trying to make contact as often as she could. She successfully cut my face during the fight, which is exactly what she set out to do. Soon after, I heard someone in the crowd scream "There's blood!" At that point, a dollar van driver grabbed the ringleader and pulled her off me while one of the other five girls grabbed me and held me steady. Just as swiftly as she was pulled off me, she broke free, ran up to me, and (I thought) punched me in the face. But it wasn't a punch at all . . . She'd slashed my face again. She dropped the razor blade and ran, as did the rest of her group and members of the crowd who didn't even have anything to do with it. Everything seemed surreal at that moment, but one thing was clear: We were alive! I turned to Dahlia and said, "Can you believe it? We made it through this okay!" But her response told a different story. She looked at me in absolute horror and said, "Oh my God, Gia! Your face!" and fell to the floor in tears.

It took a moment to process her reaction. So much adrenaline was pumping throughout my body that I hadn't felt the full impact of the pain. I then realized that my left cheek was wet and warm. I slowly raised my hand to touch my face, and when I looked at my hand again, it was covered in blood. I looked down at my clothes and saw my uniform skirt and leather jacket were covered in slashes and dripping with blood. Immediately, my vision went blurry. I was convinced that I was immersed in a dream. I literally pinched myself as proof. But I felt the sting; this was actually happening. This was real.

My mother had cautioned me several times, and again just two weeks before this day, to be very careful when I was away from the house. Her concern was warranted, given that at this time in New York, slashings were rampant. Kids were blatantly carrying razors and using them to settle disputes. Some hid them in their mouths in between their teeth and cheek. It was even considered cool by some.

I was witnessing the pandemonium occurring around me, but in those moments, the world stood still. In the background, "Where are the police?" "Somebody help her!" "Call an ambulance!" and the sounds of strangers crying. It was the day before Thanksgiving. It was cold and it began to snow. I leaned against the fence and slid down to the ground. I didn't even feel the snow beneath me. A kind woman approached me and handed me Kleenex, one after another until there was a mound of bloody tissues beside me. Reality resonated for me in that instance, and I took that opportunity to thank God that I survived. I counted the slashes throughout my clothing. There were thirteen altogether. I didn't realize it at the time, but one had gone through my skirt and cut my right inner thigh. There was so much blood that I had no idea how many wounds there were and where it was all coming from. The adrenaline began to wear off, and the pain that crept through was excruciating.

The police arrived quickly, while the crowd was still in an upheaval. They chased anyone who they saw running. They brought several people back to me, none of whom had anything to do with the incident . . . except one. I said to the officer, "That's the girl that cut my face." They arrested her and took her to central booking. I overheard the kind woman say to the police, "Look at what they've done to her. She looks like a carved pumpkin!" It was then that I understood exactly how bad it truly was. I desperately needed to see my face. The police officer put us in his car and told us that he was going to take us to the hospital. In the back of the squad car, I looked around to catch a glimpse of myself in the rearview mirror. When he noticed, he frantically ripped the mirror from the windshield. "I can't let you see your face like this," was all he said, with tears in his eyes. He was somber, and I didn't want to burden him with a reaction or with any questions. I decided that, despite the outcome, I was going to be okay. I was determined to remain calm, maintain my composure, and keep a level head.

Even at the hospital, they wouldn't let me see my face. It almost felt like this covert pact to keep me from learning what everyone else already knew. The anesthesiologist visited my room to ascertain my wounds. It was then that he discovered the slash on my thigh. He told me that it was likely going to take about a hundred stitches combined to close all three wounds, and I would need several shots of anesthesia in the open flesh of all of them to dull the pain in preparation for stitches. He warned me that those shots would be extremely painful but assured me that they would be far less painful than having the stitches without them. He left to prepare and told me that he would be back soon. There was no way that I was going to let them work on me before I had a chance to see what had brought so many to tears. So I cracked the door open, peeked outside, and when the coast was clear, bolted down the hall in search of a bathroom. When I finally found one, I opened the door, flicked on the lights, looked in the mirror, and was horrified at my reflection. I didn't recognize the girl that was looking back at me. My badly beaten, butchered, and bloody face told the story of what happened on that day better than I ever could. I stood there and cried. But after I wiped my tears, I decided that would be the first and last time that I would cry about what had happened. I did not plan on allowing my attackers to own or ruin me with their hate. I steadied myself and returned to my room. I calmly asked Dahlia to take pictures of my face. I was grateful we carried cameras with us, always ready to document our teenage years. Those pictures would prove to be helpful. This was not a simple fight between kids. I had been targeted and attacked. More than anything, I needed justice.

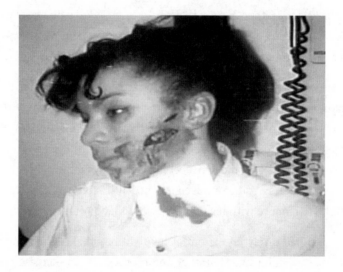

As the day's events were taking place, my mother was on her way home from Brooklyn to our house in Queens. My father picked her up as he usually did and later described her as silent and solemn the entire way home. She said to him, "Something happened to Gia . . ." She was able to feel it. When they arrived home, a dreadful message awaited them on the answering machine. My parents rushed to the hospital. Thankfully, by the time they arrived, I had already been stitched up, and they did not have to witness the state that I was in just an hour before. They were briefed on what had transpired before they were brought to my room. When they walked in, the look on my mother's face told a story of horror, shock, sadness, and revenge. She angrily said to me, "Where is the bitch that did this to your face?" She did not hug me—no kiss, no consolation. My mother knew that I did not need it. She turned around, stormed out of the room, and was gone. She was my hero in that moment. The anger and hurt that she felt *for me* allowed me to experience her love in a way that no one should ever have to. I interpreted her resolve as a sign of strength; there was no time for emotion, only time to *do*. She was off, on her way to the police station.

My mother entered the building and there my attacker sat, with a smug look on her face, as though she was proud of what she did. Disgusted, my mother lunged toward her and was restrained by officers as she shouted, "You're going to pay, you little wretch, you!" She meant those words with every fiber of her being. She told my father that, on that day, she needed to look into the face of the person who hurt her child so that on the day of reckoning, she would be able to bear witness as that smugness disappeared.

RaaShaun couldn't even look at me without crying. He felt an immense amount of guilt for not being there when it happened. A series of "what ifs" plagued his mind. At his young age and with more empathy and compassion than you would expect someone of his experience to possess, he was more of a support system than I could have ever hoped for. My face was disfigured, but he assured me that he found me even more beautiful on that day than on the day that he fell in love with me. I felt true love that day and every day since.

If RaaShaun had rarely let me out of his sight before, it wasn't happening at all from that point on. My father and brother felt an increased level of protectiveness as well. One afternoon, I walked downstairs to find my father constructing a bomb. My genius-level, tech-savvy father was in our basement plotting my attacker's demise with extreme tunnel vision. He'd gotten her address off the police paperwork and decided that a father's justice would be more "just" than a court's justice. I begged him to abandon that way of thinking, assuring him that there was a better way. He only saw red, and his need for revenge outweighed reason. Exasperated, I told him that I couldn't bear losing him to a jail cell; that if he followed through with his intentions, I would have to manage my way through the loss of my life as I had previously known it as well as the loss of my most significant confidant, him. I begged him to put me and my wishes first. Ultimately and unwillingly, he did.

The attack hurt the people I love, but it especially changed my mother. In many ways, she was never the same after that. "You bring this perfect baby into the world, and one day, someone gets to decide to hurt her, disfigure her, and change her forever," she said, with a brokenness in her voice. I was by no means perfect, but I was perfection to her. All children are irreplaceable to their parents, and my mother's fear of not being able to keep me safe is a fear shared by many parents. Your children go out into the world and you can't protect them at every turn. You just pray they'll be safe. My mother's greatest fear had come true, and it was impossible for life to be the same for her thereafter. Even though it wasn't my fault, in some way I felt responsible for her feelings. I had to let her know that I was going to be fine. I had to let everyone know I was going to be fine. The idea that my perceived pain was everyone else's burden left me feeling stifled. The only way to do that was to keep moving forward. I wasn't going to give this situation power over my life, and I hoped that, by following my example, those who loved me wouldn't give it power either.

When the school called and offered me weeks to recuperate and heal, I rejected it. I was back at school on the Monday following our Thanksgiving break, bandaged face and all. My schoolmates were shocked to see me. They stared—no, they gawked. Regardless, I walked through the halls of my school and my neighborhood with my head held high. I chose not to hide. I had no reason to be ashamed. My attacker wanted my disfigurement to resort me to a shell of who I formerly was. That wasn't going to happen.

She was right about one thing though. I wasn't the old Gia anymore. I was a better Gia. The new Gia had a better outlook on life, knowing that beauty is only skin deep and can be taken from us at any moment. Understanding that bad things don't only happen to "other people"—that sometimes, we are "other people," and embracing the kindred hurt of others that have experienced the disappointments of life—allowed me to learn and experience true empathy and compassion. My views had broadened because my life experience had broadened. This may be difficult to understand, but I feel grateful for that. Character had been built within me that I was able to stand upon.

Taking control of my life meant that I had to prepare for the fight ahead. I pressed charges and saw the prosecution all the way through until the end. Getting to justice was a long journey. My attacker was said to be a family member of a well-known actor, and he was speculated to have bankrolled her defense. But she was not the only defendant. It was a time- and energy-consuming process, but we found the identities of the other four girls who attacked me. That included staking out their high school, scouring through their past and present yearbooks, and revisiting that same McDonald's on random days on the off chance that they would return. And one day, they did. I walked into the restaurant with the detectives in tow, approximately twenty feet behind me. I was stunned when I saw them sitting there, laughing and having a good time, as though they had no cares in the world. But they were about to care, alright. I made myself seen. One of them looked up at me and said, "Hey, Gia [pronouncing my name wrong]. You look great," followed by laughter. I let a few more taunts continue before I raised my hand, giving the detectives the signal, and saying, "There they are, all of them." Within seconds, they were all in cuffs. This was only the first step, but I would be lying if I said that I didn't feel a small sense of justice as I stood there, watching the complacent looks of self-satisfaction disappear from all of their faces as they were escorted out of the same place where it all began.

Growing up, my parents instilled in me the importance of treating others the way that I want to be treated. Apparently, everyone isn't taught that, and some people need a little help getting there. Whether it is in our community or through the courts, we have to help people understand that they don't have the right to harm others; that there are consequences for actions. I'm proud of standing up for myself and not allowing the role of victim to consume me.

Two years after the attack, when I was seventeen and my attacker was nineteen, the incident went to trial. It took several weeks. Many witnesses testified, including the kind woman who gave me the Kleenex. The picture that I had Dahlia take in the hospital was used as evidence for the prosecution.

As the photo was passed around the jury box, several were reduced to tears. They would have had no true concept of the evil that took place that day without that picture. Words could have never sufficed. After that, all was clear and they were left doubtless. As the verdict was read, the defendant sat there—newly pregnant, expressionless, and emotionless. Even after all this time to reflect and to regret, she was too "bad" to care, not even for herself. She was found guilty. I will never forget the look on my mother's face. She could have exploded with satisfaction. She let out a resounding "Yes!" that came from the depth of her soul, and everyone felt it. I wanted the guilty verdict more for her than I did for myself.

At the sentencing, my attacker was given an opportunity to express remorse to the court before the judge made his final decision. She adamantly declined, refusing to say a word even at the encouragement of her attorney. The judge had several words reserved for her before he sentenced her to five to fifteen years in prison. In separate court appearances and procedures, the other four girls were given probation. I was content with the outcome. After that day, I was able to let go and begin the next chapter of my life. We have to remember that we're our own best advocates and know that protecting ourselves begins with seeing ourselves as valuable and worthy.

I'm often asked where that kind of strength came from at such a young age. My parents consistently told me that I was beautiful, smart, and strong. I believed them. They built me up on a daily basis and poured love and confidence into

> "We have to remember that we're our own best advocates and know that protecting ourselves begins with seeing ourselves as valuable and worthy." —**GIA**

me. They crafted my esteem and self-image. They never dictated; they taught instead. I recall hours-long conversations with them individually, trying to suck up as much information as I could, learning my way through their experiences and stories. They led by example, and I admired them both tremendously. To me, being compared to either of them was the greatest compliment. My mother let me know that whenever hard times arise in my life, God would never allow me to endure anything that I couldn't handle. That I can make it through any-thing with Him. So I leaned heavily on my faith throughout the physical heal-ing process to make sure that my internal healing was just as strong.

My doctor warned me that my face would be scarred forever. He compared it to a broken vase. Once it is broken, it can never be unbroken; you will always see the seams. I had to live with that. I had to decide to view my scars as an outward representation of all that I had learned through this process and the resolve that I had gained. Even still, disappointment is real. I was upset that I went through it. We have to admit that, but even as we do, we can't allow these disappointments to dictate the trajectory of our lives. As women, we do that often. Too much so, if we're being honest.

There have been things that have happened to us all that have shaped our lives. They are a part of our stories, but they're not the full story of who we are. They do not define us. But when we don't face these issues head-on, they become the mirrors in which we see ourselves. We become women unable to overcome things that happened to us when we were little girls. We become lovers who can't allow our partners completely in because past traumas are holding us back. We become parents who raise our children out of fear, rather than love. This doesn't mean that what happened to us wasn't real or painful. But it does mean that we are responsible for how we respond to it, and we *do* possess a certain degree of control over it as well. We have to take ownership of our destiny. There's so much at stake when we don't allow ourselves to evolve into our best selves. Not allowing ourselves to do so is particularly detrimental, in part because our best selves transition into the best partners and the best parents consequentially. But we have to get there first.

Sometimes, the first step to becoming better is to admit that you're not. It's okay to be honest with yourself and others in recognition of the fact that you may still be affected by someone or something that once hurt you. For me, it means understanding that true evil exists in this world, and praying that my six beautiful children never have to experience it for themselves firsthand. It means that if my prayers aren't answered, I have to be the strength that guides them through. It's impossible for you to overcome anything if you're unwilling to face it. These are some of the hardest conversations we will ever have, but they are among the most necessary. For some of us, it will mean that we have to confront the people who hurt us. For others, it may mean that we find the courage to tell others how we feel. For all of us, it means that we need to tell the truth. Our honesty is at the root of our freedom, and before we can even begin to think about being better partners and parents, we need to take stock of ourselves and seriously consider what it means to be the best we can be for ourselves.

> "Our honesty is at the root of our freedom, and before we can even begin to think about being better partners and parents, we need to take stock of ourselves and seriously consider what it means to be the best we can be for ourselves." —**GIA**

What happens when we're honest about pain? Then, and only then, are we able to get to the source of how our pain has made us feel and how we react to others. I've spoken to other women who have been attacked like I was. The ordeal made them afraid to trust women and leery of forming deep friend-ships. When something that's negative and life-altering occurs, it can cloud your judgment and lead you to believe that everyone is out to get you—or at least has the potential to. That's an honest and understandable reaction to a traumatic experience. But do you know what that does? In this case, it allows the women who harmed them to become the spokeswomen for all women in their world, and that isn't fair. It is disproportionate to reality. Some of us have been burned by women in our lives, but we know that every woman isn't like the one who hurt us. We live in a world that loves to pit women—especially women of color—against each other. But we can't allow those experiences to command the narrative. We deserve good friendships and healthy relation-ships with other women. We shouldn't let the ones who hurt us rob us of them.

> "We can't allow our past heartbreaks and heartaches to force us to believe that we are doomed to a lifetime of unfulfillment and pain. That's just not true. It will never be true." —**GIA**

21

The same goes for men. I know that we don't want to admit this, but entirely too many of us hold some men responsible for pain that was there long before they came into our lives. Sometimes, every little thing a new man does reminds us of the one before—and we make sure we tell them about it! Or sometimes, we've become so closed off from the pain that we don't even give a new man the opportunity to love us because we've already decided that they're going to hurt us. We find ourselves stuck and repeating the cycle all over again. This can be a hindering part of our common denominator that needs to be identified. Here's the truth: good men exist. I know that social media and gossip blogs want us to believe differently. However, in the spirit of giving everyone a fair shake, we cannot hold the whole responsible for the actions of a few. Furthermore, we can't allow our past heartbreaks and heartaches to force us to believe that we are doomed to a lifetime of unfulfillment and pain. That's just not true. It will never be true. In being our own best advocates, we have to take deliberate care of ourselves. That often means setting boundaries that

"We have to take deliberate care of ourselves. That often means setting boundaries that we never previously considered. By that, I mean boundaries within ourselves. We cannot allow ourselves to see the world through the eyes of the people who hurt us. They will never deserve that kind of power in our lives, and we must see to it that they never get it." —**GIA**

we never previously considered. By that, I mean boundaries within ourselves. We cannot allow ourselves to see the world through the eyes of the people who hurt us. They will never deserve that kind of power in our lives, and we must see to it that they never get it.

Once we acknowledge the ways we've allowed these hurts to shape our actions and our thinking, we can change our responses and reactions. Faith and prayer matter deeply to me. Trusting God to help me handle the big things gives me the confidence to face them. It's all about taking baby steps. Sometimes you have to coach your way through. If you find yourself having a hard time trusting women because of something that happened to you, look at the women you admire in your life and lean a little bit more into those relationships. If there's a coworker who's been reaching out and making an attempt at friendship, go out for lunch or coffee. Strike up a conversation with one of the moms in your child's playgroup and schedule a "mommy date." If you're finding it difficult to trust men again, think about the men in your life—family or friends—who are worthy of being trusted, and take a small step toward believing they're not the only ones. If you're in a current relationship, own up to and apologize for the ways you've held previous trauma against them and commit to doing better. If you're single, give others in your life who've been reaching out to you a chance. Allow yourself permission to be happy and loved. It won't happen overnight, but you can take steps toward the life you want. That is always within your power.

I can admit that the entire ordeal forced me to confront parts of my personality that I needed to confront. Looking back at that young girl, I would consider myself to have been a bit vain. My looks and my appearance mattered a lot to me. It matters to most young girls. But what would have happened if I didn't do the work to fully recognize the beauty within myself that went beyond what was on the outside? How would I be different if my strength hadn't been

"Allow yourself permission to be happy and loved." —**GIA**

tested in the way that it was? How would that have impacted my relationship with RaaShaun, my relationship with the world? How would the lessons that I have passed down to my daughters be different? How would the lessons that I teach my sons regarding society's value system of women be different?

When teaching your children that beauty is only superficial, it comes across differently when you're a parent whose "beauty" had almost been stripped from you, as opposed to a parent that is just repeating a cliché. How would my life have been different had I not fully embraced that I am far more than what others can see? To be clear, I was always more than that. I have always been smart, kind, and compassionate. But we live in a world where image seems everything happens for a reason, I was able to see how this situation brought to the surface parts of me that I may have never had the chance to explore fully. For many of us, it's not just about doing the work to heal from what others have done to us. It's also about confronting the truth about what some situations expose in us that was already there. There may be a lesson waiting to be learned, an anger or insecurity present within you that can no longer be ignored. What better gift can you give yourself than to confront and address it? If you do the work, you will be liberated, and you and your loved ones will eat the fruit from that branch.

When I think back on that day now, I am grateful to have survived, not only physically, but mentally and emotionally as well. I can only hope that those who attacked me have done their work to be better as grown women than they were as young women. They deserve that, and the people in their lives deserve the best versions of them as well. Regardless of our mistakes or transgressions, we are never too far gone. We can always find our way back to the roots of goodness. Sometimes, all we need is for someone to remind us of that, to believe in us and make us feel as though we are worthy of forgiveness.

When I look back, there are no tears, because it did not define me or who I was destined to become. I have a successful career and a beautiful family. I have friends who love me and whom I love in return. I am genuinely happy because I decided that I would be. I did not allow myself an alternative. It was deliberate then and still is now. What happened to me is only one chapter in the story of my life. And I can say that because I did the work to make sure that it was never anything more. Your dreams about the place you want to hold in this world and the reality of who you become are determined by so much more than what anyone has ever subjected you to. That is a life truth. It is up to you to believe it. And once you do, you will have the power to take control of what is yours—YOU! Yes, you belong to you. And you are your own greatest gift. Honor yourself and take advantage of all the wonderful things that life has to offer. If you do so, you will be on the road to healing, and just as importantly, blossoming. Life is to be lived. We owe it to ourselves to live it well.

———

3. When "Protect and Provide" Goes Too Far (Envy)

Have you ever stopped to think about the dumb things you used to do when you were younger in relationships and just shake your head? There was this one time, in college, when I had to deejay at a party in Richmond. Being from New York and going to school in Hampton, Virginia, I didn't know many people outside of those two cities. I arranged my boys to come with me for protection and reinforcement. Though Gia attended all of the parties with me while we were in school, this particular time, the car was filled with my "security," and that meant she couldn't come. Because I was going to be away, I told her that she needed to stay home. She laughed and told me that she was going out that night to a party at the Armory with her girlfriends. I made it clear that under no circumstances was she "allowed" to go anywhere that night and that was the end of the discussion. Gia finally gave in, and my friends and I headed to Richmond. I was well on the way to my party when my boy Shaun Evans, whom we all call "Lil Shaun," called and told me he saw Gia at the Armory. I knew this couldn't be true because she'd agreed not to go. I took the next exit to head back to Hampton so I could see for myself. I didn't know who was going to deejay the party that night in Richmond, but I knew it wasn't going to be me.

When I got to the Armory, I walked in and all I saw was Gia grinding on some random dude. She looked up at me and I was furious! In less than two seconds, I went from seeing them dance to picturing them in bed together. I could see the fear in Gia's face as I barreled toward her. Next thing I knew, I was carrying Gia out of the club over my shoulder like I was Tarzan, unleashing on her. Yelling. Cursing. I was mad. How could she do this to me?! No response was sufficient. I told her we were going home right then. She said she couldn't because she drove, and her girlfriends weren't ready to go. I told her I didn't care how they got home but we were leaving.

No matter how much I yelled and had a fit, she didn't leave the club without her girls that night. And her girls weren't in a hurry to leave either. So for the rest of the night, I walked around the club with my arms around Gia or standing still, holding her in a bear hug, letting everyone know that she was my girl.

Looking back, it would be easy to explain this away as the actions of a twenty-year-old kid who didn't know any better. When we talk about it now, even though we laugh and I cringe a bit, I know that's exactly who I was at the time. But if I'm being real, that was evidence of something deeper in me that had been around for years and would be there for years to come. I now realize that, whether I wanted to admit it or not, I was selfish and controlling.

Fellas, we know what it means to be selfish and controlling. When we were younger, a lot of us thought that's just what you do. You stick your chest out and show your girl who's the boss. And even though every guy didn't act like that, you knew someone who did. Some of us didn't grow out of it. When our wives and girlfriends are out having fun and we're trying to dictate their every move, we know what that is. We try to say it's just us being men and the "head" of our households, but we know there's so much more to it than that. Growing up with a cop as a father, I saw my dad being overprotective and strict. If you ask him, he would tell you that he was firm but fair. If you ask me, our house was a dictatorship. Whatever my dad said goes. Before I even understood what gender roles were, I saw them in my home and understood that men and women played very specific parts in a relationship. And although roles and positions vary depending on the relationship, I didn't know that at the time. I thought my experience was universal. We don't just see it in our homes, it's reinforced in our communities and through entertainment. Men take the lead. They take charge. It's understood and expected. It may be unpleasant, but for many, it's the way of the world.

Seeing my father and the other black men in my community, I created my own mantra of manhood: "to protect and to provide." As black men in America, we are already Public Enemy #1. Consequently, everyone attached to us is vulnerable too. Protecting and providing for your family means putting a roof over their heads and food on the table. It means giving them what they need so they don't have to go to the government for handouts in the streets. Protecting and providing doesn't mean your family has everything they necessarily want, but for us, "wants" are luxuries we can't always afford. We saw the men in our communities live this out, going to work every day and putting twenty, thirty years in at the same job. They made sure the household had enough, and because of that, nobody asked any questions.

Back then, you knew a man was a "good man" based on whether he provided for his family or not, and that's it. If he cheated on his wife or ruled his house with an iron fist, it could be excused as long as he was providing for them financially and doing whatever he could to protect them from society. On one hand, we can recognize the positive images of black men being providers when the world wanted to say otherwise. We may have known a few deadbeats here and there, but that wasn't the whole story for black men. At the same time, we need to be honest about the lack of accountability some black men had for how they ran their homes and how the way they were in relationships set us up for failure. Some of us saw that and believed we could say and do anything to keep our women in line, as long as we were taking care of them—because that's what men do.

I was controlling. That night at the club and so many other nights were about my need to control Gia's every move, and all of it was rooted in my insecurities. There was another time when Gia was ironing her clothes to head to the mall with her friends, and I thought her outfit was a bit too revealing. It would have been fine if I were going, but I wasn't, so she needed to change. Gia told me that I didn't get to tell her what to wear, and she continued ironing. I waited until she was fully dressed, her hair done, her makeup complete, and she was ready to head out the door before I grabbed her by her arms and pulled her into the bathtub and turned on the shower. We were both soaking wet—her clothes and her hair were ruined, with mascara running down her face. Suffice it to say she didn't go to the mall. Instead, we stayed home and argued. She tried to break up with me, just as she had tried to do several times after I pulled selfish stunts like this. But I never let it happen. I always found a way to get her to see the good in me—the parts of me that were worthy—to keep her by my side. I think that she may have understood me better than I understood myself and recognized that my actions stemmed from an insecurity that only she could make me feel. Seeing that outfit, just like the thought of her going to the club alone, made me afraid that she was going to go out, find a better guy, and leave me. I could never see my life without her. Not even to this day. I never thought I was good enough for Gia. That insecurity and fear plagued our relationship for years to come.

Growing up, I always felt like I had to prove that I was worthy of everything I had. I always felt behind. For years, I was the short kid with the glasses and braces. When I made the basketball team with all these tall kids, I felt like I

"It took a while to realize that it was never about how I saw Gia but what I didn't see in myself. When you don't recognize your own worth, you hold on to people in ways that are suffocating." —ENVY

had to work extra hard to prove that I earned my spot and it wasn't given to me. Because I was an only child who was given the world by my parents, I felt I had to prove that all things didn't just come easy to me because my mom and dad had good jobs and a little more money than most in our neighborhood. I've always felt like the underdog who isn't necessarily seen and has to make others see me. Sometimes, that fear of being the underdog and being unseen can make you feel that, when something or someone better comes along, the people you care about will forget you and run toward that. Gia was this beautiful, intelligent girl with a bright future ahead of her dating a guy everyone laughed at because he wanted to be a professional DJ. Of course I was afraid a dude with better looks, a better job, and a more stable and certain future would steal her away from me. It took a while to realize that it was never about how I saw Gia but what I didn't see in myself. When you don't recognize your own worth, you hold on to people in ways that are suffocating. You start to think that, if you let up even just a little bit, everyone and everything will disappear. And when you realize this, you know you have no choice but to confront the insecurities that make you believe it's okay to behave this way.

There's a big difference between being protective and being controlling. Being protective says, "Go out and have fun but make sure you're safe." Being controlling says, "You can't go out without my permission." One is rooted in a care that recognizes, even as your girl is having fun, you still want her to be safe. The other is rooted in a fear that, the longer she's away from you, the sooner she'll realize she needs to stay away from you. And if we're honest again, a lot of us who are controlling know these women should have left us a long time ago. Shoot, some of you may be skating on thin ice right now! Making the shift to abandon our controlling ways can mean not losing the best thing that's ever happened to us as well as unlocking a new, beautiful dimension in our relationships. When I understood that being controlling robbed me of the ability to recognize that people *want* to be in my life, I saw just how much I was cheating myself. Gia wasn't there because I was making her stay. Gia was with me because she wanted to be with me. I had value beyond the protection and provision I was taught that men provide. She saw more in me, and that enabled me to see more in myself.

I can't remember the exact events that led to my acceptance that I had to change. I just know that, one day, I looked in the mirror and realized that who I was wasn't who I wanted to be. Stripped down from being a husband, a father, and having a successful career that many doubted, I wasn't the person that I knew I could be. I needed to change but I didn't know how. Gia's college friend's husband, Rasheed McWilliams, showed me how.

I wouldn't say that Rasheed and I were close; actually, we weren't even friends. We spent time together because of our wives, but to be honest, Rasheed didn't really like me for Gia because I was so controlling and domineering in our relationship. And I really didn't like him because I thought that he was too self-righteous. It's both ironic and full circle that he'd be the one to help me on this journey to becoming a better man. Rasheed straight-up told me that I would never be the man I could be until I got my life right with God. Growing up, my faith was pretty much nonexistent. I went to church with my grandmother on major holidays, and that was it. I wasn't the church-every-Sunday-and-Bible-study-every-Wednesday kind of kid. And, honestly, I was never going to be that guy. But, at the worst time in my life, the church-every-Sunday-and-Bible-study-every-Wednesday kind of kid. And, honestly, I was never going to be that guy. But, at the worst time in my life, Rasheed showed me that it was possible to have a personal relationship with God. I'd made a huge mistake in my relationship with Gia—one that almost cost me everything—and Rasheed could've seen it as an opportunity to say "I told you so," but he didn't. Instead, he told me it was possible to be a better man, and that possibility would only come with a relationship with God.

Rasheed helped me develop my own Bible study and prayer time. Talking to God was going to be the only way I could figure out who I wanted to be, and reading His word was the only way I could learn who He wanted me to be. The closer I got with God, the more cognizant I became of who I wanted to be as a person. I wanted to be a man of integrity. Goodness and righteousness became the goal. It was in my alone time with God that I began to see what it meant for me to lead my family from a healed place instead of one crowded with my own insecurities. Gia and I are a team; there are things that she's better at than me, and yes, there are even a few things that I'm better at than her. But as a team, we're unstoppable. It doesn't make me any less of a man to admit that. The "my way or the highway" attitude doesn't honor the idea that we chose each other to be partners and need to listen to and respect each other.

"The 'my way or the highway' attitude doesn't honor the idea that we chose each other to be partners and need to listen to and respect each other." —**ENVY**

What may be the hardest thing for some of us to admit is that we have to change. Some of the ways we learned to do things have to go. On a practical level, fellas, we've got to do better because these aren't the women of earlier generations who had no options and silently went along just to keep the peace! Gia has never been that kind of woman, and neither are many of the women who listen to our podcast. Many of today's women have no problem telling you to check yourselves and no problem leaving if you can't get it together.

They're making their own money and have their own careers. They don't *need* us for that. They *need* us to be willing to create lasting relationships, healthy marriages, and families. Sometimes things don't work out and people break up. That's hard and it's real. But would you rather end the relationship because it honestly ran its course or because you were too stubborn to make the changes you needed to make for it to reach its potential?

We're also going to have to get real with ourselves about the fact that who we are in the corporate and business arena doesn't translate to our personal lives. When it comes to making sure my family is self-sufficient and experiencing

> "I learned 'I'm sorry' is manly, and insisting that I'm right when I clearly know I'm wrong is actually a sign of weakness." —**ENVY**

financial freedom, I am unstoppable. As a black man who moves in the spaces that I do, I see how the deck is stacked against us—the expectation is we won't succeed. Because of that, we can get tunnel vision about our professional and economic goals. We're going to prove to the world that it's never a good thing to bet against black men. That shrewd precision in the boardroom is necessary, but that won't fly at the kitchen table. The kind of pride that we have to have in the world, that signals we aren't pushovers, actually keeps us from being effective communicators and better listeners. Shedding that kind of pride, for me, was essential. I learned "I'm sorry" is manly, and insisting that I'm right when I clearly know I'm wrong is actually a sign of weakness. Realizing this and making healthy changes add up to us being worthy examples that our families can be proud of.

When I look back at the night of that party at the Armory, what I was trying

> "You can't make someone stay who wants to leave." —**ENVY**

to do was stop something from happening. I believed I was making Gia stay with me, but you can't do that. You can't make someone stay who wants to leave. I've met many men who keep repeating this cycle in their relationships from that, you've got to figure out what parts of you need to be worked on so you don't keep pushing people away. And there are some who find that, once

> "We try to be better than our fathers and hope that our sons are better than us. That's the only way we build lasting legacies of manhood." —ENVY

they let someone go, that person actually stays. That was us. Gia wanted to be there. I could rest assured in the fact that she truly loved me. For so long, I'd seen Gia as out of my league, but I could finally accept that she, in fact, just wanted me. She was created for me and I was created for her. I could honor and enjoy my wife but, more than that, I could enjoy the relationship with myself.

I still believe in the mantra "to provide and to protect." I believe that's the hallmark of a man. I just know there are some other attributes too. Compromise and compassion. Humor and empathy. All of these and more make up a "good man." Good men aren't perfect; we still mess up. Believe me, there are days when Gia's side-eye is strong, and I tread lightly. And there are days when I know I'm right about something and will defend it until my last breath. We're human. We get it right as much as we get it wrong. The key is that we try. We try to be better than our fathers and hope that our sons are better than us. That's the only way we build lasting legacies of manhood.

———

4. Perception Isn't Reality

Have you ever been unfairly judged or sized up before someone even got the chance to get to know you? And can you admit to yourself that, before you ever got to know someone, you made assumptions about who you thought they'd be? If we're honest, all of us can say yes to one or both of those questions. We've been victims of other people's perceptions of us all our lives, and it hasn't always been pretty. As lighter-skinned black people, we've always endured the "black enough" attacks. Because of the effect of white privilege in our community, through colorism, we have automatically been perceived as thinking we're better than other people because of our complexions.

GIA: When I was attacked by someone I'd never even met before, I was called a "piss-colored bitch." Immediately, I was being judged by something that was completely out of my control. And it wasn't the first time I'd heard such things. People would automatically assume I thought I was superior. "Oh, she thinks she's all that because she's light-skinned." While my parents raised me to be kind and caring, I grew up overcompensating because I didn't want to ever give the impressions that I *wasn't* nice. That experience followed me throughout adulthood.

I'll never forget attending lunch with a friend and some of her friends that I didn't know. Initially, the women were apprehensive toward me. One basically gave me the cold shoulder. To loosen everyone up, I started asking them about their children and family life. Eventually, I won them over and we had a great time. Later that day, while debriefing with my friend, she confirmed my worst suspicions: her friends were surprised at how nice I was. When I pressed a bit further, my friend told me that they'd been around women like me before and it didn't always go well. *Women like me.* It just echoed the same experiences I'd had before. People weren't seeing me for who I was. They were seeing me for who they'd decided I was.

The same thing has happened to us in business. Our family has been approached for much more visible opportunities, such as reality television. After discussing it as a family, we thought it would be a wonderful opportunity to showcase the beauty and fun in our family. But on one occasion, when we got into a meeting, executives began suggesting ways to make our experience appeal more effectively to black audiences. RaaShaun and I had heard this before. As everyone who attempts to broach this subject with us always does, the executives began to stumble over their words. Ultimately, we're a lighter-skinned family of means, and there was the concern that our lives wouldn't be black enough for black viewers. I was so offended. Not only had we not sought out this opportunity, but we were being assessed on whether we could be black enough for black people?! It was infuriating. The black experience is the only experience I know. The black culture, the only culture I know. To suggest that I could possibly not be black enough to live my own life simply because of my complexion, well, there just aren't enough words.

ENVY: I have words. It's fucking bullshit. None of us can help what we look like. One of the dope parts of being black is that several different shades and hues can exist on the same branch of a black family tree. That's actually why I hate all the "beige" jokes. I am a black man. I'm married to a black woman. Together, we're raising black children. To say anything else is simply disrespectful.

It's also disrespectful when people make ridiculous assumptions about the source of our financial means. I think this pisses me off more than anything. People assume that we were both born with silver spoons in our mouths. Nothing could be further from the truth. My father was a police officer and my mother worked at Guardian Life Insurance. We weren't rolling in dough. Add to that, I went off to college in hopes of becoming a professional DJ. The loan my parents took out for me to attend Hampton University? I had to pay every dime of it back. What you see is the result of hard work and effort. Granted, I know it looks different because I'm part of the entertainment industry and there are so many assumptions made about hip-hop artists and those affiliated with the culture. But I'm just like every other hardworking man who provides for his family. People don't realize, when they're attacking that, they're going after my humanity and manhood. And like I said, it's fucking bullshit.

* * *

We live in a world that feeds off assumptions and how people adjust their lives according to those assumptions. One of our friends admitted to us that, because she's a larger woman, in every conflict or disagreement, she's always assumed to be in the wrong. Because she's bigger, she's automatically presumed to be the bully. As a result, she spent so many years of her life apologizing when she wasn't wrong to avoid further conflict. For much of her life, she went without receiving apologies she was owed because people would find a way to make things her fault. It wasn't until recently, in therapy, that she was able to connect the dots and see how she'd been living her life in response to other people's perceptions of her.

That has been a lot of us, if we're willing to tell the truth. We've either acquiesced to what people think of us or we've developed a thick-skinned, middle-finger-to-the-world attitude because of it. We can say we don't care, but we'd be lying. We weren't built to live on islands—we need each other. What we think of each other matters.

At some point, all of us should do a bit of inventory and ask ourselves:

What past experiences shape how I view myself?

What experiences and ideologies shape how I view others?

If we're totally honest, the answers may surprise us. It may cause some of us to admit that we've been seeing ourselves through the negative perceptions of others—who they said we couldn't be, what they said we couldn't do, and the worst of who they said we are. As a result, we've become bitter and cold, mistrusting of everyone and second-guessing if people can really like or care about us. Some of us even became self-fulfilling prophecies, afraid to try because people already said we wouldn't succeed, and we ultimately failed at personal relationships, in business, or in any other area of our lives where engaging with people is important.

In that same manner, it's impossible for us to see other people for who they truly are. It's why gossip and bad news are so easy to consume and can always travel fast. When we're feeding into people's negative perceptions of ourselves, it's easy to transfer that energy onto others and sow seeds of negativity. It's a never-ending cycle, and nothing good comes from it.

GIA: Being nice is a good thing. It is a Godly thing. We should all strive to be kind. Being overly nice and accommodating, however, was rooted in my experience of being judged as a result of other people's projections. This was something that I internalized. It takes real courage to be that honest with myself. But in doing so, I was able to say that I can be kind and compassionate and I can also possess a confidence about who I am that doesn't bend to other people's opinions of me, especially people who don't know me. As I hold that space for myself, I get to hold that same space for others.

ENVY: I agree. I'll admit hearing people question my blackness or suggest that I didn't work hard to get to where I am will always rub me the wrong way. But that's not going to stop me from being my black-ass self or helping others experience financial freedom through teaching. I realize that when people are projecting onto us, whether they know it or not, the goal is to make us less of who we truly are. I know who I truly am. And I've worked very hard to get here. No one is ever going to strip me of that.

* * *

When we look at our lives, we have to ask ourselves if we are the people we truly want to be. Are we self-actualized? Self-actualization is the full realization of one's potential and of one's true self. It is the intrinsic growth of what already exists within us. Allowing that growth to take shape leads to self-fulfillment. When we focus on our potential, our growth, and our own fulfillment, we create fruit that we, as well as those around us, can eat and be nurtured by.

Right now, it may be helpful to go back to your life's common denominator and ask yourself how you got here. All of us are the sum total of our experiences. Have we ever taken any time to evaluate how those experiences added up and ultimately shaped us? That's going to be key to really getting to the heart of who we are, especially if we possess some behaviors that don't serve us well in our current relationships.

Maybe you've become willing to admit that you're controlling and it's a result of some insecurities you need to address. After digging deeper, maybe you've discovered that those insecurities are rooted in people telling you what you couldn't be and couldn't have. Your insecurities may be in response to people laughing at your dreams and now, when you get into a relationship, you feel you have to dictate every single aspect of it so you won't lose it and can prove those naysayers wrong. But what you don't realize is you're actually proving them right. Your controlling and manipulative ways will push away the love you say that you want because you've allowed your personality to be in response to negativity and not rooted in who you truly, *actually* are.

Or maybe you haven't been speaking up in your relationship because you want it to work. There haven't been many successful relationships in your family and you haven't been successful in past relationships yourself. At the beginning, you heard things like "I wonder how long this will last" from friends and loved ones who led with negativity. Consequently, you've not said what you needed to say about things that bothered you because you don't want the relationship to end. On the outside, it seems like you're in a happy and fulfilling relationship. But inside, you're unhappy and suffering in silence because you don't want to prove those people right yet again. You've allowed the perceptions and projections of others to dictate your happiness—making you beholden to them. Those perceptions and projections are poisonous fruit. And sometimes when we consume bad fruit, we regurgitate it and are left to look at the mess we produced.

There are a million other examples we could use, but the point is that we have to recognize how we're allowing what others think or say about us to keep us from the lives and loves we want. For some, this necessary work can happen by standing in front of the mirror and telling ourselves some hard truths. For others, it will take the accountability of friendships or the safe space of therapy. Either way, the work has to be done, because if it isn't, the root of it all will start to show. There are some people who have mastered the art of living their lives in response to what other people think. And haven't you noticed how these people always think that nobody notices, but we all do? Unfortunately, they have no idea exactly how transparent their lives actually are. You know when someone is living a life of authenticity and when people are moving in a way that's trying to please or spite others.

Over time, our relationships will show the wear and tear of that kind of living. They won't be full of the deep love and joy they could be. Instead, there will always be "something." You know how it feels to not be able to put your finger on it but be frustrated by the fact that your relationship is always going through *something*? Or that the same issues keep surfacing? Or no matter how much you keep trying to push past something, you can't seem to let it go? And when you finally talk about it, when you finally address it, you realize that the root issue has nothing to do with you or your partner? That's when it's time to sit down and really evaluate how deeply the thoughts and opinions of others have affected you. The goal isn't to have a relationship that *looks* good; it's to have a relationship that, at its core, *is* good.

This may bring up unresolved issues from your childhood. It may mean that you have to think about those painful things said to you by strangers, parents, family members, teachers, former friends, or people who are still in your life. You may even have to establish some boundaries that have been overstepped for years and never enforced, knowing that it's never too late to assert your-

> "The goal isn't to have a relationship that *looks* good;
> it's to have a relationship that, at its core, *is* good."

self. Whatever you have to do so that your life is the most authentic it can be, you *must* be willing to do it. Remember, you're not doing this for anyone but yourself. The people we love will be able to benefit from this growth and evolution. But it's us who have to live with us every day. If anyone should be happy and enjoy inner peace because of us, it's us.

We can't stop people from making assumptions about us because of the complexion of our skin, how much money they think we have, or other things that they draw from our appearance, just as others can't stop people from assuming things because of their complexion, financial status, socioeconomic status, size, or sexuality. People will think what they want, and even though we can't change that, *we* can be different. We can choose to base our opinions of others on who they are to us. And we can give them a bit of grace and breathing room when they mess up, because we already know what kind of world they're dealing with. And we can extend that same goodness to ourselves, refusing to root who we are in what others project onto us. We know what's at stake when we do this, and too much happiness is available to us to act otherwise. And we're not leaving any happiness on the table.

———

5. Ladies, Don't Fall for the "Mind-Bleep" (Gia)

We all know what mind-bleeping is. It's when a person in the relationship takes a dominant position and uses that dominance to convince their partner to believe an untruth. While this happens in all types of relationships, we've seen it play out time and time again with men and women as sexism and gender roles take center stage in many areas of our lives. We also see mind-bleeping when men act like they don't understand why we're upset about something after we've clearly explained ourselves. "You're overreacting." No, I'm not. "I didn't say that." Yes, you did. "Who are you going to believe, me or your lying eyes?" You, I guess. "You're crazy." Wait . . . Am I? Mind-bleeping causes us to doubt our own thinking, perception, and reality. Our confidence, power, and authority are stripped from us, leaving us vulnerable and more susceptible to control. The byproducts then become low self-esteem, anxiety, and learned helplessness—all of which can lead to depression and the doubting of one's own sanity. Some would say it's another form of gaslighting, but I think it's much worse. It is a deliberate manipulation. When a woman is mind-bleeped, she will disregard all reason and abandon intuition and common sense for something that she knows is absolutely ridiculous. This will cause her to make bad decisions that are detrimental to her, but benefit her partner or, better said in this instance, victimizer. It is inherently emotionally abusive but may not seem that way because it can take place in a somewhat subtle way. It will have her asking herself, "How did I get here?" She knows she doesn't like it but doesn't quite know how to identify what just took place. I do . . . she's been mind-bleeped.

It's like a Jedi mind trick, and we know why we succumb to it. For as long as there have been women on earth, our identity has revolved around us being "chosen." To society—and even to some of us—being single and without a family isn't a good look; it can be embarrassing actually. Even when we know it's a lie, we will accept what they tell us just so we can hold on to that "dream," all while convincing ourselves we're the ones in control. But, when we do that, we're not in control at all.

The world raises us to make excuses for men and accept what they say without even questioning it. We don't lose our identity as women when we aren't chosen. We lose it when we abandon our God-given common sense and intuition just to say we have "a man."

It's so easy to believe the lies and make excuses when you're looking at your goals and watching your life's clock tick away. There are societal expectations of us as women, and we have been wired to satisfy those expectations. It can be easy to accept the things you know don't make sense to you when you refer back to the relationships in your family that are dysfunctional. We may have been programmed with a false sense of normal, compelling us to allow destructive behavior, which we've seen the women that came before us allow. We can be reluctant to break those chains of dysfunction that bind us, but we shouldn't allow ourselves to be crippled or held captive by fear.

We've all been there before, and it doesn't feel good. I'm a quick study. Once I realized my intuition would never steer me wrong, I refused to let anyone talk me out of it. When RaaShaun still tries it on occasion (because even the best men do), I make it clear that I am fully aware of the tactic and that he is wasting his time and effort. And when he pretends he still doesn't understand after I've explained myself thoroughly, I tell him I'm his wife, not his teacher, and it's on him to do the work and figure it out.

As women, we have to regain trust in ourselves. We need to honor that we know better when we do, and we must refuse to shrink because the world tells us it will make men feel better. We deserve the truth; our relationships thrive on honest communication. The men who love us should be willing to give us that. So the next time he tries to mind-bleep you, cut him off at the pass and let him know you're not falling for it.

And let's be real: women are capable of this mind-bleeping as well. So it's important for everyone in a relationship to recognize these signs and honor their gut instincts.

———————

6. How I Became DJ Envy (Envy)

In high school, I was zoned to attend Andrew Jackson High School in Queens. Many people know it from the cover of LL Cool J's *Bigger and Deffer* album. The first school in the United States to implement metal detectors, and one of the worst schools in the country—my parents were adamant that I wouldn't be going there. They enrolled me in a Catholic school, but to get there, I had to take the city bus every day.

One day, I was at the bus stop and a kid I knew named Ernesto Shaw pulled up, driving a Honda Accord. Back then, if you had an Accord, you were the shit! You were on top of the world and making it. He was an acquaintance. We lived on the same block, across the street from each other. Though he's just a few years older than me, growing up, we used to ride bikes with each other and played basketball together a few times. We were neighbors but not necessarily friends. When I saw him pull up, I ran over to him. "Yo, what are you doing to pay for this car?" I asked him. "How are you making all this money?" Sensing that I was serious, Ernesto told me to come to his mother's house after school.

Ernesto's mom's house was about six houses from mine. I hopped off the bus and headed straight there. His mother answered the door. "Is Ernesto home?" I said. She replied, "Yes, he's downstairs, come on in." When I entered the basement, I saw all kinds of records, tape decks, CD players, microphones, and some machines I'd never seen before in my life! It looked like he had a Guitar Center store in his crib. "What the fuck are you doing down here," I asked him. "I'm a DJ" is all he said to me. "Dude, I thought you were selling drugs." Ernesto shook his head and laughed. "Nah, I'm a DJ." "Well, what's your DJ name?" I asked him. He replied, "DJ Clue."

Finding out Ernesto was DJ Clue was crazy, because I'd been bootlegging his mixtapes and selling them for extra money. See, the thing is, Clue's identity was a mystery. Hence the name "Clue." He never put his face on his mixtape covers, so no one had any idea who he was. He played so many new records that were exclusive, unreleased, or leaked that he never wanted people to connect him to his mixtapes. If they did, it would have created beef with artists and made him a target. For him, it was about the music and building a brand that didn't center on his identity. Nobody knew Ernesto was DJ Clue; that was part of the allure. It was genius! Seeing all he had and his accomplishments at such a young age inspired me. "Yo, this is what I want to do."

One of my best friends at the time, Renan Thybulle, was a talented musician. Like his father, he played every instrument. His father also had DJ equipment, so Renan knew a little bit about that, as well. We decided that we'd do it together and formed Envy Productions. Two black boys at a predominantly white high school, where we'd always get into trouble. Whenever we did, we'd always say it was because everyone "envied" us. That's where the name came from. He was DJ Mono and I was DJ Shrimp, a name I got for being five foot four in high school.

We were doing mixtapes and parties, trying to do everything we could to make money, but we weren't making any. One day, Mono came to me and broke the news: "Look, we ain't making no money. You can keep deejaying if you want to. I'm going to holla at these girls." At the time, I was super slow and wasn't focused at all on chasing girls. I decided to stick with the deejaying. Plus, even if it wasn't paying off right now, I knew that it would eventually. Clue was proof of that. I just kept practicing in our basement and creating mixtapes. When we were Envy Productions, our mixtapes only said "Envy" on the cover. When I'd take my mixtapes to the bootleggers, they'd ask, "Yo, you got that new Envy?" And the name just stuck.

So I dropped Shrimp and officially became DJ Envy. Despite becoming taller eventually, I'd like to think it was a good move.

REFLECTIONS

Dahlia Haynes

I've known Gia since we were fourteen and sophomores in high school. I came directly from Jamaica and transferred to a private all-girl school in Brooklyn. Being a predominantly white institution, it had a small group of black students to connect with culturally. When I started high school here, I was very quiet and reserved. Funnily enough, Gia was instrumental in bringing me out of my shell. She would go out of her way to connect with me, sneaking up behind me at my locker and tickling me all the time. Then she'd run down the hallway laughing! It used to drive me crazy, but that was just Gia recognizing a shy, quiet girl and reaching out to pull me into being social.

Eventually, she invited me to sit by her at lunch, which led to us realize we had even more in common—her being Jamaican, our love of reggae music, fashion, and jokes. We quickly became best friends. When I think back on that time, Gia was and still is the person who makes it her responsibility to make people feel comfortable and included: a rare trait in the bullying world of high school. It's interesting that, because of how Gia looked, people didn't take it at face value—they wanted to assume the worst. But I am a direct example of experiencing her goodness and her heart and the strength that she had facing all those challenges.

Gia is one of the strongest women I know. Growing up together, seeing her face so many challenges, I watched her rise above it all. From being viciously attacked- which stemmed from jealousy about her physical appearance, the loss of her father and mother, the constant bullying she endured, her positive outlook on life has never wavered.

Watching Gia navigate the cruelties of life, I have seen firsthand how she has managed to look at what life has thrown her, still manage to laugh and smile, and still put people first in her thoughts and actions. Where many would have crumbled under pressure, Gia has only persevered and risen to be the woman she is today—successful, strong, beautiful, kind, considerate, and loving. She is my best friend forever!

Rasheed McWilliams

In the fall of 2000, my wife, Sasha, and I moved to Queens Village, New York, so that I could attend law school at NYU. As I was spending almost all my time studying, I wanted to encourage my wife to engage with friends. The only friend she had who lived close was Gia, whom she'd met in freshman year of college. She always described Gia as her friend who was both extremely intelligent and extremely pretty and happened to be in love with a guy named RaaShaun, who was professionally known as "DJ Envy."

At the time, I was commuting to school in the Village on the F train, and every day I would hear mixtapes playing from the bootleg stands, stores, and vehicles on Hillside Avenue. In Queens, the mixtape game was completely dominated by two names—DJ Clue and DJ Envy. I honestly thought RaaShaun might be a little Hollywood because of how big his name was in New York.

At our first meeting, I quickly realized I was apprehensive for nothing and we had a lot in common. We were the same age, born roughly a month apart, and both ambitious graduates of HBCUs, Morehouse and Hampton, respectively. We would get to know each other better over the years as we became closer as couples. He and I were not always close friends, but over time we have become more family than friends.

What I want others to appreciate about RaaShaun is that he is so much more than an entertainer. He approaches his life with an intense desire to be the best in everything. And watching his growth as a man of God, husband, father, businessman, and entertainer has been inspiring. RaaShaun is a man of faith who leads his family as God leads him. By putting God first, he has been blessed with a very large and loving family. I know that he is extremely proud of the life that he has built with Gia for his family and works hard to not only provide for his family, but also be a better person for them. Despite how hard he works, RaaShaun is always present as a dad, whether attending ball games, community plays, or equestrian events.

Without a doubt, RaaShaun is the hardest-working man I know. I have watched him live off of naps for more than twenty years to fulfill his ambition to be the biggest DJ in hip-hop and an extremely successful businessman. He is loyal to his friends and family; the same people who are close to RaaShaun today have been around the entire time I have known him. His faith and loyalty are two of the main components of his success, allowing him to achieve his dreams—including being inducted into the Radio Hall of Fame as a member of *The Breakfast Club*.

RaaShaun's extraordinary journey shows you what a kid from Queens can accomplish with faith, ambition, hard work, discipline, and talent.

Sasha McWilliams

I truly believe that God placed Gia Grante at Old Dominion University, in the fall of 1996, with a purpose and plan to transition a beautiful, intelligent, and confident seventeen-year-old girl into a classy, fearless, and purpose-driven woman.

Gia Casey would reenter my life in September 2001 as a wife and mother-to be. From that moment, I would witness her growth, which truly has been amazing to watch. She has faced the highs and lows of life with grace, dignity, and strength. She has always found a way to balance her role as a wife, mother, daughter, sister, aunt, and friend. The knowledge she has gained navigating the rigors of life has only made her stronger, and now she inspires women through the *Casey Crew* podcast with her knowledge about familial and marital relationships. I believe that through the trials and tribulations she has faced in her life, she has learned that life is not a fairy tale and situations are not always black or white. She has demonstrated that forgiveness is the key to repairing any broken relationship. Her recent growth has also come from the development of her personal relationship with God.

I knew that Gia would be a great mother from the first moment I watched her in the hospital singing "Happy Birthday" to Madison to celebrate her first twenty-four hours in the world. That was a moment of pure joy and love. Through the years, I have witnessed the bond she establishes with each of her

children, spending individual time, providing emotional and physical attention, and showing a nonstop dedication to their growth and development. The
nurturing care that Gia received from her parents, Tony and Norma Grante,
has been reflected in her daily parenting methods. For example, Gia is the
"chief cuddler" of the family. Gia's compassion for the people she loves is one
of her greatest qualities.

I have seen Gia's inner strength, especially during the various difficulties that
have arisen. Watching her climb out of the deepest pit of her life, while pregnant with London and under public scrutiny, left me in awe. She became
determined to climb out of the pit, while holding on to God and to RaaShaun's
hands, for better or worse. I admire her willingness and commitment to
rebuild the dynamics within her marriage, especially with God as the foundation, with four balanced pillars, which are spiritual, mental, emotional, and
physical components, versus the "fire and desire" roller-coaster relationship
she and RaaShaun had in the past. Gia has had to learn that sometimes,
ultimately, the battle is the Lord's, in turn strengthening her faith in God.
Her fortitude to prevail through life's difficulties over and over is inspiring,
especially as she walks toward her purpose and destiny.

Recently, I again witnessed a tough time in Gia's life with the sudden death of
her mother, while she was in the first trimester with her sixth child. Through
it all, this amazing woman was able to remain present for her husband, children, family, and friends, all while grieving. The knowledge and life skills she
has gained will be a tremendous advantage for her children as they mature
into adults and begin to maneuver through all that life will throw at them.
Gia constantly demonstrates an inner strength that is astonishing when you
reflect on all of the ups and downs that she has faced in her life. God has truly
blessed Gia with beauty, brains, and a kind heart.

———————

Part One Q&A

I've realized I'm the type to become consumed in my relationships and have lost touch with a lot of my friends. How do I apologize and attempt reconnection?

ENVY: My wife is my best friend, and my friends are also my wife's friends. When you are as wrapped up in your relationship as I am, it may seem like you don't have time for your friends, and that's understandable. There is, however, a happy medium. If you bring your friends into your relationship, and bring your relationship into your friendships, there is room for everyone to coexist and to cultivate all the relationships simultaneously. My wife and I do a lot of couples' nights, because it's the best of both worlds. And if you have friends who don't have significant others, then you need figure out a way to ensure your partner feels comfortable around them and they don't feel like the odd one out. Your friends should understand that your spouse is the priority. I don't believe that an apology is necessary, just thoughtful and intentional consideration of your friends' role in your life.

GIA: The truth is that it is perfectly natural to be caught up in the whirlwind of a new relationship. And to be honest, most, if not all, of us would consider ourselves lucky if that whirlwind continues to swirl years later. Friends should, first, be understanding and happy for you and champion the success of your relationship; second, be supportive in their words and actions; and third, be tolerant, playing their position in the hierarchy of interpersonal relationships by realizing that once a person finds a potential life partner, that partner typically becomes number one on the list. You should be honest by communicating to your friend that being in a relationship puts you in a position to have to negotiate your time and attention. Explain that while you may not have much experience doing that, you are willing and eager to learn, in order to reverse the hurt you have caused. Commit to leveling out your relationships so that you will be able to maintain all of them in a healthy way, but never by compromising your priorities.

I love my husband and my children dearly, but it seems that being a wife and a mom has completely taken over my identity. How do I find "me" again?

GIA: First, you begin by internalizing that being wife and a mom is, in fact, part of your identity. Understand that there is nothing wrong with that and be very proud. Catering to that part of your life doesn't necessarily mean that you lost "you." It simply means that you have been prioritizing the newer you that emerged when you took on those roles. You don't have to find "you" again. You just have to learn how to *balance* "you" so that you are not only fair to your husband and children, but fair to yourself as well. The goal is to become even-keeled. What we all must understand is that when we are happy within ourselves, we are at our best for those whom we love. Because of this, it is pertinent that we engage in things that enrich our minds, bodies, and souls. This may mean that, on occasion, we put ourselves first. This may include setting aside time for reading, working out, traveling with friends, taking a class, going out on Friday nights, sleeping in on Sunday mornings, meditating, reconnecting with your "inner sexy," or doing *whatever* it is that makes you feel solid. Know that these are not things to feel guilty about (like many wives and mothers do). Rather, you must view it as insurance that you will show up as a *whole* you when your family needs you—not an impatient you, an irritable you, an exhausted you, a resentful you, or a you that is mentally spent. So rejoice in enjoying life, aside from your family, because those who love themselves first (but after God) are best equipped to give to the world.

ENVY: When you're married with a family, it's hard to find "me time." You are more likely to have "we" time. And if you have kids, especially six like we do, both "me time" and "we time" are damn near impossible. Not to sound all stiff and formulaic, but scheduling "me time" is probably the only way you're going to get it. Gia and I always try to find time for ourselves. It could be something small like watching my favorite TV show or getting a couple's massage. Those are things we like to do together, and in my mind, that fulfills my "me time" itch. But I'm not gonna act like I don't get time to myself when I need it. Gia can sense when I am overworked and overwhelmed. In those cases, she will do things to make sure that I have alone time to unwind, like taking all of the kids out for the day or setting up the guest room in our house with dinner, candles, a scented diffuser, and other creature comforts, so that I can have an early night's sleep. Efforts like this show true partnership and understanding of your loved one's needs. And as her husband, I return the favor when I know that she needs it as well.

Recently, I've accepted that I'm too controlling and domineering with my family. They've given me countless chances to change, but I never did, and now I'm about to lose them. What should I do?

ENVY: Men get a bad rap for being controlling. Yeah, I said it! But a lot of times, we are. Admittedly, I was controlling in the past. I always thought I was gonna lose my wife, and I thought being controlling would keep her home and away from another man. That was my way of making sure she never left me. I know now that my controlling attitude was pushing my wife away from me. I had to learn that my wife loved me just as much as I loved her. I had to really trust in our relationship. I'm not gonna lie. It took me years to figure this out. But once I did, it unlocked new levels like a game of Super Mario. Learning more about myself (I know, adults call this *growth*) gave me a new kind of power. Not the dominating, controlling power that I initially sought when I was insecure in my relationship. But a power over my own actions. I had to conquer my own insecurities, and once I did that, there wasn't a controlling bone left in my body. Am I exaggerating a little? Maybe, but Gia knows how much I've grown. Being controlling in your relationship is usually a sign of your own weakness. It can mean that you're insecure about something in your life, or that you have an unhealthy amount of fear inside of you. Let it go. You have to look at yourself and be complete, so that you can put trust in your relationship. Many men want to wear the pants in their family; I get it, but those times are long gone. As real men, we must explore constructive ways of making and keeping our relationships healthy.

GIA: First things first: You must start by coming to terms with *why* you are controlling and domineering. Consider nature versus nurture. Try to figure out how much of your personality is attributed to each. How much is a result of your natural personality versus the amount that was shaped by unpleasant things that you have endured? We experience things in our lives, both consciously and subconsciously, that are largely responsible for the people we ultimately become. Once we identify the root, we are in a better position to rectify the problems that have subsequently developed. You have pushed your loved ones away and have become seemingly unbearable. It is *your* job to figure out why this is your reality, how to *stop*, make amends, encourage the forgiveness of those whom you've offended and commit to changed behavior. The key is figuring yourself out first.

I haven't been in a significant relationship in more than ten years. My friends say I'm asking for too much, but I don't think there's anything wrong with having standards. Am I the reason I'm having a hard time finding love?

GIA: Ten years is a very long time for a person who wants to be in a relationship to *not* be in a relationship. At this point, you must stand back, take stock, and access what role you have played in this outcome. It is likely that you bear some of the responsibility. While having standards is necessary, so is being realistic. The expectations that you have of a potential mate cannot simply be reduced to a punch list. Their value cannot be assessed by your ability to check items off a list. "The Two Cs" (as I like to call them), chemistry and connection, do not inherently come along as the bonus prizes because your "candidate" met every *other* piece of your criteria on your list. They are not a given. They must simply exist. A big heap of your expectations must rest right there. Pay attention to the important things. Give a person a chance by appreciating and enjoying them as an individual. See if the the Two Cs can live in a relationship between the two of you first, before you start deducing everything that person is not.

ENVY: Having standards is not a problem, but having standards that are unattainable is a different story. It's okay to be picky—to a certain degree, and it's certainly okay to have a preference. But don't fall in love with the idea of who you think someone is, their representative, or the idea of a relationship. You're picky about what you want, but do you really know what you are in pursuit of during this process? Having standards and being picky are two different things. Having standards is reasonable. Being picky comes from a place of negativity. I believe that most people want to be with someone who is attractive, intelligent, sexy, loyal, and in possession of goals. The list of what you want grows as you get older. But once you figure out what it is that you like, make sure the person you "pick" truly possesses those qualities. Don't get your standards confused with seeking perfection and fooling yourself into believing that what you see is going to be exactly what you get. No one is perfect. Perfection is an illusion that you can get caught up in when you are scrolling through your Instagram feed and photos. They may look nice with the filter and go well with a snarky caption, but in real life, the imperfections are loud. I think a lot of times people are looking for the perfect person, and perfection doesn't exist in human form. Give that less-than-perfect person a chance, and it might change your view on life or your life altogether.

———

PART TWO:

Love
and
Relationships

There are some who would say that falling in love is the easy part. *Staying* in love and choosing your partner each and every day is what takes work. We're inclined to agree. Unlike most couples, the biggest challenge in our relationship played out in public and threatened everything we'd worked to build and create. These essays tell the truth of what happened and how, through forgiveness and faith in God, we were able to get back on track. Every relationship will be faced with hard times. How we respond to them says everything about the love we want and what we're willing to do to get it.

7. What Happened (According to Him)

"When are you coming home?" Gia asked. It wasn't an uncommon question. We talk several times during my commute between our house and the radio station. Usually, to tell each other about our days. She could also need a number of things, from asking me to pick up something from the grocery store or having one of those weird pregnancy cravings. At the time she was three months pregnant with our third child. I told her I was about fifteen minutes away; she was heading home too. "Well, when you get home, we need to talk." During our entire relationship, I can count on one hand all the times Gia said we "needed to talk." She rarely said it, and it was always reserved for something serious. Immediately, I got nervous.

"Talk about what," I asked her.

"We'll talk about it when you get home." Gia was insistent and eerily calm.

Whatever she wanted to talk about, I didn't want to wait.

"Where are you right now?"

Gia told me she was about to pass a Home Depot about thirty minutes from our house, and I told her to pull into the parking lot. She did and I raced to meet her, pushing that Dodge Charger to its limits. While driving to meet my wife, I wondered who'd told her. She had a friend who was well connected in the industry. I despised that relationship for this very reason. I knew the closer the two of them became, the more obligated she'd feel to tell Gia if she'd heard anything. Social media apps and black celebrity gossip blogs were starting to become more and more popular. Thankfully, Gia was on none of them. She wasn't on any forms of social media and was hyper-focused on being a mother. Taking care of Madison and Logan and preparing for the new baby kept her pretty busy. But that didn't mean something hadn't hit the blogs and someone else hadn't informed her. I called my manager, Carl "June" Blair, to see if he'd seen anything. He did a quick internet search, checking the apps and blogs. There was nothing. And truthfully, there shouldn't have been; my indiscretion was almost three years old at the time. As I was approaching Gia, I still had no idea what she knew, how much she knew, or who told her. But after learning that my antics weren't in the digital streets, I figured I could lie my way out of it. When I got out of my car and hopped into the passenger side of Gia's Range Rover, I had only one mission: Deny! Deny! Deny!

Honestly, I have no clue what Gia said to me in that car. For me, it wasn't about listening to what she said as much as it was about coming up with a defense. If I had a response for everything she said, hopefully that would show her how ridiculous this all was, and my wife would believe me instead of whatever she'd heard and whoever she'd heard it from. "Do you know how many of those bitches would love to be where you are?! They're lying because they're jealous and they don't want to see you happy!" I pulled out all the stops, every single trick in my bag. I yelled. I cried. I turned it around on who-ever had told her this foolishness and on her for believing it. I did whatever I could to make myself the victim. In many ways, I (wrongly) thought I was. I was guilty of what my wife had always referred to as "mind-bleeping." I felt as though I had no choice. I'd been completely blindsided with no ability to form a proper defense. I couldn't even face my accusers. I didn't know who they were, and Gia wouldn't tell me. I couldn't keep it up anymore. Her demeanor was calm and collected; it almost seemed sinister and it scared me. "I'm sorry," I said. Even though I don't remember much of what she said, I heard the most important part. Gia said the "D" word. "Divorce." Immediately, I stopped all my unsuccessful denials and studied her face. She was steadfast. She never cried, and she was clear. My wife didn't want to be my wife anymore.

I knew that I wasn't going to be able to get out of this by denying everything, so I decided to give Gia something. A partial truth was better than a com-plete lie. I confessed to Gia that I'd cheated but said it had only happened once. I told her that it was the biggest mistake of my life and I would never do it again. Gia thanked me for being honest and told me that she was still proceeding with the divorce. In fact, she told me that she was heading back to our home to tell my mother that the Christmas holiday was canceled. My mom was there, preparing for our family and friends to arrive in a few days. Gia made it clear that was no longer happening. It felt like all the air left my body. I was struggling to breathe and comprehend what was happening. Everything I'd worked so hard for was gone in an instant. I'd been with Gia since we were fifteen and sixteen years old. She was my best friend. She was the love of my life. We'd created a beautiful family together and it was still growing. I'd thrown that all away, and for what?! Ego? Insecurity? I'd disappointed the one person who had always had my back. When Gia drove off, I sat on the curb crying and thinking about just how irreparably I'd fucked up.

That drive home felt like the longest drive in my life, as I thought about what I'd done and why. The truth is, as I mentioned before, I was riddled with insecurity. Growing up, I wasn't the guy that the girls ran after, and to wind up with someone as beautiful as Gia kept me on edge. I always thought that it was only a matter of time before she found someone who was better than me. And truthfully, I had a deep-seated resentment toward her for "making me" feel this way. In all actuality, she had never done anything to feed that feeling. I was subconsciously holding her responsible and punishing her for the way I felt inside. Even though she'd done nothing to make me believe she'd leave, I was angry that I felt that way, and the only one I could blame was her. Add to that, right before I cheated, Gia told me she'd been faking orgasms for a number of years in our relationship. With that confession, she called my ability to please her into question. I needed to feel desired, to feel like a man who could satisfy. And the opportunities were right in front of me. Gia was far removed from the industry and my life outside the home, so there never really seemed to be a threat of her finding out. Or so I thought.

A pain formed in the pit of my stomach. I knew that by the time I got home, Gia would have told my mother and I would have the two most important women in my life disappointed in me. I'd done some stupid things before—the coming-of-age bullshit that some young men do when they're trying to find themselves. Even though she knew she'd taught me better, what would my mother think of me now? I wasn't just her son who messed up. I was a man who'd broken the heart of a woman and destroyed my family. That story was a tale as old as time, and women stood with each other in moments like these. I'd already broken Gia's heart and trust. The reality I'd done the same with my mother was another hurtful blow. When I got home, Gia and my mother were in the kids' playroom. When I saw my mom's face, full of sadness and disappointment, I broke down. I apologized to her. I apologized to Gia again. I knew I didn't deserve their forgiveness, but I wanted it. I needed it.

We don't talk a lot about black men and depression, and we talk even less about the dark thoughts black men have about life when they've failed or fucked up. I was moving through depression and some real darkness. Every day, it became a chore to wake up. I couldn't eat. I couldn't sleep. I couldn't work. With each new day, I had to face the reality that I was losing my family.

"We don't talk a lot about black men and depression, and we talk even less about the dark thoughts black men have about life when they've failed or fucked up." —**ENVY**

It was excruciating. I sat down with Madison and Logan, ten and eight at the time, and told them Daddy made a big mistake and cheated on Mommy. I decided to tell them because, ultimately, my actions affect them too. Their mother was hurt, and what I did was going to potentially destroy the only home they'd ever known. I owed it to them to tell the truth, even if it meant losing their respect and admiration. I made my bed and had to lie in it. Watching them react to hearing what would be their new normal—me no longer living there and them being shuttled between two homes—I couldn't look at myself without complete hatred.

My career was on the rise, but that shit doesn't matter when home isn't good. I would go to work, do *The Breakfast Club*, and in between takes, I would lie on the floor and pity myself. Other times, I would find a quiet space to be alone because I didn't believe I deserved to be around anybody and had nothing worthwhile to contribute. At the time, I wasn't able to be good at my job. I wasn't able to be good at anything. Gia showed me compassion by letting me know that she didn't hate me, she just no longer wished to be my wife. One thing that I knew about her is that when she said something, she meant it. She didn't mince words about her is that when she said something, she meant it. She didn't mince words and didn't bullshit. But even knowing that, I hoped with everything I had that she still had room in her heart for me. That hope was crushed when my manager informed me of a conversation that he'd had with her.

Gia made it clear that, even though our relationship was ending, we still had three children who would need both of us. Although we wouldn't be together, she wanted to act as a unit. She was willing to be more than amicable. She was willing to be friends.

In that moment, I saw an opportunity. I asked Gia for some grace. "Give me two weeks," I said to her. All I needed was two weeks to remind her of who I was at the core, prove to her that I'd changed, and convince her that I would never break her trust again. She turned me down. I begged and begged. Finally I told her that if I wasn't able to make her fall in love with me again during that time, I would let her go (even though I knew I would never be able to do that). She felt my desperation and reluctantly agreed. I knew there was still some love left.

If you ask me, the next two weeks were amazing. We were back to dating again. We were going out to parties and industry events together. As usual, we were having mind-blowing sex. But, more importantly than that, we were talking. We were talking about the insecurities that had caused me to cheat. Gia asked pointed questions, and this time, I didn't do any of that partial-truth shit. I told her everything, and I mean everything. I wanted my family back, and I wanted her to trust me again. The fact that she didn't call off the two-week trial after I told her the full truth—that I'd cheated and why—gave me some hope. Whatever painful moments were happening now wouldn't last long. I was getting my wife back. Or so I thought.

Gia and I spent an evening partying together at an event I had to host. I felt good about the night; we were getting back to us. The next day, my manager called and told me that it wasn't looking good for me. "She still wants a divorce." Initially, I dismissed it. I love June; he's my man. But he didn't know what he was talking about. He was insistent. He had learned things about Gia that I had already known but was scared to come to terms with. She'd told him plan was already in place. She was only giving me time—those two weeks—to get myself together before she moved on to next steps. He warned, "Bro, she's serious. It's over." He continued, "To her, those last two weeks were only the last hurrah." He said that Gia told him the night before that she was still moving forward with the divorce. I could hear the conviction in his voice. I was devastated. I went to work the next morning feeling numb. If I wasn't sure of it before, I was sure of it now and was desperate. I was willing to do anything.

My cohosts knew something was wrong, and it was Charlamagne tha God who finally asked me; I told him the truth. "You should call her on air and apologize," he suggested. Angela Yee told me that was the worst thing I could do. I should've listened to her. Instead, in despair, I called Gia when we went back on air. This was my *"anything."* At the time, Gia was pregnant with our third child, and instead of mentioning the affair and apologizing for cheating, I apologized for the ways I neglected to be as attentive as I could be to her during her pregnancy. I told her that I loved her. Surely, professing my love across the airwaves would let her know that I adored her and buy me some more time. When Gia said, "We'll talk about this when you get home," it was clear it hadn't. I *really* should have listened to Angela.

The days to follow were absolutely shitty. She was livid about the on-air call.

Nothing I could do was right, and nothing I could say would change Gia's mind. She was adamant. We were financially secure; I'd done everything I could do to make sure my family would be taken care of in case anything ever happened to me. To be honest, they didn't really need me; at least not in that way. *I don't deserve her. I don't deserve my kids. They'd be better off without me. See, she is too good for me after all.* These were all the notions that were creeping in and beginning to fester. Dark thoughts about how killing myself was the best option for her and the kids weren't just thoughts anymore. I made them known. I continuously told Gia that she and the kids would be better off without me. Without her, I didn't want to be here anymore; I didn't want to live. I was never able to imagine life without Gia. I needed her—in every sense of the word. She was my lifeline, and that life was imploding. What I wasn't able to accept within myself was that I was the one who had lit the match. It's able to accept within myself was that I was the one who had lit the match. It's crazy because I felt two competing emotions: I wanted my old life back, and I wanted to end my life at the same time. Having both wasn't an option. I didn't know what to do. I'd never felt so low in all my life.

The depression and darkness were drowning me. I was fighting against these forces at the same time as I was fighting to get my family back. When I learned that there was nothing I could do to bring us back to who we used to be, the darkness won. I was ready to go. Everyone I loved would be better off without me, and I would feel relief if I were just dead. In my mind, the pain would be gone. Gia would find someone else who would treat her better than I ever had and would be a better example for my children. In the moment, suicidal thoughts made all the sense in the world; when you are that broken, nobody can tell you otherwise. I don't remember what I said as I stormed past her into our garage. Maybe that doesn't even matter. But I do remember Gia beating on the garage door and trying to open it while I turned on every one of our

> "In the moment, suicidal thoughts made all the sense in the world; when you are that broken, nobody can tell you otherwise." —ENVY

six cars. As I lay on the floor next to one of them, I closed my eyes and readied myself for what would happen. For whatever reason, the roar of all the engines still couldn't drown out Gia's screams. It seemed like the last thing I would hear would be her voice. That felt like a little bit of karma. My phone rang; it was Rasheed. He and I weren't friends. We were just the husbands of best friends. I didn't know why he was calling me. Nevertheless, something made me answer. That's another one of those conversations where I don't remember what was said, but I ended it quickly. I had a job to do, and I needed to focus.

There were no words to express how disappointed I was in myself, and I was ready to end the pain. A few minutes later, I heard the sirens and the sounds of the garage door being pried open. It was the police and paramedics. Calmly, I surrendered to their custody. As I was being carted into the ambulance, eyes, even as Gia and I tried to convince them that everything would be okay. Even if I didn't know if that was true.

I couldn't believe Gia called the cops on me. My anger at my life's circumstances was now directed at her. Here I am having to give these people my cell phone, belt, and shoelaces. All I could think about were the headlines: DJ ENVY TRIES TO COMMIT SUICIDE. I was in a bad place, but this wasn't the way to handle it; she should've just let me go. Even as the doctors began to tell me how long they were going to keep me for observation, I was planning my escape. I couldn't rely on my parents for assistance. Gia had already rallied them and they were on her side, believing I needed to do whatever was necessary to get well. But help for me didn't include a hospital. I had two cell phones, though, and they didn't ask if I owned a second after I gave the first one to them. So I texted my friend Lil Shaun and told him to pull up to the back of the hospital and leave the back door of his car open. When Lil Shaun got there, he texted me that he was waiting and the door was open. The security guards did their shift rotations, checking on all the mental health patients. As this was happening, there was about a ten-second window for me to make my move. While the guard was distracted, I jumped off the bed and ran like my life depended on it. They began chasing me. Gia and my parents were screaming. I ignored them, ran into an orderly, knocked him over, and sent his tray of food flying into the air. I ran right through the door, not waiting for its motion sensor, colliding with it and taking it off its hinges. I jumped in Lil Shaun's back seat, headfirst, and he sped away with my legs still dangling out the door. I hid out with him that night. I didn't answer Gia's calls or any from my parents because I knew I wouldn't be able to lie about where I was. I couldn't go home because the police would be there waiting for me, and the next morning, I was given a heads-up that the police were at the radio station. I was scheduled to deejay an event that night that I was never planning on making it to. The promoter called me. He asked me if everything was okay. I told him everything was straight but that I wouldn't be able to make it. He told me that he already knew because the police contacted him looking for me, expecting me to be at the club. He said that there was a BOLO out on me.

said that there was a BOLO out on me.

"What the hell is that?" I asked.

He responded, "Be on the lookout for."

Apparently, leaving the hospital the way I did, as a mental health patient, is not allowed. There was no place I could run. I had to go back to the hospital. The last place I wanted to be was in the hospital. Gia spent two days there with me. This is one of the reasons I loved her so much. Regardless of what I had put her through, she always put me first. She was strong enough to do that. And I wasn't always that strong for her. She is a nurturer. Feeling her arms around me gave me a sense of comfort that I never wanted to lose. I would have lain in that bed forever if it meant that time could stand still. She was able to make me realize that, despite what I was feeling, my life was important to all who loved me and still worth living.

I successfully convinced Gia that I would never let the depths of despair consume me again. She saw fit to sign me out, believing I was no longer a risk to myself and others. On the way home, Gia told me that Rasheed would be staying with us for a few days. What?! Why?! If he was coming to the East Coast for business, I would gladly put him up in a hotel. Coming home from the hospital, plus having my depression and suicide attempt known to others—let's just say his visit was the last thing I needed. Gia was insistent that he was coming to help us. What could Rasheed help us with?! He didn't even *like* me—probably because he also believed that Gia was too good for me. Well, I couldn't blame him. But I wasn't in a position to put my foot down about anything. Honestly, I didn't want to fight. Not right then.

When Rasheed came in from LA, he was insistent that God sent him to us to help us through this and save our marriage. I wasn't so sure about all the God stuff, but I was open to anybody trying to help me convince Gia that we needed to stay together. Over and over again, Rasheed made it clear that the Lord had spoken to him, and God didn't want us to end our relationship. But if we were going to get back on track, we needed to be willing to do the work. I was ready to do whatever it took. Over the course of those two weeks Rasheed was with us, he led us in Bible studies and prayer time. Religion and church attendance weren't big in my house. Being an active churchgoer, who had a relationship with God, wasn't a priority for my parents. Essentially, all of this was new to me. Prayer and Bible study brought Gia and me closer together, but it did so much more than that. Rasheed introduced me to scriptures that talked about what it meant to be a Godly man and how Christian men should lead their home. I'd never had conversations like that before, and with Rasheed, I could be honest about that. The more I studied and the more I talked to God, the more I wanted to be better. I'd made the decision to stop cheating on Gia long before she ever found out about it—years before, actually—and I thought that was good enough. But my budding relationship with God showed me that was just the beginning. I had to peel back layers of insecurity and controlling behavior. I had to find the courage to be the man I'd been pretending

"I had to find the courage to be the man I'd been pretending to be." —ENVY

to be. Part of that meant accepting responsibility and accountability for my actions. It meant facing myself again and finally being honest with myself.

As my star began to rise, I began feeling myself a bit. The culture of hip-hop—mainly the money and the women—was more than I ever bargained for. And here I was, the guy who lucked out and got the prettiest girl in high school, and now I was the guy hanging out with some of the most successful names in entertainment. RaaShaun, the quirky kid with braces and glasses, was now DJ Envy, and that name meant something. I'd realized that, in this quest to get Gia and my family back, I'd not done anything to get back to myself. I needed to decide who I wanted to be and then do the work to be better. Had Rasheed not come and introduced me to a relationship with God, I don't believe I would have learned the difference between a good man and a Godly man. All my life, I'd been trying to be a good man—one who provides for his family and makes sure that they can live the life they desire. For some, that's enough, that's everything. But once I was introduced to the idea of a

Godly man—a man who allows integrity and principle to lead him—I wanted to be that. I wanted to regain the adoration of my family, especially my children. More than that, I wanted to be someone *I* could be proud of.

I was slowly trying to conceive of and process a life without Gia around the time when I got a call out of the blue from Tyrese Gibson. He and I weren't friends—aside from radio interactions, we'd never talked. But he reached out and told me he'd heard about what Gia and I were going through and wanted to do something special for us. We got the private room at the restaurant Philippe Chow, and, accompanied by a violinist and background singers, Tyrese performed his hit song "Stay." Then he sat and talked to us for hours. He offered Gia perspective on the thoughts of men, what leads us to cheat, and how a couple can bounce back from it if they are willing to put in the work. I have no idea why our marriage mattered so much to Tyrese when we didn't even know him. But he said God sent him, and I was grateful to anyone who was on the side of keeping my marriage and family together. Even though I was grateful to Tyrese, he wasn't saying anything I hadn't said, Rasheed hadn't said, and plenty of others hadn't said. Gia's mind was made up. We were done. While it was devastating to accept, I was trying to wrap my head and heart around it and begin my journey to becoming a better man, in hopes that one day she would respect me again. So imagine my surprise when Gia, while sitting at the table, looked at me and told me she was willing to give me another chance. This is one of those times when I wish my memory weren't trash, because I'd love to tell you what specifically was said that caused Gia's change of heart, but I can't. And maybe that's not important. What matters is that she told me that she was willing to forgive me and move forward. I made a vow to her that day that I'd never make her regret giving me another chance, and I'd spend the rest of my life living up to those words.

While I would love for someone like Rasheed and Tyrese to come to the rescue of every man who has fucked up like I did, I know that's not possible. And even though these brothers were there during the worse time in my life, there were still some things I should have done for myself. First, I didn't seek help for my suicidal thoughts. Black men have always been taught to bury our emotions, to keep pushing as if nothing happened. I don't know how it's possible to do

If you're experiencing suicidal thoughts—whether you want to act on them or not—you need to talk to a professional. Black men's mental health matters, but in order for us to be our best selves, we've got to let go of the ego or whatever fear we have that will keep us from being honest about the help we need and getting that help. We owe it to ourselves and the people who love us to be better.

Maybe you're reading this right now and you've been caught. My suggestion to you is to fully come clean so that true forgiveness and healing can take place. Maybe you're reading this and your wife or partner doesn't know what you've done. I have two words of advice for you: *Come clean.* You can't keep dishonoring the person you love and expect your relationship to last. At some point, it's likely to come out, and trust me when I say that you're not ready to come face-to-face with that kind of devastation. And even if it never comes out, it is a poison that will eat away at your relationship from within. If you need accountability, reach out to someone in your life that you trust and respect. They need to be someone who will hold you to your word and the life you say you want. They need to be someone who is strong enough to tell you to get your shit together.

Gia deserved so much better than what I did to her. I know that now. I knew it then. I wish it didn't take all the pain I caused her to see that. Forgiveness isn't guaranteed, but I thank God I got it. And I hope every man in my position, who's messed up but is willing to do the work to repair what they've broken, can get it too.

---

8. What Happened (According to Her)

I was at home, putting away the week's laundry when I remembered that RaaShaun had recently done a photo shoot and the pictures should have been available on the promotional sites by now. I grabbed my laptop, searched "DJ Envy," and waited for the most recent posts, which would undoubtedly be those pictures, to appear. I didn't find them. Instead, I found much more than I was looking for. A link to a thread on a gossip blog popped up. That was confusing, given that the thread itself wasn't about RaaShaun or "DJ Envy." This is probably how RaaShaun missed it when he googled himself to see if there was any information out there about his indiscretion. In the thread, two young women were going back and forth insulting each other. These gossip sites were known for this. That was fine; to each their own. But what did any of this have to do with my husband?

I continued reading, and it became clear. As the young women continued the name-calling and attacking each other's character and integrity, in one sentence—and one sentence only—one of them demeaned the other by accusing her of having performed a sex act on RaaShaun while knowing that he was married. And when accused, this woman didn't deny it. I sat there, stunned at this revelation. Two women I did not know were discussing my husband on a gossip blog, for public consumption. If I believed what I was reading, he had cheated. I closed the laptop, trying to make sense of this news and what it meant. It was difficult to digest, being that, in the eleven years of marriage that we had enjoyed up to that point, even with all its ups and downs, cheating had never been an issue. RaaShaun was loving, attentive, and affectionate. He always put my needs first and prioritized anything that would make me happy. Since the very beginning, he would say, "If you like it, I love it." Or, "Nothing makes me happier than being the one to put a smile on your face." And it was true. Because of him, I was always smiling. We had an amazing sex life; the chemistry between us was palpable. He was a doting husband and father who, along with me, rarely, if ever, missed our children's practices and games. He was a family man who was home for every holiday and would take three planes to get home in time for a special occasion if work was trying to keep him away. He was sweet, thoughtful, and generous. And the truth is that he was more romantic than I ever was. He never missed an opportunity to show me exactly how much he loved me.

These are just some of the many reasons I showed patience and understanding when it came to parts of our relationship that needed work. I *never* had a reason to suspect him of being unfaithful because, as that well-known saying goes, he always "took care of home." Even with all of the flaws (that I was aware of), he was an incredible husband who put me on a pedestal and made me feel adored and appreciated. Still, that didn't negate what I had just read, and I wanted to think through a strategy for bringing this up and getting to the truth.

When I asked him about it, he dismissed it. He didn't even flinch. The idea that he could be cheating was so illogical and far from our reality that he didn't even make any attempt to explain it away. In fact, he surmised that they'd probably gotten him confused with another popular DJ whose stage name also begins with the letter E. And it was a fair attempt on his part, considering I'd been with RaaShaun on several occasions when people came up to him and mistook him for the other famed New York DJ and radio personality. We'd always joke that the two of them look nothing alike, to be confused in this way, but people did it more often than you'd expect. Nonetheless, his rationale just didn't sit right with me. I had a nagging feeling about it that wouldn't go away. It was my intuition. The facts didn't add up, and I was like a dog with a bone. This wasn't simply a case of mistaken identity. My husband was lying to me. I didn't know to what extent, but he was lying. He firmly stated that it wasn't true, but logic and common sense dictated otherwise.

One thing that he—and anyone that knew me well—was aware of is that cheating was a deal breaker, under any circumstances. It is a line that cannot be uncrossed. I've always been good at follow-through. If I say that I am going to do something, I damn well do it. And I had always said that if the day ever came when I found out I'd been cheated on, that would be the last day of my marriage. I meant it. My mother raised me that way. I'm not weak and am certainly not someone to be played with or for a fool. Divorce would be the only option. And it would never matter how I actually *felt*. I couldn't allow that to be a factor. I have the ability to separate how I feel from what I do. Feelings? See, feelings cloud your judgment. And I had to be clear—very clear. It *did not matter* if I cried my face into a pillow every night for the rest of my life riddled with pain and longing, at least those tears would come along with self-respect and the fact that I did exactly what I always said I would do. There's a strange sense of power and pride that comes along with that. If he knew the consequences and did it anyway, there was nothing else to consider. Simple. This was my way of owning my emotions. Why waste time, energy, and tears? Not me. I was good at being deliberate, and he was going to learn exactly how good.

Because I couldn't let this go, I began turning over every aspect of our marriage in my head. That's what lies and secrecy do. In an instant, it can erode trust and make you question everything you knew to be true. It is like a fruit that is beautiful at first, then begins to rot until there is nothing left. Well, the rotting had begun. Is he really capable of this? Was he actually at a party that night or was he lying? Who else knew and covered for him? The endless questions you can ask yourself will drive you crazy, but more than that, the inability to get answers is the most frustrating part.

I couldn't look at any particular moment and see any signs or "red flags." RaaShaun was never different—always consistent. When he was away, he'd call me no less than every two hours, to tell me something that had happened, to check up on me, or just to tell me that he loved me. So much so that many of our friends made fun of us—constantly—thinking that we overcommunicated and were too "mushy." We often spoke to each other in an adoring way and used pet names regardless of who was around. That was always endearing to me about RaaShaun—he was always proud of and stood on his love for me. He talked about it openly to friends, amongst family, and on the radio, as well as other public platforms. It was obvious to me that he was a man that was proud of his wife and family.

I completely understood the nature of his profession and loved that I married someone who would work hard to provide for his family. We he came home, he was as into us as he was his profession—maybe more. So when I learned the possibility of his cheating, I couldn't make sense of it. How could he be so devoted to me and the life we created together and betray me at the same time? With such a beautiful life, why would he want to? How could someone who has repeatedly made it known that he couldn't live without me do the one thing it would take to ensure *that he would live without me?*

Here I was with two young children and one on the way, trying to make sense of the bomb that had just blown my life into pieces. Nothing was the same for me, and RaaShaun was holding fast to (what I believed to be) his lies. I needed to know the truth, and I needed to know it now. I knew that RaaShaun would never admit what I suspected to be true, so I would have to get creative. I had to devise a plan and back him into a corner, and I had to be convincing. I could never let him call my bluff. Even if he refused to tell me the truth, I could never alert him to the fact that I didn't actually *know* if any of this was true. All I had was my intuition, and for me, that was enough. So I had to commit. It was going to be a blatant accusation with the essence of certainty. I took a deep breath, called RaaShaun, and asked when he would be home from work. I'd had a doctor's appointment earlier that morning and was heading home. He told me that he was as well. I told him that when he got home, we needed to talk. Immediately, he was apprehensive. Even though I assured him that the baby was okay, he still didn't calm down. He kept asking me what we needed to talk about, and I insisted that we'd talk about it when we got home. But he wanted to talk about it right then. He asked for my exact whereabouts. I told him I was passing a Home Depot. I obliged when he asked me to pull into the parking lot and wait for him. As I sat in my car, I steadied and prepared myself for whatever would come from and after this conversation. I loved RaaShaun, but I couldn't stay with someone who would disrespect and take me for granted like this. We'd been through a lot—everything, in fact—but this was likely to be the beginning of the end.

When RaaShaun got in my car, I was calm and resolute. My voice never wavered, and I was sure. "Is there anything you want to tell me?" I asked him. RaaShaun looked at me, confused, and said no. I asked him again and, yet again, he said no. After giving him the opportunity to come clean, it was clear that subtlety had no place in this conversation: "Some things have come to my attention, and I know that you have been unfaithful. I just want you to know that I know and I have contacted a lawyer to begin divorce proceedings." First, RaaShaun just looked at me, bewildered. Then, he became utterly belligerent. He ranted and raved about how these women were jealous of me and would do anything to be in my shoes. He screamed, punched the side of the steering wheel repeatedly, and slammed his fists against the windshield and dashboard. I laughed . . . hard. He stopped and recoiled from me. Not this time, buddy. He looked at me with fear and confusion in his eyes.

Over the course of our entire relationship, RaaShaun had perfected obnoxious outbursts to quickly turn any anger about his behavior into sympathy. On many occasions he threatened his life, assuring me that I was all that mattered to him, and without me, he couldn't fathom the idea of living. Outside of our relationship, RaaShaun was extremely secure, competent, and self-reliant. But inside our relationship, and only when it came to me, he was very insecure, obsessive, and dependent. Even though I knew that he felt this way, I also believed that, at times, he used my sympathy as a way to manipulate me. For years, it worked. He controlled situations, playing on my tendency to nurture, knowing that I never wanted to see him hurt. The situation would shift from the matter at hand to doing whatever was needed to calm him down—which meant reassuring him that I wasn't going to leave him. That wasn't happening today. As I watched him pull out every trick in his playbook, I saw him and myself differently. What I didn't know for sure had been confirmed through his actions, and I wasn't going to be manipulated like that ever again.

When RaaShaun finished his performance, I told him that I wasn't *asking* him if this was true. Rather, I was *telling* him it was true. I wasn't interested in his confirmation or denial. I was simply informing him of what I knew as fact and my plans for proceeding. I urged him to stop his theatrics because he was only embarrassing himself. He sat with that for a few moments, understanding the seriousness of his response. Finally, and under duress, he told the truth (or at least part of it). "It's true, I cheated, but it only happened once." While I didn't know specifics, I was too smart to believe that this only happened once. But once, ten times, or twenty—it made no difference. Our trust had been breached and we were at the point of no return. In my mind, "It worked, it friggin' worked!!!" Because in all actuality, I knew nothing *at all*. I was only armed with suspicions. It was all a bluff. I resorted to this tactic because my intuition told me that I had to go the distance to reach peace of mind. The feeling of relief that came over me was almost tangible. This may be difficult to understand, but I honestly felt so happy. The months that I suffered though uncertainty, doubt, and the cruelness of my imagination were over. I was right! My intuition hadn't let me down. As women, mind-bleeping can leave us feeling crazy, as though we live in the twilight zone. But no, it's not all in your head, you don't have a persecution complex, and mistakes don't just happen. Nevertheless, I thanked him for his honesty. To even confess to cheating had taken more than what I believed he'd ever give me. But it didn't change anything. Divorce was imminent.

He was beyond devastated; he was ruined. In complete disbelief, and with all of the urgency imaginable, he begged and pleaded with me to let him explain. He wrapped his arms around me, buried hid face in my chest, and soaked my shirt with tears. I felt all of his raw emotion. But this time, I had no desire to make him feel better. I pried myself out of his grip and asked him to get out of my car. When I pulled out of the parking lot, I saw him in the rearview mirror, sitting on the curb with his head in his hands, processing all that he had lost.

The first order of business was figuring out what, at this point, would be best for my children and unborn baby. The next order of business, though, was to go straight home and tell his mother, who was helping me decorate, that Christmas would not take place at our home this year. Aside from ensuring that our children had an amazing holiday, I would do nothing to uphold the charade that my marriage and family were okay. I wouldn't give him the satisfaction of not having to deal with the consequences of his actions.

When I got home, I found my mother-in-law knee-deep in decorations and preparations. I told her she could stop. She looked perplexed as I explained why. My mother-in-law allowed me to speak my piece before she dismissed it

WHAT HAPPENED (ACCORDING TO HER)

all. "These girls are lying! They're just jealous because they don't have what you have and would say anything to destroy what the two of you have built!

> "I wouldn't give him the satisfaction of not having to deal with the consequences of his actions." —**GIA**

That boy loves you! He loves you more than anything!" Almost verbatim, she repeated the very same things RaaShaun had said in the car. She believed the best of him; so did I. I told her I would have agreed with her but for the fact that he had just confessed to me several minutes earlier. My mother-in-law, unable to comprehend all she'd just heard, moved into the kids' playroom so she could sit down. She was hurt. She was disappointed.

When RaaShaun came home shortly after and they saw each other, they both broke down. For a moment, I found myself consoling them, telling them that everything was going to be okay. I couldn't help but think how much this moment explained so much in my life. Here I was, comforting the man who'd

> "I couldn't help but think how much this moment explained so much in my life. Here I was, comforting the man who'd cheated on me and his mother while there was no one to comfort me." —**GIA**

cheated on me and his mother while there was no one to comfort me. Christmas came and RaaShaun couldn't bear the thought of coming downstairs and watching the kids open gifts because it would be too harsh a reminder of all the Christmases to come that we would not spend as a family.

As disappointed as I was in RaaShaun, and although I knew that I didn't want to be his wife any longer, I still loved him dearly. We'd cultivated a love that could never be duplicated, walking each other through more than half of our lives. In retrospect, we'd been two young and inexperienced teens—virgin and virgin-ish—who tried to take on the world together. And we did. His career began to flourish, and he found himself in a world that he

Pook and Daddy—husband and father—but when he was working, he was Envy—famous and flashy DJ. RaaShaun took out the garbage, picked kids up from school, and hosted barbecues, like he always wanted in his picture-perfect dreams. Envy was in three cities in three days, deejaying celebrity events, and constantly in the studio. RaaShaun was insecure and believed that I was too good for him—thinking that he had to *hold on* to me, rather than believing that I *wanted* to be there. In his mind, he couldn't loosen that grip, because if he hid, I'd soon be with someone "better"; while Envy was that guy who was "better"—on top of the world with girls who would be grateful for just one night with him. RaaShaun had me, two beautiful children, one on the way, and hopes of more, while Envy had groupies and girls stroking his ego every time he went out. Girls even wanted to sleep with his friends *just* because they were his friends. So imagine the "opportunities" he had.

As his friend, I understand the allure, confusion, and weight of all that—especially for someone who got married young, at twenty-three, with two and a half children and a wife that he felt he didn't deserve. In hindsight, he didn't possess the maturity to balance the juxtaposition between both. Being that I was his only significant sexual experience and relationship, how could he not be curious, especially given his lifestyle? I know that I was curious, and with far less exposure to the world than he'd had. I trusted him completely because I prioritized our love over curiosity and believed that he did the same. As a result, I encouraged him to take on more opportunities, to position himself for more desirable spots at the station, and to travel more to expand his brand. I wanted him to be his very best and acted as the driving force behind that. As his wife, I wanted to be his support system. I never complained that he worked too much or spent too much time away. I didn't want him to have the burden of having to worry about a needy wife at home or someone holding him back. I needed to be strong so that he could be strong.

I cherished him, not only as a husband, but also as a brother and friend. When I found out the truth—as his wife—I was confused and devastated. But as his sister and friend, I got it. If your boyfriend or husband cheats and gets caught, you respond to it with confusion and devastation, but if your brother cheats and gets caught, you respond to it with compassion and protection, cheats and gets caught, you respond to it with compassion and protection, thinking, "He messed up, but how can I help him get out of this?" As his wife, I wanted to see him suffer; as his sister and friend watching the torment that he was going through, I wanted to protect him and empathize with his feelings. Wearing many different hats in my relationship with him allowed me the advantage of many different perspectives. Clearly, from any perspective, he was wrong, but it allowed me the understanding to move forward with love and a continued friendship, rather than hate.

Unfortunately, he didn't want that friendship—not exclusively. If he couldn't have our relationship in the way that he'd grown accustomed to, he didn't want anything—not even life. I struggled to temper my need to leave "us" behind and feeling responsible for his well-being. Eventually, RaaShaun and I had a very specific conversation about his insecurities and how they fed into bouts of self-doubt and even moments of depression. Whether it was authentic or not, I could never ignore the threats. The one time I ignored him could be the time something actually happened, and I would never forgive myself for that. I heard the things he said to me. He was so ashamed, especially knowing the pedestal I had reciprocally put him on and how far he had fallen. He believed the kids and I would be better off if he were gone. He didn't feel as though he could face us. As we were going through the motions, he would hide out in the house, spending full days in the guest room, with the lights off and no food. He constantly spoke about himself in the past tense, but when he spoke of me and the kids, it was always in the present and future. I did my best to affirm that I still loved him and we needed him, even if we weren't going to be together. But that didn't work.

I was kind to him, believing that if I showed him that coparenting and coexisting could be much like marriage, he may see a bright side. I explained to him that as friends, we could still spend time together, raise our children, travel, and make future plans; that he could come over, spend the day, watch movies, and celebrate occasions with us. The only thing that would change is that we wouldn't belong to each other exclusively any longer. We wouldn't have an intimate, nor sexual, relationship. I emphasized that I did not hate him and still viewed him as a brother and friend. RaaShaun got up from the table, ran him get clean. He told me that the thought of me being with someone else sexually made him sick to his stomach. I was at an impasse. He left me and went back to the guest room.

Later, that evening, he appeared in our room to explain that he didn't take my friendship for granted and appreciated the kindness I extended to him, acknowledging that anyone else would have likely kicked him out by now. He took this opportunity to ask for one more expression of kindness. He asked for two weeks to convince me of his commitment and dedication to me. He said that if, in those two weeks, he wasn't able to remind me of why I fell in love with him in the first place and make me fall again, he would let me go and accept the next chapter of our lives without each other. He said that he would pull himself together emotionally, knowing that he was being given a chance. While I appreciated his sentiment, I knew that there was no way that this would work. I knew why I fell I love with RaaShaun, just like I knew why our marriage was over. A two-week whirlwind of nostalgia and romance wasn't going to change that. But here I saw an opportunity, an agreement that, by design, would free me of the weight of responsibility that I was carrying. Against my better judgment, I agreed.

Over the next fourteen days, RaaShaun pulled out all the stops. He wined and dined me and lavished me with gifts. For some women, it would have been all about making this man pay for what he did with emotional and material things. Not me. I just wanted RaaShaun safe, physically and mentally, because in my heart (but mainly my head) I was done. However, I did have questions; eager to make this work, RaaShaun answered every one of them. It was then that I learned that this began and ended years before I found out about it. I'm sure RaaShaun wanted me to be proud of him for changing on his own, without any prompting, but I wasn't. He said he changed his behavior because he was disappointed in himself and wanted to be a better man. He realized that his actions left him feeling empty and unsatisfied; they didn't benefit his ego in the way that he expected. They did not build his security in our marriage or make him feel any more deserving or worthy. He explained that, in his mind, I only looked at him as RaaShaun, but everyone else looked at him as special. He didn't learn until later that in doing this, he didn't feel special at all. He only hated himself.

until later that in doing this, he didn't feel special at all. He only hated himself.

He continued to say that the thought of me ever finding out crippled him, knowing the hurt that it would cause and the disaster that would follow. Again, that would have been enough for some women. Not me. To say that you ended something because you didn't want to hurt the other person, to me, takes the onus off you. I didn't want RaaShaun to stop cheating because he didn't want to hurt me. I wanted RaaShaun to stop cheating because he didn't want to hurt himself and corrupt the roots of our marriage. He had to want integrity for himself because, if he didn't, this same lesson would show up again, just in a different way.

One evening, during this two-week farewell, I accompanied RaaShaun to an industry event he was working. I hadn't done that in a while, but that night, I had fun. It was always great seeing him in his element. I looked at those moments with pride because I'd been there from the beginning, when it was just a dream. And now he was living it. Even though he'd disappointed me and broken my heart, I was still proud of everything he'd accomplished. He'd done more than many ever believed he could, and we'd done it together. It would take some adjustment to get used to not being with him every step of the way going forward, but that didn't mean he wouldn't have my support. That night, RaaShaun's manager, June, came up to me and asked how long would it be before I forgave him and took him back. I told June that it was over. June dismissed it and said to me, "You're going to give up all this?!"

> "He had to want integrity for himself because, if he didn't, this same lesson would show up again, just in a different way." —GIA

He continued, "Come on, you know you're not going nowhere." It's expected that women, especially those married to men in the industry and/or men of means, overlook their men's misdeeds to maintain their lifestyles. You hear about it all the time. These men get to openly cheat and disrespect their wives while these women stand beside them and continue enjoying the perks of being connected to them. That's what I felt like June was asking me to do that night. I felt like he wanted me to ignore my own intuition and self-worth to stay by RaaShaun's side because that has always been the example and what was expected. But I wanted more for myself and for my children. I knew I was capable of finding a love that honored and respected me. I wasn't going to be anyone's doormat, not even the love of my life's. I expressed to June my level of seriousness. No matter what happened within these two weeks, I was resolute and clear. My marriage was over.

I knew that June was going to tell RaaShaun what I'd said, and I was okay with that; there were only a few more days until our two weeks were up. At some point, he would have to come to terms with the truth.

"You told June that you're still filing for divorce?!"

I replied, "Yes."

"How could you? These last two weeks were amazing!"

He questioned those days together as though they'd meant nothing to me. "Our communication was amazing," "The sex was amazing," "There was magic, our magic!" The truth was that I'd felt all of those things, but for me, it was the last dance.

The next morning, feeling overwhelmed, scatterbrained, and desperate, RaaShaun called me while he was on air to apologize, as a last-ditch attempt to do something "big." He expressed remorse for the wrong thing. The issue wasn't that he wasn't being an attentive husband during my pregnancy but clearly he thought it would impress me. It did the exact opposite. I was appalled. This had nothing to do with him not rubbing my feet enough! He'd cheated on me! In fact, he was wonderful to me during my pregnancy. He simply wanted to apologize to me without divulging to the public exactly what he was apologizing for. But it wasn't difficult for the public to read between the lines. Not only that, he'd now made our personal business a talking point on the blogs and social media. Perhaps unknowingly, RaaShaun had now put me in a position where I had to deal with the complications within our marriage *and* the public's perception of it, all at the same time. I didn't ask for any of this, and the fact that I was upset only made him slip further into depression. But this was more than depression; RaaShaun was suicidal. No matter how angry I was at him, I still loved him and he was still my best friend. I wanted him alive, and I would do anything to ensure that.

Word traveled quickly, and one of my best friends, Rasheed, husband of one of my other best friends, Sasha—also godfather to all our children—had heard the news all the way in LA. He called, thinking that it was just gossip to drum up publicity, knowing that we had been approached to do a reality show. I responded by saying, "No, it's all true." He was shocked. I let him know that RaaShaun was in a bad way and that I was very worried about him. To say that Rasheed was mad would be an understatement. See, Rasheed never *really* liked RaaShaun much, and RaaShaun felt the same. It was never spoken on, but you could feel that the closeness was never there. They would only spend time together on "couple things" and holidays. Rasheed was the *only* person in the history of my marriage who ever had anything negative to say about it. He witnessed RaaShaun's obsessive nature firsthand and was always concerned that it would go too far.

RaaShaun was dragging his feet regarding the divorce, so one day I approached him, urging him to hire a lawyer so we could move forward. That conversation put into motion a series of events that I wish never happened. It put everything into perspective, gave him a feeling of finality that he wasn't able to accept. After a huge blowup, he grabbed all our car keys, headed into the garage, locked the door, and started each car. I didn't know what to do. I didn't know whether or not this was another attempt to hide from the reality of what I'd said or if this was really it. I pleaded with him to unlock the door and turn off the cars. He refused. It was in that moment that Rasheed called. Even is the midst of the chaos, something compelled me to answer. Frantically, I told him what was going on and that I was debating whether to call the police or not. This felt more real than it ever had in the past. Rasheed told me that he would call RaaShaun and call me right back. Although it felt like an eternity, less than five minutes later, Rasheed called back. "Gia, call the police." I asked Rasheed if he was sure. "I just called him and that wasn't RaaShaun, Gia. That was the devil. Call the police." I hung up, dialed 911, and prayed they would get there in time.

As RaaShaun was being taken to the hospital, our nanny was coming home with Madison and Logan. We did our best to calm them down and tell them that Daddy was going to be fine. But how was I going to explain this to them? What would I say? I couldn't even make sense of it myself. I struggled for the words when I called RaaShaun's parents. Up to this point, I never involved them or told them about any of the times when things had gotten out of hand. But this was different. I explained as best I could and asked them to meet me at the hospital. Thankfully they were there, because RaaShaun wouldn't even look at me. He was so upset that I called the police, he couldn't even recognize it for the lifesaving action it was. To be honest, I didn't care. He was alive and he was safe. He never had to say another word to me. He was still with us and that's all that mattered to me.

He was alive but wouldn't be "with us" for long. There all of us were, waiting for him to be further evaluated and for the doctor to give us the next step in this process, when RaaShaun jumped and bolted out of the hospital room. We can laugh about it now, but can you imagine a psych patient running down the halls of the hospital, knocking people over, with security chasing him? That's exactly what RaaShaun looked like. When he ran through the automatic doors and leaped into the back of Lil Shaun's car, I couldn't believe it. As Lil Shaun sped off, you could see RaaShaun's feet hanging out of the open car, flailing in the wind.

I had no idea where RaaShaun went; I assumed he was hiding out with Lil Shaun. He wasn't answering my calls or texts. The police assured me they'd find him soon. They'd have someone at the radio station that morning and at an event he was supposed to deejay that night. When I got the call that RaaShaun turned himself back in to the hospital, I was relieved. At least I knew where he was and that he was safe. This time around, RaaShaun was talking to me. His tone was soft and gentle. He knew this was serious and he wasn't going to get out of it by running away. In the hospital, I got in the bed and snuggled up next to him. I rubbed his head, caressed his face, and told him that, no matter what, I loved him and would always be there for him. He told me that he loved me too and thanked me. He said that, in the hospital, he felt like he was in a cage and was stifled; he couldn't think, couldn't feel, and was desperate to get out. He promised that if I signed him out of the hospital, his days of threatening and attempting harm to himself were done. He just wanted to go home. More than being in the hospital, RaaShaun said he needed to be with his family. I believed him, agreed, and signed the paperwork.

He was then released into my custody, which was the only way the hospital would allow him to go home. While I was worried about RaaShaun, I genuinely believed that what he needed wouldn't come from remaining in the hospital. He would be resistant to the process and that wouldn't be good for anyone. However, I assured him that if we ever came down this path again, I would do the same thing.

After RaaShaun came home, Rasheed called back to tell me that he'd had a breakdown at work after speaking to RaaShaun. Once he'd collected himself, he'd walked into his boss's office, told him that he had a family emergency, was taking a leave of absence, and didn't know when he'd be back. He was flying to New Jersey from Los Angeles to be with us. I couldn't let him do that. I knew how stressful things were at work for him at the time. Furthermore, I needed to be alone. I didn't want him here. I didn't want anyone here.

Since my childhood, I dealt with my problems by myself. I was never the type of girl to call a friend when I needed someone to lean on. In fact, I rarely if ever needed someone to lean on. I figured things out on my own. I always preferred my friends to lean on me. I prided myself on my ability to be there for them, staying up till all hours of the night immersed in conversations about whatever it was that had them down. I was the friend that would show up to their house in the middle of the night with two fuzzy blankets, chips and guacamole, their favorite movie, and a box of Kleenex so they knew that someone (even if it wasn't *him*) loved them. The odd thing about that is that I never wanted that type of care or concern for myself.

In retrospect and after some soul-searching, I've come to realize the reason why. In life, some people lead with their hearts, while others lead with their heads. Neither is necessarily preferable to the other. However, it's been my experience that leading with my head has always produced better results. If something doesn't make sense in my head, it doesn't matter what my heart has to say. The heart is more susceptible to making wrong choices because it considers so much more than the facts. The head is more objective. While the heart may say, "But he loves me," the head may say, "So what?" With this mindset, I have been able to simplify my life by letting go of people and experiences that weren't good for me. And not looking back. It allows me more control of my life and conviction in my decisions.

The only people that I ever confided in or sought advice from were my parents. By this time, my father had already passed away and my mother was suffering from dementia. I was alone to figure this out—just the way I liked it. This was my comfort zone. I believed that Rasheed's presence, on the contrary, would make my comfort zone uncomfortable. When I expressed this to him, he said that he was coming and there was nothing I could say to change his mind. He informed me that he had already bought his ticket and that he would tell me what time to pick him up from Newark International Airport. And there I had it. Rasheed was flying in from LA. Lo and behold, this was the best thing that could have possibly happened.

When Rasheed arrived, I asked him why it was so important for him to come. Rasheed had a deeply personal relationship with God, one that was nothing like ours, so I took his response very seriously. He said that when he spoke to RaaShaun in that garage, my husband's emotional state wasn't a game, a ploy, or a manipulation, but that it was, in fact, real. That RaaShaun was under the influence of something that wasn't Godly and that he heard it for himself. When he hung up that day, he dropped to his knees in his office, cried, and prayed with fervor; he believed that RaaShaun may have lost his life there in that garage. He felt that it was critical that he show up immediately. On his flight, he paced the aisle, Bible in hand, reading scripture and praying, overcome with emotion and desperate to spiritually intervene.

As he described to me what brought him here, I was confused, to say the least. I believed in God, went to Catholic school my whole life, but I asked, *"What in the world are you talking about?"* He told me that God sent him here to save our marriage.

"*You???* You don't even like RaaShaun! You told me that maybe we should go our separate ways on more than one occasion. God would have used anyone but you—you've got it wrong."

He explained, "That's exactly why he's using me. If *I'm* telling you, you know it *has* to be true."

The fact that Rasheed was there to help us get back on track and not to help me pack was proof that there was a higher power at work.

He had my attention, but I needed further explanation. He said that God had spoken to him and he had no choice.

"God *spoke* to you?" I asked "So, what, you're hearing voices?"

He responded, "When God speaks to you, he puts an overwhelming feeling on your heart and you know that it's Him; and when He tells you to do something, you don't ask any questions, you just do it."

Those words would turn out to be more important than I could have ever imagined. Rasheed asked our permission to share what was going on with a pastor he knew and trusted completely, by the name of Sister Nancy, and we agreed. After much prayer, the word Sister Nancy sent back to us, through Rasheed, was that God wanted us to stay together—same as him. But how could this be? Sister Nancy did not know me, had never met me, and was completely unaware of my existence until Rasheed called and confided in her. Still, I agreed to meet with Sister Nancy and invited her into our home. RaaShaun was excited to pick her up, eager to expose me to anyone who would fight for him. When Sister Nancy arrived at my house, she introduced herself and explained to me her relationship with God. She took the time to counsel and pray with us. She also prayed over our home and asked God to restore our family. She said this was an attack sent by the enemy to get the two of us off our purpose and destiny. If we divorced, we let the enemy win. If we fought through this, God would get the glory and we would make it through to the other side.

Sister Nancy and Rasheed told me that the enemy had been after me since I was a child, and I always bounced back stronger. Because of this, the attacks would persist until I was broken, unless I made a change. These attacks weren't attempts to destroy RaaShaun; he was just a tool. According to them, I had to remain in my marriage, develop a strong relationship with God *together*, and become a united front. They reassured me that only good things would follow. Not being spiritually equipped to digest this information, I asked, "And what if I don't?" I didn't like the answer. They told me that God had done something special by sending people to me with his message, possibly to divert me away from a far worse outcome, and it would be in my best interest to listen.

I was left feeling that even though I'd been hurt by my husband, if I didn't stay with him, I would be hurt again—all through no fault of my own. If I believed what I was being told, my free will was being stripped from me. I was mad and having trouble processing. While I'd had a Catholic upbringing, I didn't grow up "in the church." I prayed, generically, and without much connection or meaning. I never *felt* God and had no understanding of hearing his voice. If someone asked me if I believed, I would think to myself, yeah, I believe, but you never know. I didn't have true conviction, and my faith certainly wasn't rooted in anything of substance. I was morally sound, but it is safe to say that I was spiritually inept. I later came to learn that this wasn't just God knocking on my door, but God kicking my door down.

There were moments when I felt so overwhelmed. I had so many people in my ear telling me what they thought I should do. Some were even telling me what God wanted for my life. One night, frustrated, I began to cry in the shower—the first time since this all unfolded—and it was a good cry. I told God that it felt impossible to make this monumental of a decision about my life based on messages sent through other people. I told him that if this was, in fact, what he wanted me to do, to please send me a sign that I could interpret for myself.

Rasheed was instrumental during his stay. He led us in Bible studies and prayer sessions and heart-to-heart talks that allowed our connection with God and each other to grow deeper. He pointed out parts of the Bible, such as those on marriage and pride, that enlightened us. By nature, I was resistant. I still loved my husband, but I wasn't going to be anyone's fool. It would hurt to end things, but for the sake of my dignity, I was ready. At the same time, I didn't want to make a decision solely rooted in my ego. I realized that the only way I was going to make the right decision was to be led by God.

My insistence on a divorce was my initial response to RaaShaun's infidelity. I wasn't going to be one of *those* women. Fool me once, shame on you. But I loved him, and I loved the family we'd created. There was something in me that was encouraging me to fight—still, there was also something in me that

> "I still loved my husband, but I wasn't going to be anyone's fool." —**GIA**

wouldn't let me fight. That saw staying with someone who cheated on me as weak. And the last thing I am is a weak woman. God felt my resistance and was about to give me what I needed.

While at home one day, the phone rang. When RaaShaun picked up and asked who it was, the person on the other end of the phone said, "Tyrese." RaaShaun responded, "Tyrese, Tyrese. As in *Transformers* Tyrese?" The person on the phone responded, "Yes." RaaShaun was caught off guard by the call. Tyrese told RaaShaun that he'd had to go through several people to get his telephone number, but he wanted to reach out. Tyrese had heard about our troubles and wanted to help in any way that he could. This didn't seem to make sense, considering that RaaShaun and Tyrese were not friends or acquaintances by any stretch of the imagination. They had never interacted, outside of a radio interview or two. But RaaShaun was willing to take help from whoever he could get it.

Tyrese instructed him to rent a private room at Philippe Chow in Manhattan on the following Tuesday night at 7:00 P.M., order appetizers, and wait for him to arrive. RaaShaun planned a special day and at the end, brought me to the restaurant. After appetizers, Tyrese walked in with a guitarist and a backup singer and serenaded us with his song "Stay" as though he were onstage at the Grammys. It was incredible. He sat down, had dinner with us, and engaged in conversation for about four hours. During that conversation, he offered insight on the male perspective and helped me understand what RaaShaun may have been feeling when he decided to cheat. He was insightful and informative, but most importantly, he cared. Tyrese told us that he was scheduled to be in a wedding the following day and was supposed to be at a rehearsal dinner that evening, but he'd canceled his plans and changed his flight to be there with us instead.

While I appreciated the sentiment, I was skeptical. Tyrese didn't know us. He had never even met me before. Why was he so invested in us? I asked him and couldn't believe his response. He told me that there was a sense of urgency for him to be there. He said that God sent him there to help save our marriage—that God had spoken to him and given him this mission. My heart almost stopped. He said that God had spoken to him, so he put everything else on hold. I was in complete and utter shock.

"Wait, God *spoke* to you???"

"Yes."

"So . . . were you, like, hearing voices?"

He looked at me, and with as much seriousness as he could muster, he said, "When God speaks to you, he puts an overwhelming feeling on your heart and you know that it's Him; and when He tells you to do something, you don't ask any questions, you just do it."

My eyes widened, my heart started beating uncontrollably, and tears started rushing down my face. Tyrese said the exact same thing Rasheed had said to me, verbatim. The two of them had never met each other, and Tyrese didn't know about our private conversations. I didn't know many things when it came to this situation, but one thing that I *did* know was that there wasn't that much coincidence in the world! This was my very clear and unmistakable sign—one that I could interpret for myself. This was God answering my prayer. It *was* possible that we could get over the worst thing that ever happened to us. First, I just needed to do one thing. I looked up with tears in my eyes, holding my arms up to Him, and said out loud, "Okay, okay, I understand! Thank you! Thank you!" I looked over at my husband, the man I'd loved since I was fifteen years old, and told him that I was willing to forgive him, to move forward and not look back!

I look at our life now. Had Rasheed not come to visit and Tyrese not called, I don't know where we'd be. Actually, I do: divorced. For that, I will always be grateful to them. Many of us know what it feels like to be hurt by the people we love, but very few of us know what healing and forgiveness look like. It's daily work, a choice we constantly make, to live in the present while looking ahead to the future and not be bound by the past. RaaShaun and I live there now, and it is beautiful. Aside from having children, forgiving him was the best decision that I ever made.

I'm asked all the time, "Why did you stay?" The question pops up regularly in my DMs, in podcast listener letters, and whenever someone sees me and finds the courage to walk up and ask. There are typically two kinds of people asking this question. First, there are the people who are just nosy. They believe they're owed every detail of our lives simply because they know some of the worst ones. They want you to explain yourself to *them* so they can decide whether your explanation is a valid one or not. But, more times than not, they're ready to just pick you apart because, in their minds, if you're not

> "Many of us know what it feels like to be hurt by the people we love, but very few of us know what healing and forgiveness look like. It's daily work, a choice we constantly make, to live in the present while looking ahead to the future and not be bound by the past." —GIA

leaving your cheating spouse, you're making the wrong decision altogether *or* you're staying for the wrong reasons. It's easy to spot these people, and I ignore them.

But the majority of women who ask me this question are a second kind. They are lovers and wives who genuinely want their relationships to work. They're brokenhearted and trying to move forward but can't figure out how. So that's really the question. These women aren't really asking me why I stayed; they're asking me *how* I stayed. They want to know how I was able to move past the pain and find a way to true healing. These women deserve my full attention and transparency.

I give it to them. I tell the truth. At various stages in our relationship, I stayed with RaaShaun for different reasons. When we were kids, I stayed because I had a warped sense of what love and devotion truly meant. The fact that RaaShaun would be so distraught over the possibility that I would leave him signaled to me how much he loved me. Foolishly, him being "crazy in love" flattered me. As I matured and realized that healthy love didn't look like that, it also meant that the reasons I stayed with RaaShaun didn't look the same either.

Early in our marriage, I stayed through his obsessive, possessive, and controlling ways because, despite them, I loved him and really wanted our marriage to work. I genuinely believed that we were created for each other and destined to be together. But after he cheated, I stayed with my husband because I was convinced and truly believed that it was what God had intended for us. I don't necessarily believe in soul mates, but I do believe that the inseparability that both RaaShaun and I felt, after only weeks of being together, was the glue that He formed between us, holding us together through high school, college, and then, through marriage. I believe that it was all part of His plan, like there was something special only the two of us could be together, and ways that we would move through this world that only the two of us could do together. More than anything, this is why I stayed. It's why I keep staying, because I believe remaining committed to your marriage is intentional and a decision you make daily.

My experience was a gift and a curse. In hindsight, I realize that it was far more the former than the latter. The curse—pain, struggle, and darkness—was only temporary. The gift—the ever-feeding fruit—lasts a lifetime. A newfound relationship with God, a genuine love for Him, a clear understanding of who He is and His purpose for me on this earth are the gifts that will keep on giving. The truest beauty of all is that I am now equipped to arm my children with this knowledge and His love, in a way that I wasn't before.

There is a difference between *knowing* because your parents and religious upbring tell you of God's greatness and *knowing* because you've experienced God's greatness for yourself. God had to break me down and bring me to my knees so that I had no choice but to look up and recognize Him. For that, I am forever grateful. I wouldn't have been exposed to His fruit if I hadn't been made to suffer. I believe that God may have been reaching out to me throughout my life, but I couldn't hear Him. I wasn't rooted deeply enough in my spirituality to accept His hand, and I didn't have the discernment. I do now. My life has changed for the better in every aspect since this trial. I thought that my life was extraordinary and happy before the devastation unfolded. The truth is, I had no idea that this level of happiness even existed. I did not possess a lens through which to see the possibilities of what a Godly life had to offer—*true* unadulterated happiness. "Who knew?" I'll tell you: "He knew." I can now teach my children from a place of sincere *knowing* and confidence, and they can teach theirs. That is the definition of true legacy.

Now, *how* I stayed took a little more effort. It meant genuinely forgiving RaaShaun. A lot of us say we forgive our husbands, but during every fight or frustrating conversation, we're always bringing up or alluding to the very thing we say we've forgiven. Anytime we see or hear something that even remotely reminds us of cheating, resentment and angst build up and we go for the jugular. We do not always know our triggers or for how long we will be triggered, but what we do know is that we were *put* in the position to feel this way by someone who was supposed to protect us. We didn't do this to ourselves, so we are allowed to go through the motions. For some, it only happens during the beginning stages; for others, well beyond that point; and for many, all the way through. They are unchartered waters that many never conceived of navigating until they got thrown in without a life raft. We may feel destitute, hopeless, and alone; often there's no one to confide in, out of fear of judgment and embarrassment.

As her partner and the offender, it is your duty to be understanding and patient, and show grace as the effect of her trauma is rearing its ugly head. A woman may say that she forgives you without truly knowing the meaning of forgiveness. For many, it simply means, "You cheated and I didn't break up with you, therefore, I forgave you." Nothing could be further from the truth. All of the trauma created by the infidelity has to be dealt with and reconciled. That can take an unforeseen amount of time. Many men will say, "She said she forgave me. How long do I have to go through this?" as though he is the victim. That is laughable. The answer is *until*. Until. Until. Until. Until she is healed, until she can trust you again, and until she can fall in love with you again. The list goes on. He may not realize it (and she may not either), but she used the word "forgive" as an expression of intention, possibly with no understanding of execution. She wanted to forgive you but didn't know how. This can thrust a couple into a cycle of dysfunction. Frustration begins to set in for the man because, for him, there is no end in sight. But what he must realize is that he can't put a "due by" date on healing. In fact, he has no right. You don't get to impose your expectation of healing upon your partner. And remember, you didn't fulfill her expectation of fidelity in the relationship, so who are you to dictate expectations to her? You may have done what you *thought* was appropriate and acceptable to induce healing, believed that you've "paid your dues," and are now left wondering, "What more can I do?" Well, here is the answer:

1. **Be accepting.** Accept that you are the cause of the destruction in your relationship. Come to terms with the fact that you created this mess and it is *your* job to clean it up.

2. **Be responsible.** Take responsibility for that destruction and be willing to do the work to rebuild. Process that you may be responsible for her feelings of inferiority to other women as a result of your infidelity. Reinforce her security and her belief that she doesn't have to be something else to be desirable or worthy.

3. **Be supportive.** Support her by letting her know that you understand her natural reactions to the trauma, as extreme as they may be. Know that "throwing it in your face," hurling insults, crying, and constantly needing to "talk" may be part of the package. Reassure her that you are willing to do all that is necessary according to her needs. Expressing that you are there for the long haul will help you go the distance.

4. **Be a truth teller.** Be willing to be forthcoming and answer all questions truthfully. Remember, additional lies to cover up hurtful details and telling half-truths will only undo the good work that you have already begun. Don't undermine yourself.

5. **Be proactive.** Come up with different ways to demonstrate to your partner that her happiness and well-being is the primary concern. Don't wait for her to tell you how to fix the relationship. Come up with those ways yourself. Showing initiative will signal that you are invested. It indicates that you are someone who *does*, as opposed to someone who *reacts*. Being a doer is a sign of manliness, which is always attractive.

6. **Be understanding.** Internalize that forgiveness is a process and will take all of the above to achieve.

If you are making every effort to rehabilitate the union, remember that you have earned the right to be fair to yourself. Just because you have made a mistake does not mean that you deserve to be her personal object of punishment. Recognize and understand that that may come naturally to her, along with the rationalization, "I suffered, therefore he must suffer." While that sounds reasonable in some ways, the truth of the matter is that the two of you decided to stay together because, ultimately and to some extent, you believe in each other and believe that you are better together than apart. There is a certain amount of respect that allows that to happen, which is a good thing. In this journey to the other side of forgiveness and healing, we must not take each other for granted or be abusive.

True forgiveness is required for true healing, which is the end goal, regardless of whether you stay in the relationship or move on. As the victim, forgiveness must be achieved to relieve *yourself* of all the burdens that came along with the trauma, not to relieve *him* of the burden of creating them. Insecurity, low self-esteem, and worthlessness are examples of those burdens. Feeling like one is not "good enough" because their partner chose someone else (even if it was only for a night) is real and common. The feelings of inadequacy can lead to embarrassment. Other women may say anti-woman things like "You can't even keep a man," which supports the narrative that having a cheating spouse is *our* fault. As though we didn't do enough to *keep* him.

The truth is that every person is responsible for their own actions. The person who cheats has the opportunity and freedom to leave the relationship if they are, in fact, not satisfied. They compromise their own integrity and worth by engaging in deceitful behavior. You were "good enough"—so good that he couldn't bear to leave you. Instead, the boy in him made him want to have his cake and eat it too. He simply wasn't man enough to exercise his decency and do the right thing. This is a testament to his own lack of righteousness and honor. You are not to be judged and have nothing to be ashamed of. Forgiveness is the first step toward shedding these insecurities and should be desired with the understanding that it is not sought for your cheating partner's sake. Rather, it is sought for your own sake, selfishly, because as the victim, you stand to gain the most once it is achieved.

Once I decided to forgive RaaShaun, the true test began. I had a host of harsh realities that I had to grapple with. I did not know how to forgive because it wasn't necessarily in my nature, but I had to figure it out and was resolute to do it the right way. RaaShaun was patient with me through all the pains of this of this process. I had to grow in the space of maturity and as a Godly woman in order to resist the urge to punish him and make him suffer. I had to grow in the space of respect, acknowledging that he had earnestly changed and was doing everything within his power to make sure that I chose him every day. I had to grow in the space of compassion, giving value to the fact that he sincerely regretted his actions and was suffering knowing what he had done. I had to grow in the space of pride shedding, understanding that pride had no place here and would only work to antagonize our progress. Ego shows up as a protective armor defending us against hurt and disappointment. It prevents you from letting down your guard and allowing the newfound love and forgiveness to seep in.

Once I grew in all of these spaces, I was able to appreciate that RaaShaun was worthy. He was a beautiful man who, even in his weakest moments, was strong enough to be vulnerable. He exemplified what it meant to "show and prove" and was never too proud to wear it. He left no stone unturned in his pursuit of redemption and continued his pursuit *until*. When I wondered to myself, "What more could he do?" he showed up every day with the six answers in his hand. I love that man and am so glad that I chose him back.

It takes courage to truly forgive and believe that you can have a better life than the one you had when you were in a darker place. This doesn't dismiss the experiences of women who left their cheating spouses. Without the intervention of God, I would have certainly landed in that group. Most men choose selfishness over thoughtful reconciliation, all while dragging their partner along for the painful ride. Many women don't have the strength to leave those men. That takes true courage, as does finding the courage to forgive. I did, and leaning into it was truly life changing. It will not happen overnight, and it will force you to summon all the strength you didn't know you had. But if he is worthy, you can do it.

———

9.   The New Deal

For six years, beginning in 1933, President Franklin D. Roosevelt authorized the creation of various programs and initiatives that helped get the country back on track after the Great Depression. Several federal agencies were created, all to provide support to various groups in society, especially the elderly and the unemployed. Roosevelt's "New Deal" focused on the three *R*s: **relief** (providing immediate assistance to those in need), **recovery** (ensuring the economy returned to normal), and **reform** (overhauling systems to ensure the Great Depression didn't happen again). The country was able to rebound, thanks to the New Deal, and we still benefit from many of those programs and federal agencies today.

When our marriage faced its most crucial moment, we knew that things needed to change. We couldn't continue with business as usual and expect that things would be different. We were at the brink of disaster. We were headed for divorce, and there were some painful experiences that we couldn't pretend didn't happen. We needed a new way of being together, a way that brought us closer than we'd ever been before. Then, and only then, could we ensure that certain mistakes would never be made again and we had what we needed to face whatever storms would come our way in the future. Like America in 1933, we needed a New Deal.

GIA: When RaaShaun desperately wanted to fix what he'd broken, he asked me to tell him what I needed him to do. Whatever I said, he would do it—no questions asked. While other women may appreciate this, I didn't. I told RaaShaun that I wasn't the one who put us in this position, and therefore, I wasn't about to come up with the solutions. This wasn't about me giving him an angry "honey-do" list, him checking items off and feeling good about himself. He was going to have to dig deep, ask himself the hard questions, and chart a path forward accordingly. While our New Deal *does* include aspects that we collaborated on together, a great deal of it was a result of RaaShaun's intention to take inventory within himself to be a better man and husband. We're the better for it.

> "We needed a new way of being together, a way that brought us closer than we'd ever been before." —**GIA AND ENVY**

Envy: I was the one who fucked up, so I was the one who needed to do whatever I could to fix it—and I wanted to fix it. There's a difference between putting a Band-Aid on a wound just to stop the bleeding and cleaning it from infection, getting stitches, and taking the time to really heal. You can be someone who's pissed because they got caught, or you can be someone who takes being exposed as an opportunity to become the person you've pretended or always wanted to be. If you are the latter, we invite you to use our New Deal as a guide to create yours and get your relationship back on track.

Relief

In 1933, it was important to provide immediate relief to stabilize the economy and give families whatever they needed. This included financial assistance, food rations, and anything else that met the needs they had as a result of the Great Depression. For us, in the wake of infidelity and mistrust, our immediate need was believing that it was possible for us to make it beyond this moment. In order for us to do that, we had to have faith. In order to have faith, we needed God.

God hadn't been a central focus in our relationship. We believed in God and endeavored to be good people, but to say that we were Christians deeply rooted in our faith wouldn't have been the truth. After Rasheed and Tyrese came to us, at the urging of God, we knew that we owed it to Him to begin developing a solid relationship with our Lord and Savior that would become the cornerstone of our relationship with each other. We began reading the Bible together and praying together, something that hasn't stopped to this day. Our day starts as early as 4:00 A.M., and before we're off to the radio station and getting the kids ready for school, we take a moment to pray together. Every single morning. We thank God for our family, friends, and loved ones. For our health and the opportunity to make a positive impact in this world. And we ask God to help us remain close to Him, close to each other, and close to our children. Though we have many moments and conversations throughout the day together, nothing is more beautiful than when we're praying as one.

Not only do we cultivate our relationship with God together, we're also doing so on our own. Reading scriptures and praying, allowing God to speak to us individually, has been essential. The truth is, while one person's actions can destroy a relationship, the relationship itself is composed of two imperfect people. We each have our own flaws, imperfections, and growing edges. There

"The truth is, while one person's actions can destroy a relationship, the relationship itself is composed of two imperfect people. We each have our own flaws, imperfections, and growing edges." —GIA AND ENVY

are ways we can grow and become better, fully realizing our purpose and the calling of our lives. But we can't do that if we're not connected to the One who gave us this life and calling.

Faith is extremely important to us. God has to be at the center of our relationship. It has been God whispering in our ears to extend grace and forgiveness when we've been unwilling to let the pain go. And it was God who nudged us to keep going when we didn't believe our relationship could ever be what it was before the pain entered it. We believe God will sustain anyone if you ask for forgiveness, if you choose to forgive, and if you push forward to create a relationship that will actually be *better* than what you thought were your best moments. To get back on track, you've first got to give this relationship and yourselves over to God.

Now is the time to take inventory of the role God plays in your life and your relationship.

Do you pray?

If so, how often?

If not, what's holding you back?

How often are you reading your Bible, listening to sermons, and reading resources that will help build your faith?

How are you incorporating your spouse or partner?

Is God important to your spouse or partner?

Have the two of you ever talked about the role of faith and God in your relationship?

Asking these questions is a crucial exercise to providing the relief your relationship needs in order to adjust to what has happened and equip you with what's needed to do the work of reconciliation and restoration.

We recognize that not everyone is Christian and there are a number of faith traditions in which to ground one's life, relationship, and home. We honor that and encourage you to root your relationship in whatever faith or spirituality grounds you both. There are also people who don't subscribe to a faith tradition at all, and that doesn't mean they're incapable of having healthy relationships, because they absolutely are. At the same time, it's important to agree on what ethical behaviors will be the foundation of your love. Without that clarity and consensus, you will never be on the same page.

Recovery

The main focus of the New Deal was to get America back to where it was before the Great Depression took place, at least, and at best, to take America to new heights. It didn't mean that people would ever forget that the Depression happened. But with these programs and initiatives in place, the country could return to normal and still thrive. In order for our relationship to get back to "normal" or to exceed that "normal," we knew what we had to do: communicate.

This may sound trite. Every relationship book, every relationship podcast, every piece of relationship advice stresses the importance of communication. If you're going to have a healthy relationship, you have to talk to each other;

you have to talk about what's happened and how it's affected you. Admittedly, we took for granted that because we'd known each other since we were kids, we knew everything about each other. That since we talked to each other every day, several times a day, we knew all that needed to be known. But both of us were keeping secrets. We weren't telling each other everything. In the wake of our marriage implosion, we learned this painful truth. We learned that we couldn't just talk to each other: we had to have directed conversations that would get to the heart of our issues. We couldn't just have *idle* conversations; we had to have *deliberate* conversations.

These conversations are not easy. That's why people don't want to have them. Unfortunately, we live in a world where people don't like to be held accountable. And because many have unresolved trauma from previous relationships and childhood, it's easier for them to shut down than engage. But these conversations have to happen. You must be willing to hear what led your spouse or partner to make the mistakes they made. Sometimes, it may have been in reaction to something you did, knowingly or unknowingly. That gives you the opportunity to apologize, talk through your rationale, and course correct. Sometimes, their mistakes may have absolutely nothing to do with you and they now have the opportunity to make that clear to you. Because you've decided to salvage the relationship, you now are equipped with information that allows you to hold them accountable and ensure their words and actions align.

The key to effective communication is respecting your partner in word and deed. Too often, communication goes awry due to what we call **"right fighting."** It's when a disagreement or argument takes a sharp turn and there's really no desire for true resolution. One or both parties just want to be right. You're arguing to win rather than talking to express your perspective or listening to understand. Right fighting can involve deliberate tactics such as insults, condescension, mind-bleeping, and other attempts to make the other person feel insecure or inadequate. Make no mistake: right fighting is deeply rooted in ego and a need to be right at all costs. Some may approach right fighting from their competitive nature and believe the feeling of winning is gratifying, but truth be told, right fighters always rack up more losses than anything else. If you resort to right fighting, you will always lose a little of the respect and adoration of your partner, and over time, that adds up. It's never worth it.

Both of us have been guilty of right fighting. For a long time, neither of us realized it was a problem. We're both naturally competitive, and we're always attempting to best each other in sports and other fun competitions. That drive spilled over into our arguments. And though we didn't know we were right fighting at the time, once we discovered that's what we were doing, we made the necessary changes. Humility and learning to listen go a long way. Our communication drastically changed as a result of saying no to right fighting, and yours can too.

Though we were able to have these difficult conversations without a third party, we strongly advocate for couples counseling. There are so many opportunities available for couples counseling now than there were for previous generations. When working through the pain and disappointment that have derailed a relationship, many couples benefit from an impartial third party who will be able to be objective and hold you both accountable to the great-

> "Conversations matter."

ness that is possible together. For too long in our communities, counseling has been dismissed as something for people with "real" problems or what white people do. But it's through counseling that couples are able to develop new communication and conflict-resolution techniques that will restore the character of the relationship.

Conversations matter. We can't stress that enough. What's also important is that a safe space is created for these conversations to take place. To create a safe space for a difficult conversation, here are a few suggestions:

> ***Pick a room in your home that's comfortable and conducive to a tense conversation. We recommend the bedroom.***

> ***If you have children in the home, schedule the conversation for when they're away or sleeping.***

Dress comfortably. Pajamas, preferably.

Subscribe to the idea of reciprocity. Lead by example. Show respect during these conversations and expect to be respected in return.

Set the ground rule that neither person will interrupt the other. Everyone gets a chance to say everything they need to say. Remember, patience is a virtue.

Questions are encouraged. In this space, there's no such thing as a "dumb question." If a clarifying question offends you, state that respectfully.

Trust that your spouse or partner loves you and has your best interest at heart in the conversation.

Identify some action items and desired outcomes. How are you going to measure growth in that particular area of your relationship?

When you've decided to spend the rest of your life with someone, you can never talk to them too much about what can make your relationship better.

Reform

All of the efforts of Roosevelt's New Deal were ultimately to ensure that a Great Depression never happened again. When there has been destruction in a relationship, the point is to instill security and do the work to make sure the two of you will never have to experience that kind of pain again. This requires three things.

First, the person who caused the pain has to stop doing whatever they did that created the dysfunction.

Second, that person has to replace those behaviors with new actions that can enhance the life of the relationship. Here we'd like to introduce **"Envy's Phone-Up Relationship"** plan as an example.

ENVY: When I told Gia I'd do anything to make it right, I meant it. She told me I needed to decide exactly what that was. She wasn't going to do the work for me. And this wasn't the time to drop the ball. This was my opportunity to show her that I had a full and vivid understanding of what I stole from our relationship with my infidelity. She had to both know that I was well aware of the void that I had created and feel my urgency to fill it back up. This is part of the "show and prove" part of healing. The root of my infidelity was about secrecy and creating situations that made it easy for me to be sneaky and dishonest. My first step to regaining Gia's trust was eliminating all suspicions.

Because I had been secretive and couldn't be trusted, I knew that Gia needed unlimited access to my life as a whole, no exceptions, no questions asked. She needed access to my phone, email, calendar, and all my social media accounts. This is what I call a "phone-up relationship." If you notice, so many people will be in a relationship, and they sleep with the phone under their pillow (I mean, they might as well put it in a safe, right?), take their phones to the bathroom with them, or as soon as their partner walks into a room, put their phones facedown on the table. And if they're not placing their phones facedown, it's because their wives don't have the passwords to unlock their phones at their own discretion. The husband's secrets are safe. He's made sure of it. Most people will defend this by saying they have a right to privacy. But what are they supposed to say instead—that they don't want you to see the latest nude that they've received? Ask yourself this: What type of privacy is required or necessary between two people who make love together, have possibly created children together, and have pledged to *share* a life together before God (or plan to)? Not the type of privacy that prevents her from seeing the latest pictures on your phone, people you've been texting, emails you've been receiving, or DMs that you have sent. If you are apprehensive about your partner gaining eyeshot of any of this information, let's be honest, it's because you have something to hide. And a solid, healthy relationship is not a place for hiding your life. A distrustful, deceitful one is. You may be in the wrong place. If the person you want to spend the rest of your life with can't open your phone to send herself the plumber's contact info without being debriefed, why are you with them, or anyone, for that matter?

I gave Gia everything. All the codes and passwords. I know that, whenever she wants, she can get my phone and go through it. At any moment, from her own phone, she can check my email and DMs. She can see it all. Although she's often answered my phone and looked at something on it, I don't recall her ever actually going through my stuff looking for anything. The point is she *can*. If she chooses to, she can check up on me and see what I've been up to. This is easy for me because I have no desire to lie to Gia or do wrong by her ever again. There is peace and openness in that. But for someone else, this holds them accountable and ensures they do what they need to do to rebuild broken trust. It may be difficult to surrender control, but if you want to have a better relationship, you've got to give up them passwords. It's just that simple. Now, ladies, this doesn't give you permission to abuse the person who hurt you and the best foot that they're putting forward. Even though they caused the damage, you must recognize and show respect for the level of intention and commitment that they are exemplifying. We are all adults and respond well to knowing that our efforts are appreciated. Make sure to take care of each other during this healing process. Remember that it is a joint effort.

Third, you have to prove that you are willing to do whatever it takes for as long as it takes to restore trust to the relationship. This demonstrates to your partner that they are your priority and that you are worthy of their forgiveness. Here, we'd like to introduce **"Envy's Create a Comfortable Environment"** plan. My main goal was to remove all situations that had the potential to create doubt in her mind. If I'm being honest, that would be the entire music industry as a whole, but I offered a series of suggestions to that end:

1. I told her that I would stop deejaying clubs. Although the club wasn't where my indiscretion occurred, it's seen as the devil's playground by many. Alcohol, objectification, and music that glorifies womanizing run amok. I imagined that after my indiscretion, she may not have believed that the club was a proper place for a husband trying to make amends.

2. I offered to only communicate with her via FaceTime so that she could, without doubt, account for exactly where I was, what I was doing, and who I was with.

3. I asked her to accompany me whenever I traveled for work or
    appearances. This way, she would be in the thick of it, right there
    with me.

4. And if the above three weren't good enough, I was willing to give
    up my career as a DJ and radio personality altogether. I told her that
    I would call my boss in that moment and resign if she saw fit. I was
    fully prepared to leave my life's dream behind, because my dream of
    remaining her husband was bigger. I would create alternative streams
    of income to support our family. And if that didn't suffice, we could
    downsize and live a more modest life.

In addition to creating a comfortable environment, I wanted to show her the
level of sacrifice that I was willing to endure just to ensure our future together.
"There is no progress or accomplishment without sacrifice." I was willing to
put that to the test—ten toes down. While she appreciated my sentiment, she
didn't take advantage of any of my offers. She told me that she was working
on forgiveness in the truest sense of the word, and that our relationship was
not only in God's hands now, but subject to His review. She couldn't trust in
my faithfulness to her, but she could trust in my faithfulness to God. And if,
after pledging my life and marriage to Him, I fell short, I had bigger fish to fry
than her. She was right: I would never dishonor my wife, nor God, with infidelity again. I now live life with the freedom that I was able to exercise before
because I made those offers, made myself vulnerable to what she wanted to do
with those offers. She was able to identify my sincere intention, and for Gia,
that was all that mattered; intention is everything. She knew that I certainly
intended to do right by her for the rest of my life. Your ways of creating safety
and comfort don't need to be as intense or drastic as mine. All you need is to
design your own set of *offers* to prove your intention to your partner. This was
just my way of proving to the love of my life that I was all in.

* * *

The New Deal lasted for six years. In the grand scheme of things, that's not
a long time to get a nation back on track. Here's the truth about the New
Deal in your relationship: It will last *as long as it needs to* in order to get

your relationship where it needs to be. This is the harsh reality of what happens when you hurt someone. It may take a long, seemingly unbearable and unforeseen, amount of time to rebuild the trust and love that are necessary to make your relationship grow. But if you're willing to provide the relief, recovery, and reform your relationship needs, you can revive and restore it.

———

10. "Faking It" in a Real Relationship

GIA: One night, RaaShaun and I had an argument. He said or did something to offend me and, in typical RaaShaun fashion, tried to initiate sex to "make it all go away." This was a tactic of his that he used for two reasons. One, because it worked, and two, because if I remained upset, we wouldn't be having sex that night, which was a big deal to him because we rarely went a night without having sex. At first, I turned him down, but after several attempts, I gave in. During the act, I couldn't enjoy myself because I was consumed with the notion that I had been duped . . . again. This carried a lot of weight that night, because the conflict had never been resolved. A resolution hadn't been reached, and I finally realized that he didn't care. That wasn't his priority. He was far happier to put it to bed and pretend like nothing had happened, thinking that sex would be my muzzle.

Frustrated and angry at myself for not recognizing that sooner, I made a hasty decision that would change our dynamic forever. As I climbed off of him, I looked into his eyes and said, "I've been faking it." Moments passed and RaaShaun's face went from confusion to horror, but all I felt was relief. I'd been holding that in for so long, and on that night, it felt like a balloon had popped. "How long have you been faking it for?" RaaShaun asked. I told him the truth. "Since we started having sex." His glare was cold. "So, you've been lying to me this entire time—for eleven years?" He was despondent and angry. There was a shift. I had never felt that energy from him before. He went from madly in love with me to almost hating me in an instant. I experienced immediate regret. I tried to explain, but he was short with me. I'd opened Pandora's box and created a distance between us that would begin to unravel something that was wound so tight.

All my life, I'd been living up to a certain ideal that's expected of women—to be everything. When I was young, I didn't experiment like other girls my age did. I had many boyfriends, but they never went further than a kiss (and first base with one boy). My friends considered me a prude. I took pride in that though; I was waiting for the one. And even though I didn't wait until I was married before I had sex, I was only ever intimate with RaaShaun—he was the one. I was a virgin, and he was my first—my only. It was magical. He was considerate, affectionate, and patient. We had great sex. But more times than not, I couldn't get out of my own head. The stigma about young girls and sex doesn't leave once those girls become women. Instead, our thoughts and behaviors are shaped by what society tells us about sex and intimacy. Images of "sexy" women plastered on billboards, the covers of magazines, and every-

"A woman's worth isn't measured by who she's been intimate with or how she chooses to engage with her sexuality." —**GIA**

where else that you look, leaves a subconsciously imprinted message behind in the minds of most girls—that women are here for the pleasure of men; that we are objects of desire and toys. Many women spend their lives trying to live up to that expectation (just open up your Instagram app). As a result, we desire to be beautiful; we desire to be sexy; we desire to please. But, at the same time, we receive conflicting messages. To be reserved and conservative is to be a lady. To be wild and uninhibited is to be a freak—and freaks aren't respected. They are the loose women who don't become upstanding wives and who endure the whispers and chatter behind their backs. Of course, we know this isn't true. A woman's worth isn't measured by who she's been intimate with or how she chooses to engage with her sexuality. We know this *now*. But when we were young, that was what was instilled in us. Young girls have to decipher, through the noise, what makes sense for them and their sexuality. What made sense to me was that I gained pleasure through pleasing.

I was a wife and a mother. I had a healthy dose of self-confidence, and my husband loved me at every juncture of our relationship. My capacity for sex and sexuality, as well as my performance, was very important to me. I knew what to do to please RaaShaun and make him happy. I knew his body inside and out in a way that I never knew my own. He was like an instrument to me. I knew exactly what to do to hit each note. It feels good to be enjoyed . . . I would feel like the guy in the movie who would roll over and smoke a cigarette after his sexual feat. Pleasing RaaShaun was my strong suit, and part of his pleasure came from thinking that he pleased me as well. Once I realized that, I was committed to continually giving him that feeling. I couldn't take it away. That was, until years passed, and it began to take a toll on me.

Not once did I ever let on that I wasn't satisfied. The truth is that I *was* satisfied in many ways; I always enjoyed sex with RaaShaun because he was so attractive, sexy, and attentive. Our passion and intimacy were through the roof. What was missing was my orgasm. I knew there could be *more*, but that would require undoing something that I had already set in motion. The problem was that I was so preoccupied with pleasing that I never prioritized my own pleasure. I was always so busy performing that I never took the time to completely figure out what made me tick.

What tends to happen to those of us who are pleasers is that we don't give ourselves a chance to understand sex from our own perspective first. Everything revolves around the satisfaction of the men in our lives. Even if we enjoy sex, it's either because *they* know what to do and they are doing the pleasing or because our fulfillment comes from pleasing *them*. The truth is that I was programmed to value his pleasure more than my own and then, the next thing I'd know, I'd feel obligated to perform a climax to satisfy his ego. I didn't realize it at the time, but by faking it, I was stripping him of his ability to learn my body, because according to my reaction, he was teaching the master class. I was also robbing myself of the results that should have been mine. But, during that time, it wasn't about me. It was always about ensuring that he felt empowered, even when it was to my own detriment.

I was a big girl. It was important to ask myself hard questions that allowed me to explore who I really was and what intimacy meant for me. In order to stop faking orgasms, I would have needed to do an edit, which would have meant coming clean and communicating to my husband in a thoughtful way and in a safe space. Had he known that my faking it had everything to do with me and nothing to do with him, it would not have fed into his insecurity, and we would have had fun discovering each other and fixing that problem. If we had healthier roots of communication, we would have been able to enjoy the fruits of a satisfying and fulfilling sex life.

When I finally told RaaShaun, it was *not* in a thoughtful way at all. It was because the thoughts in my head had gotten too loud and the only way to quiet them was to tell the truth. At the time I didn't consider myself to be lying; I just hadn't found the words or the courage to tell him the truth because I was so far gone. Some may call this a lie by omission, but that's still a lie. Lies hurt and lies have consequences. I wasn't prepared for mine. I don't know what I expected to happen when I told him. I hadn't even thought about that. I think that I had built myself up and psyched myself into blurting it out because if I had given myself a moment's notice, I would have changed my mind, chickened out, and continued the dishonest cycle, like I'd done every time before. I knew it wouldn't be nice, but I definitely didn't expect the severity of his reaction. RaaShaun was irate. He was disappointed. More than that, he was hurt. I could see it in his eyes. It was one of those times when I wish I could go back in time and take back what I said. In hindsight, this warranted more cautious and considerate planning. Maybe if I would have planned for this conversation, the outcome would have been more manageable. I'd humiliated my husband and, as a result, he couldn't stand me.

ENVY: The closest I've ever come to hating Gia was that night. I couldn't believe she'd been lying to me, especially about something so important and valuable to me. When Gia and I got together, I had limited experience. Gia was a virgin, and I considered myself virgin-ish. Being the one to take her virginity made me feel like I had something that no one else could ever have. Gia was my unicorn. I could never bear losing her—never. What we learned about sex, we learned together. It was loving and special. It was an important part of our relationship that connected and bonded us forever. We grew up together, even intimately. Our inexperience was emotionally dangerous and tricky though.

Gia being a virgin and me being her first made me feel as though I was a prime candidate for being cheated on. I believed that her curiosity would one day get the best of her, especially with all the options she had, and she would leave me abandoned and heartbroken. That put added pressure on me to meet all of her sexual needs and be everything she desired. I never wanted to leave her yearning for anyone other than me. But being virgin-ish left me feeling insecure about being able to accomplish that. Using what I knew myself, combined with what I'd heard in conversations around school and the neighborhood, I did my best to keep her satisfied. And her reactions told me that she was. She made me feel like King Kong. If I didn't do anything else right in our relationship, I put it down in the bedroom, and my baby was satisfied.

So when she told me she was faking it, all of my fears had been realized. I found out that I had been given a false sense of security, my ego was shattered, and I was back to feeling like she was one foot out the door, heading toward a man who was better than me. The rug had been pulled out from under me and a void was left behind. I'm not gonna lie. What man wouldn't react that way? Consider a scenario in which you've dated someone for seven years, been married for four, and not having any problems in the bedroom only to find out that it had all been a lie. It felt like every time we were together, she must have been laughing at me. I began to second-guess everything. Every couple has those *special* nights and experiences that they'll never forget. I thought about them and wondered if she was faking then too. When I would ask her about specific instances, she would say that those reactions were real or that it wasn't as big of a deal as I was making it out to be. But it was. Everything changed after that, and I mean *everything*.

I'll never excuse my cheating or blame it on anyone else. I was wrong and I own it 100 percent. At the same time, something about knowing my wife wasn't satisfied led me to want to find someone who *would* be satisfied with me. And that's the part no one tells you about cheating. Of course the person you're cheating with is going to be totally satisfied with you. In their eyes, you can do no wrong. And that's because they're only getting stolen moments with you. They don't have to deal with you in the morning and throughout the day. Or when you're grumpy because you didn't get enough sleep. Or when you have an attitude because you're an only child and are sometimes selfish. Our spouses are the ones who have to constantly put up with our bullshit, and even though I know I was wrong, cheating was my silent way of getting revenge on Gia for crushing me the way she did, for emasculating me and sending my insecurities into overdrive. Cheating was an ineffective attempt to reinstate my manhood. It didn't fix our problems. It only ruined my life.

GIA: Faking it was only part of the disconnect. But I have to be honest about another part of the disconnect, as well. When things finally came to a head and I was honest with RaaShaun, he and I also weren't in sync. Remember, it was him sweeping my concerns under the rug that night that began this domino effect of disaster. At times, he was neither present nor cognizant of the fact that I felt a certain emptiness. More than anything, RaaShaun related his ability to protect and provide to his value as a man. He became hyper-focused on it. In his mind, it was always about giving me the life of my dreams and never saying "no." In his logic, as long as he never said "no," he was doing his job as a good husband. And he made certain that he never had to. If I wanted it, it was mine. Houses, cars, jewelry, vacations—you name it—it was all mine. It made him happier to give than for me to receive; that is because he preferred nothing more than to see a smile on my face. But as I told him many times, none of those things mean anything if the magic begins to slip away. The *magic* is what made RaaShaun truly special and irreplaceable to me. It was his manliness, along with his sweet, boyish nature, our friendship, the jokes, his charm, his kisses, his cuddles, and his *desire* to provide, not his *ability* to provide. The intention always meant more than the act. In my eyes, he was so much more than he ever gave himself credit for.

During that time, RaaShaun's main focus was his career, because that is what enabled him to provide. It made perfect sense to him. He was spending a lot of time in the studio and working parties all across the country. That was in addition to his career in radio and a new television opportunity. His dreams were coming true, but they were also distracting him from his nucleus. At that time, my life revolved around our children. We lived in New Jersey, so I felt relatively secluded from our family and friends in New York. When RaaShaun would come home, he would want to tell me all about his day and pick my brain on certain things; when it became my opportunity to do the same, he would only be halfway listening and "yessing" me. There was a certain amount of selfishness associated with that. That wasn't lost on me. Our lives had become so consumed with what was going on with him and his career that there was very little time to address the things that would keep me from feeling taken for granted and sustain us as a strong, loving unit.

ENVY: Yeah, you could say that was a time when Gia and I were disconnected, but I didn't see it like that. In my mind, I was grinding. Working hard to secure our future. Although Gia actually picked out that house, I enjoyed the fact we were away from the city. I wanted my professional space and home life to be separate. But on the commutes home, I wasn't ever preparing my mind to be present at home. I was calculating how many hours of sleep I could get before I needed to be back out the door again. I knew that I owed Gia the time that we both loved to spend together—I owed it to myself too. But the time just wasn't there. By the time I played with my kids, oohed and aahed over their art projects, and did my manly chores around the house, there wasn't that much time or energy left to be as present as I would have liked to be. I just wanted to make love to my wife and go to sleep.

The truth about hip-hop at the turn of the new millennium was that it was in uncharted territory. Nobody expected we would be able to do the things we were doing, and nobody knew when the opportunities would shift. We had to strike while the iron was hot. At the time, I was on the radio at Hot 97, had a gig with MTV, was working on an album with Red Café, and had a multitude of other projects. That was in addition to hosting parties and doing special events. At the time, I was focused on making all the money I could so that my family could have whatever they wanted. Every day, I woke up thinking of different ways to make Gia happy, because that made me happy too. I did all that I could to make sure that she didn't have to lift a finger, and I thought that compensated for the things that I lacked. At least that's what I was telling myself. The success was getting to me, and I was enjoying it.

While I was experiencing these amazing professional opportunities, my wife was at home taking care of the children. I wanted her to be with me at the parties, events, and through my travels—there's no one I preferred having fun with. But she was a super mom, feeling guilty spending time away from the kids.

She would say, "We have the rest of our lives to party together." Still, I wanted her there with me, then. I also didn't feel as though Gia fully understood my life outside the house. On one occasion, I told her about a night at the club; I had on my sunglasses and was standing on top of the couch with a bottle in my hand. Gia just looked at me like I was crazy. "You were wearing shades in the club? And you were standing on couches? Do you know how ridiculous you sound? How could you even see?" There was definitely a disconnect.

GIA: Okay, wearing shades inside the club *is* ridiculous, and if anyone should tell him that, it should be his wife. That moment captures so perfectly how distant RaaShaun and I were at the time. He was standing on couches in the club. I was running behind kids in the playroom. Our intentions weren't aligned. Yes, we had a plan and vision for our family, but how we saw getting there was diverging. That spills over into the bedroom. If you're not feeling your partner, you're just not feeling them. Sometimes they can tell, and sometimes they can't. But you always can. So much that was going on with our sex lives also had more to do with what was happening outside of the bedroom than anything else. I wasn't faking all the time. There has always been real love between us. RaaShaun *is* sexy to me, and I've always wanted him. Still, our problems affected intimacy.

As women, we often bury our frustrations until they bubble up to the surface. That's what happened the night I told RaaShaun about faking it. What would it have meant to sit him down and have a conversation about priorities and expectations? The answer is, everything. Communication is key, and to be honest, this is one of those times when I didn't do it well. When women find themselves in similar situations and ask me what to do, I'm clear that honest communication about the underlying issue is most important. Talking to RaaShaun about the ways it seemed like we were drifting apart *and* doing the internal work on my own to turn the conflicting thoughts off would have been a better approach. We weathered this storm, but damage remained. Whenever RaaShaun asks me if I was faking an experience, I know that is a response to being deeply hurt by what I said that night. When I told RaaShaun that I'd been faking orgasms, I hurt him, made him not want to be intimate—he had to learn to trust me again.

ENVY: I trust Gia. Asking whether or not she faked it is, again, about my bruised ego and hurt feelings. Gia thinks that my asking her if she's still faking it is because I don't trust her. It has nothing to do with trust. She's stood by me at my worst; this is nothing. It did teach me about being a selfish lover though. When I was really busy with work, which was most of the time, sex was about release. It was about doing what I needed to do to take care of myself and my wife. And I actually thought I was doing a good job. But after Gia said what she did, we began to have different conversations. Gia began to talk more about what she needed from me inside and outside the bedroom. Because I love her, I listened. When it came to what she needed during sex, she became my teacher, and it turned me on. More than anything, she needed me to step up. So I did.

11. Use Your (New) Words

How many times have you heard people say "Relationships take work" or "Marriage is hard work"? While they may be telling the truth, the statements don't make being in love sound appealing. But even if you haven't heard someone say this, you've seen people live it out.

You know the man who was excited about getting married but, after a few years, he doesn't call his wife by her first name or pet names anymore. When he talks about her, she's just "the wife." Or maybe you work with the woman who, after years of wedded bliss, rolls her eyes when her husband's car enters the garage and busies herself so she doesn't have to say anything to him when he finally comes in the house. Or it could be that these two are you. These people will be the first to tell others that relationships take work. In their voices, they project all of the frustrations from their situation onto others. And, unintentionally, they make a mess.

If we want lasting relationships, we have to reorient ourselves with new language and ways to better describe what it is that makes love thrive. Here are three sentences to better convey the beauty of hard work in a relationship.

Relationships take commitment.

When you prioritize commitment in your language, you develop an "At All Costs" ethic and attitude in your relationship. It means that, despite the challenges you face, there's an intention to fix the issues *no matter what*. It doesn't mean we condone mistreatment or disrespect. It means we hold each other accountable to our highest selves and standards. In our relationship, there isn't an out for us. Our commitment to each other ensures we take care with our words and one another's hearts.

If you want to stay in love, relationships take commitment. They take waking up every day and choosing the same person over and over again, through all of life's challenges, knowing that you've made the best decision possible. And that dedication to leaning into your decision will ground your love and family for generations.

Relationships require understanding.

Things change. We are not going to remain the same people we were when we got together. Now, we don't mean *fundamental* change, like you woke up one day to a complete stranger. As a matter of fact, we don't believe that can happen if you've been in tune to your relationship. But we're talking about the changes that take place over time. The subtle changes in politics, thoughts, ideologies, likes, dislikes, music, and culture. The longer we live in this world and consume experiences, the more we'll grow and evolve.

And when that happens, if we want to remain in our relationship, we'll have to adjust and adapt. Offering understanding doesn't necessarily mean we'll agree on everything. After all, we've been changing as well. But there is a willingness to listen and appreciate our partner's evolution. It may mean extra steps on our part. Those steps can include therapy, pushing ourselves out of our comfort zones to try something new, and expanding our capacity for emotional maturity. Whatever it takes, the reward for taking time to really get to *have* and *enjoy* who our significant others have become deepens trust and ensures you are always a safe place for your partner to land.

Relationships necessitate discipline.

If you want a lasting relationship, you're going to have to be disciplined and commit to following through. You must keep your word and allow all your actions to be rooted in integrity. The same focus we put into our physical health with exercise or into our professional goals has to be present in our relationships.

When we say we're going to be somewhere, we need to be there. When we see that our behaviors need to change, we need to push through until they become habits. We need to become people our partner can depend on.

When we exercise discipline in how we approach our relationships, we become steady and solid. We become strong foundations for the legacies of our families. We create new narratives for the relationships in our bloodlines where there have been none.

* * *

Practice living out the principles of these sentences every day for thirty days. Remove "hard work" from the vocabulary you use to describe your relationships and replace it with these sentences or any other positive attributes you choose. Change your language, change your perspective, and change the course of your love.

———

12. Twenty-Five Questions to Ask Yourself Before You Get Married

Nobody goes into marriage with the intention of it failing, but too often, people jump into the most important commitment of their lives without taking a moment to really ask themselves whether or not they're actually ready. We've come up with twenty-five questions that will help to gauge where you are in your preparation. Whether you're single, dating, engaged, or even already married, these questions are designed to push you to think more critically about what it will take to be the best spouse and partner you can be. Grab a notebook or highlighter and take your time going through these questions. If you're ready, it will also make a great couples' exercise.

1. Do I know what love is? If so, how do I define it? Do my partner and I have similar definitions?

2. Can I honestly say I know what I want in marriage? If so, are my expectations reasonable?

3. Will I want it for a lifetime?

4. Have I articulated what brings me joy in a relationship and what it takes to make me happy?

5. Do I know what my partner needs in order to feel secure, and am I willing to give it to them?

6. Do I know what I need to feel secure and am I willing to express it to them?

7. Am I committed to doing the big and little things to make my partner happy and enjoy life with them?

8. Am I committed to doing the big and little things to make myself happy and enjoy life with myself, thus maintaining my own individuality?

9. Do we speak each other's love languages?

10. Am I built for unconditional love, recognizing that people can change physically, emotionally, and spiritually over time?

11. Do I love my partner enough to weather the storms with them and never give up on them or their potential? Does my partner love me enough to do the same?

12. Do I understand the potential for disappointment in my marriage? Am I aware that things can and will change over time?

13. Do I have the tools to deal with the disappointment and change? If not, am I willing to take the extra steps to develop or obtain them?

14. Do I have the capacity to forgive, extend grace, and grow beyond my disappointments and frustrations?

15. Have I discussed my dreams with my partner and are they supportive of me achieving them?

16. Has my partner discussed their dreams with me and am I supportive of them achieving them?

17. Am I on the same page with my partner about children? Do we both want them; if so, have we discussed how many we want, when we'd like to start having them, how we will afford to raise them, and have we agreed upon their religious upbringing?

18. Do we have compatible parenting styles and are we in agreement about how we will discipline our children?

19. Do my partner and I have similar relationships with money?

20. Have we discussed our credit scores and financial goals? Do we have like-minded points of view?

21. Have we taken the time to create a concrete vision for our future together with tangible goals?

22. Am I secure enough to allow my significant other to be who they truly are?

23. Are we on the same page regarding faith or lack thereof?

24. Do I recognize and appreciate that marriage is a choice?

25. Am I prepared to ask my partner to ask these same questions of themselves?

———————

REFLECTIONS

DJ Clue

Out of all the people we know in this industry, Envy and I have known each other the longest. We literally grew up across the street from each other. When Envy told me he wanted to deejay too, he and his father came to my house and asked me to go with them to buy his first set of DJ equipment. When he started deejaying while still going to school, I was proud to see him following his dream.

Because of how close we were, I got to see Envy and Gia's relationship from the beginning. They've always been inseparable. First it went from hanging out and holding hands to wearing matching sweatshirts and sneakers with "I Love You" written in graffiti across the front. I used to tease him all the time about that, too!

Envy and Gia had a strong bond from the beginning and are the perfect example of soulmates who were meant to be. They are a real love story and a true match made in heaven.

Kirk and Tammy Franklin

In a society that programmed black people to misappropriate their value and the idea of true love, many were lost without heroes. So we stumbled through generations seeking examples of what healthy love looked like. Marriage can't just survive in the mall or on the red carpet, in the next sneaker drop or another Telfar bag. The ministry of it is found at the crossroads of balancing the house budget, taking out the trash, and gaining a few pounds around the midsection yet still sparking that inner fire because the love for each other is still there.

For more than twenty-five years, we have journeyed through life's mountains and valleys and found that strength can only be curated from the tension of those *same* mountains and valleys. To reject pain—necessary pain, that is—is often to reject God's tool for character. Thank God that He brings, from the ashes, authentic ambassadors of agape love like Envy and Gia. Thank God for heroes. Long live love.

———

Part Two Q&A

I'm trying to build up the courage to ask my wife to try new sex positions and introduce toys in the bedroom. Any suggestions?

ENVY: After years of sexual exploration with my wife, I can honestly say that I have reached a level of comfort that manifests itself in many different ways. Now that we have open communication about our sex life, we're both confident in our ability to please each other. But trust, it was a long road. Sex in our relationship started off a little rocky. We were both young and inexperienced. We laugh about it now, but for years, I thought my wife was reaching an orgasm when she was faking. Yeah, the stories you hear about women faking orgasms—that was me. The day she told me was probably the worst day of my ego's life. I don't think my ego has ever fully recovered from it. But my ego had to take a back seat and allow the sexual health of my relationship to triumph. Even though it was a difficult conversation, my wife was honest with me about my not getting her to climax, and that became a challenge for me. After our initial conversation, we started to explore in the bedroom. Whether it's being a voyeur, watching porn together, or trying new sexual positions, Gia and I have tapped into each other's souls. We are both down to please each other sexually, and I think that's what it's all about. I encourage you to tap into your wife's sexual soul. Feel her out and tread lightly if this is uncharted territory. You don't want to scare her. Knowing her the way that you do, make sure that you institute comfort and openness. I did and I think that Gia's orgasms are better than she ever thought they could be.

GIA: The fact that you are asking this question implies to me that you and your wife have enjoyed a more mainstream approach to sex in your relationship. That can be fine for the duration of a marriage for some, but expire after a period of time for others. Sex is, by design, meant to be fun, exciting, and pleasurable. It should not be taboo, and as sexual beings, we should not be conditioned to tiptoe around the topic. Also, by design, sex with one person over a long period of time can become repetitive and monotonous—resulting in boredom. It is a hard truth, but it is a truth, nonetheless, for many. We must challenge ourselves to keep it fresh, sexy, and passionate. The key is to keep our partner engaged and yearning for intimate time spent with us. There are many ways to do that, but for the sake of your question, we will concentrate on the two that you inquired about, the use of toys and introducing new sexual positions. I strongly encourage both. Developing comfort in these areas that transitions into skill can introduce a whole world of newfound desire to your relationship. Your partner can go from grabbing a drink after work with his or her friends to rushing home instead to experience you. Discovering a new attitude about sex can unveil a layer of desirability that neither of you ever realized could exist between the two of you.

If you have trepidation about having this conversation as a whole, I would begin by focusing on new sex positions. Some may suggest that you try it during your lovemaking. But if you are scared of talking about it, I certainly wouldn't jump out the window and put something where your wife may not appreciate it. That may create awkwardness and embarrassment, which isn't likely to end in an optimal way. Let her know how much you love her—so much so that you want to take your lovemaking to greater heights. Let her know that you think of her in your private thoughts in those ways and would like to make those ways a reality. Tell her that she is the object of your desire and that you want to experience these things with her and only her. Communicate that you want to please her in ways that will keep her satisfied and wanting you for years to come.

I can't seem to get out of my head during sex, and it's causing me to overthink things and making it less enjoyable for me and my man. I need help but don't know what's the problem with me.

GIA: In my opinion, the problem for most people who cannot "get out of their head" during sex is body image issues, performance anxiety issues, or issues associated with preconceived views of sex as a whole, which may have begun during childhood through imagery, society, or trauma. The key is to reprogram your thinking where sex and intimacy are concerned. This can be done through self-reflection and/or therapy. Without understanding the root of your anxiety, you will never alleviate it. Whatever the actual issue is, you will primarily have to become confident within your sense of sexual self. You'll have to learn how to become comfortable in your mind and body, knowing that you were created as a sexual being and meant to enjoy your sexual experiences. God gave us sexual pleasure as a gift. We are expected to make the most of it without any embarrassment or guilt attached. In addition, we are all beautiful and are entitled to confidence during our sexual acts. That confidence shows up in our sexual spaces as freedom to explore openly and be pleased without being held back by insecurity, judgment, or lies.

ENVY: Getting out of my own head sexually was a major problem of mine early on in our relationship. I was so focused on pleasing her that I wasn't just enjoying it for myself, and I came to find out that she was doing the same. This happens in a lot of new relationships, because you don't know your partner well enough to trust them with your whole being. In the beginning of our relationship, there was too much going on in my head. *Does she like it? Are my sex faces ugly? What's she thinking about?* Couple that with me holding back my excitement because I wanted to make sure I didn't become your average two-minute guy. All of this made our sex less enjoyable. One of the biggest turn-ons for me today is watching my wife enjoy me as much as I enjoy her. There is a comfort level between us that elevates our experience. The first step is learning how to relax enough so that you can be fully engaged and in the moment. After being together so long, I know that whatever ugly sex face I may be making must turn my wife on. Our sexual experience is on a whole other level now that we are comfortable enough to let go. Sex is very mental. And I think people usually get in their own way by letting their mental state control their body during sex. That may work for your everyday life, but to have a truly euphoric sexual experience, your mind has to let go of control. When you fully release control, you can fully enjoy the experience. And if you do it correctly, you're guaranteed not to make an ugly sex face. I'm lying about that last part, but it sounded good.

I think I want to have a threesome, but I'm not sure how it will impact our relationship outside our bedroom. What should I do?

ENVY: I have this recurring nightmare. I'm watching my beautiful wife enjoying the best sex of her life. I can tell because I know her that well.

Her head is lying on the pillow, and I can see her about to climax. She's so gorgeous and sexy in my vision that it's like a movie. Then it's like reality sets in. It's a three-camera setup, and when you pull out to a wide shot, I see that it's not me on top of her. I'm sitting on the side of our bed, just watching. That's usually when I wake up in a cold sweat. For me, I couldn't see my wife with anybody else. Not a man or a woman. As you can tell by my dreams, it's a fear that I refuse to overcome. That being said, a threesome for me would never work in our marriage. Threesomes are tricky. Are you okay with sharing your partner? Clearly, I'm not. But maybe you are. Is your partner okay with sharing you? Hopefully, their feelings mirror yours. I think you have to have a real conversation with your significant other if you are considering a threesome. Really discuss the pros and cons. Some are so sexually explorative that threesomes add extra spice to their sex life. I see nothing wrong with it, as long as you and your partner are on the same page. Never do a threesome because your partner wants to do it, if you don't. Ask yourself why your partner would even want to compromise your comfort level for their own pleasure. I would consider any sexual request from my wife, but I would be honest with her about the way it would make me feel if I wasn't feeling it. We want to please each other, so neither of us ever wants to sacrifice the other's comfort level. Is the sex about what you want or what your partner wants? I think it should be about what you both want, collectively. To me, that's the definition of a relationship. Now, if you don't care about what your partner wants and/or feels, then it sounds more like sex than it does a relationship. In that case, do you really even have a relationship outside the bedroom?

GIA: I am in no position to tell you what to do. I have never had a threesome, so can only offer my opinion from my perspective. I have known many people who have enjoyed threesomes inside and outside of their personal love relationships. I have also known people who have engaged in threesomes solely for a good time and the eroticism that they provided. I understand and appreciate why all the people above participated in the act(s), as I do give credit to people being free spirits and exploring their own individual sexuality in whatever ways they see fit. However, I am able to do that while at the same time acknowledging that that lifestyle is not for me. My own personal belief is that lovemaking is at its best when it is shared between two people who love each other. I enjoy the peace, intimacy, sacredness, and trust that come along with a monogamous relationship between two people. In addition, it is clear to me that when three people are involved in a love or sex relationship, favoritism, preference, insecurity, jealousy, and competition are likely to ensue if genuine feelings are involved. I have seen these feelings creep up even when genuine feelings were not involved. It can simply be a function of human nature. We inherently want to win, to be the best and not have our position threatened by others. In a threesome, there is a high likelihood that one will be left holding the short end of the stick. In many of the decisions that I make in life, I put my options on a scale and measure risk against reward. I suggest that you take your own personality into consideration, do the same, and see which way the scale tips.

How do you tell your partner the sex isn't good without hurting their feelings?

GIA: Simple answer: You don't. If I'm being honest, I cannot imagine a scenario in which a person can be told that sex with them is not enjoyable with kid gloves. Every attempt can be made to soften the blow, but it will be a blow nonetheless. My suggestion would be to determine what exactly it is that you deem as "not good" and do everything within your individual sexual power to encourage change in your partner. For instance, if your partner is too reserved and timid, that may be a reflection of inexperience and/or insecurity. You can counter that with compliments and letting him or her know how attractive you find them to be. Help to create the security in them that they may be lacking. If your problem with them is what you find to be the misuse of their body, express to them in a gentle way your preferences. It can be turned into a fun conversation during which you pick each other's brains about your likes, dislikes, and things you'd like to try. If conversation makes you uneasy and you prefer to avoid it, you can use your own body, physical cues, expressions, and sounds during actual sex acts to guide them toward your likes and away from your dislikes. The best way to achieve true intimacy is to create a safe space for yourself and your partner. As much as you may want to avoid hurting his or her feelings—gentle, thoughtful, and considerate conversation, born out of love, is be the best way to create that space. Once you achieve this, the sky may be the limit.

ENVY: There's a phrase I like to abide by: "Pacify *then* persecute." It's a technique in social interaction with others that usually provides a nice cushion of care before you ultimately deliver a blow. It's something I would utilize in a relationship that warrants a discussion about sex—especially one that may deliver a couple of blows to a person's sexual ego. I don't think it is ever easy to have a conversation with your spouse about sex, especially when the topic is that you are not happy or not getting pleased. But if you pacify first, then the persecution will be received differently. Imagine if I told you that you suck at handball. If you grew up in the parks of Any-Hood USA, you may feel less than. Now imagine I told you that you got a mean jump shot, but you suck at handball. I'm still telling you that you suck at it, but complimenting your basketball game first is going to change the way you receive the handball comment. I would think that the same would work when talking to your partner about sex. Be honest, but don't take it upon yourself to honestly be disrespectful. I would start with discussing the good things. *I like the way you kiss me—your lips feel amazing. I think about you throughout the day.* Then maybe you can tell them what your issue is. *Your legs are so sexy, but I need you to shave them, because the feeling of them brushing up against me during intimacy distracts me.* Okay, maybe a bad example, but you can figure out what your partner likes to hear before having a conversation about your wants and needs. It will make things work better in the long run.

———

PART THREE:

Parenting and Family Life

Quite possibly the most rewarding aspect of our lives together is that we get to be the parents of six amazing children. But as beautiful and bright as they are, we know we can't protect them from everything. Our journeys as Mommy and Daddy have pushed us to look back at our own childhoods and see our parents differently. It's also helped us realize that being Gen X parents to Gen Z and Gen Alpha kids is its own interesting adventure. Whether it's dating or navigating racism and sexism or making sure our kids remain safe in this digital age, we're trying our best to give our kids the room to grow and become who they want to be.

13. Like Mother, Like Daughter (Gia)

As a child, most little girls grow up adoring their mothers, and I was no different. I always looked up to her. She was the most beautiful woman I'd ever seen. Her long, flowing hair and impeccable style made her a goddess to me. Even when I was young, I knew I wanted to be that elegant and graceful when I grew up. More than being regal, my mother was the kindest soul I knew. The word "generous" fully encapsulated my mother. She would give anything of herself to make the people she loves happy. I can't recall a time in my childhood when we didn't have someone who wasn't family living with us. My mother always opened up our home to people who were down on their luck, from recent widows to a friend who could no longer afford the mortgage after her husband lost his job. I'd hear my parents discussing lending people money, and it didn't really matter what my father said about it, my mother was going to make sure that whoever it was had what they needed. If I could say one thing about my childhood, it's this: I knew what it meant to be generous.

We weren't wealthy people, but that didn't matter to my mother. She would say, "When you see people in need, you do whatever you can to help them." Perhaps that's one of the greatest lessons a mother can pass down to her children. We

> "If I could say one thing about my childhood, it's this: I knew what it meant to be generous." —GIA

live in a world that gives girls conflicting messages. On one hand, we're taught to put everyone's needs before our own, and on the other, we're taught to be skeptical of everyone and look out for ourselves. My mother cut through all the noise and taught me the most important things I could ever be are caring and kind. This didn't mean I would become a doormat or allow myself to be used. It also didn't mean that I would be naïve and not exercise wisdom when people asked for help. But what it did mean was: Do whatever you need to do for the people that you love. This idea of community and "showing up for people" filled our home and was the embodiment of womanhood to me. You take care of the people you love. That's it. And my mother loved me well.

My brother, Roman, and I were my mother's world. Our family unit was small and tight-knit. It was just me, my parents, and my brother. Our parents raised us to have everything we needed, and we were given room to be our unique, individual selves. My brother had a much more simplistic view of life and its circumstances than I did. He was easily satisfied and took life day by day. I was a child who lived in vibrant color. I had huge dreams. Even as a child, I wanted a life to fit the size of my hopes and imagination. More than that, I knew that I could work hard to make those visions and aspirations come true. When I would discuss my future, I could tell it absolutely thrilled my mother. She loved having a daughter who dreamed big. She made that possible.

When I was thirteen, my mother and I were shopping for a dress when I spotted an advertisement for the Miss Junior Teen New York pageant. Instantly, I knew I wanted to do it, but I didn't tell anyone. The application required a video entry; I set up my father's tripod by myself and recorded my application video. I came home from school and my mother asked me if I'd applied to be a contestant in a pageant. I told her yes. "Well you're in," she said. I'd been selected as one of the participants for Miss Junior Teen New York. Some parents would have gotten upset with their child for doing all of this behind their backs. My mother marveled at my initiative and confidence. She did whatever was needed to ensure that I was a strong contender. Not only was I a formidable opponent, but I went on to win the title of Miss Junior Teen New York and represent New York as I competed on the national stage at the Miss Junior Teen Cities of America pageant, where I came in as first runner-up. And who was right there beaming with pride? My mother.

I knew my mother lived for me; I knew there was absolutely nothing she wouldn't do for me. When RaaShaun and I were dating in college and got into an argument, it was nothing for me to tell him how easily I could walk away from our relationship because I still had my mother. She believed in fueling and funding my aspirations. I could tell my mother that I wanted to be a sanitation worker, and she'd say, "And you're going to be the best damn sanitation worker in New York City. Then you're going to open your own sanitation business. You're going to start with one truck and then you're going to have ten. And I'm going to fund it for you."

My mother believed in caring for her children. She believed that we were always her responsibility. That didn't mean she didn't want me and my brother to grow up to become productive humans. She most absolutely did. In fact, seeing who they become as adults is the best way parents know that they did right by their children. But even as my mother pushed us to be independent and live up to our own goals, she wanted us to know that she'd always be there. My mother didn't see her obligation to me ending the moment that I married and moved into a house with my husband. She knew that she was the only one who could ever love me without reservation or conditions.

There were ways my mother's commitment to me became even more intentional after my father died when I was nineteen. I was deeply loved by my father, and she didn't want me to lose out on certain experiences because he was no longer there. As it's tradition for the bride's father to pay for the wedding, my mother helped pay for our wedding. At the beginning of our marriage, we actually lived with my mother. As a college graduation gift for me, my mother had her basement converted into a fully furnished apartment. As newlyweds, RaaShaun and I lived there until we could afford a house of our own and move out. My mother also helped us with a substantial loan when we bought that house. These are things that Mommy knew that my father would have wanted and done for me, so she did them instead. She never wanted me to feel at a deficit because I no longer had my father.

When I became a mother, my mother was extremely hands-on. She offered to help in any way she could, and that included babysitting at a moment's notice. We loved being parents, but RaaShaun and I were *young* parents. His career was still taking off, requiring him to be away a lot and out late at night. Oftentimes, we needed time alone. I could pick up the phone, call my mother, and she'd never question it. I could be en route to her house with the kids and call and she'd say, "Yes, bring them. Their food will be ready." There were moments when I just needed a breather. My mother was more than willing to take the kids for a weekend and drop them off at school on Monday. Developing my identity, outside of being a wife and mother, mattered greatly to her. She loved my father and they had a beautiful marriage. She also loved me and my brother and was an amazing mother. Still, she wanted me to remember there were parts of me that needed to be tended to, and she would help ensure that I could do that, even if it was just by taking the kids for a few days.

In ways great and small, my mother showed her love for me. I knew she loved me, and more interestingly, I knew she liked me. Oddly enough though, my mother didn't show her love and devotion by being affectionate. She wasn't that way at all. I was raised in a home where, even though I knew my mother adored me, I never heard her use the words "I love you." It wasn't until I was in college that I realized I'd grown up without hearing those specific words.

She came to visit me at my apartment in Norfolk once, and we began talking about those years growing up. "You know what, Ma? I just realized that you've never told me you love me," I playfully declared. "What are you talking about?" For my mother, my saying that seemed to come out of the blue, and it did. I don't know what brought on that epiphany; I was joking but it was the truth. Still being silly, I stood up and told her to give me a hug and a kiss, and tell me that she loved me. It was the stiffest hug and kiss I'd ever received; you could tell she was beyond uncomfortable, and it was hilarious. Some of us just don't have overly affectionate mothers, but that doesn't mean our mothers love us any less. I knew what it meant to be deeply and incredibly loved by my mother. She loved me fiercely and protected me like a lioness protects her cubs. When I was attacked, my mother didn't come into the hospital and fall apart when she saw my face slashed open. She only wanted to find my attacker. Her love was devotion, provision, and protection.

Not only did my mother want me to be independent, but she also wanted me to be financially savvy. "I've never bounced a check in my life." I grew up hearing my mother say this often. Her integrity when it came to financial matters was very important to her. I had a mother who paid all of her bills on time and was meticulous about her credit score. She often said she could borrow hundreds of thousands at the bank, at any given time, if she wanted to. This

> "Not only did my mother want me to be independent, but she also wanted me to be financially savvy." —**GIA**

was never to brag. She didn't need to impress me or anyone else. By telling me this, my mother was reinforcing the importance of women being able to take care of themselves. Whether it's a car, a place to live, or money for an emergency, a woman should always be able to get what she needs for herself. I adore RaaShaun, but there was nothing he could do for me financially that my mother couldn't or wasn't already doing. She'd put herself in that kind of financial position because, again, she took care of the people she loved and believed

> "RaaShaun can't do anything for me that my mother didn't empower me to do for myself." —**GIA**

financial independence should be the calling card of every woman. But more than that, RaaShaun can't do anything for me that my mother didn't empower me to do for myself. She taught me that being in a relationship was not about dependency. I can love my husband and be excited about creating a life and a family with him. But as a woman, I should always be able to take care of myself.

My mother was the prime example of how kindness and strength can go hand in hand. When I was young, I interpreted that strength as not needing anyone. Essentially, my mother had put herself in a position where she didn't *need* my father, or anyone else for that matter. But that wasn't the strength my mother was showing. Her strength and kindness was always rooted in care—her care for others and her care for herself. It was as if my mother knew the secret to life was being good to yourself and those around you. It was innate, as much a

> "I can love my husband and be excited about creating a life and a family with him. But as a woman, I should always be able to take care of myself." —**GIA**

part of her as anything else. My mother was regal and beautiful because she committed her entire life to loving people.

And while I will always treasure the memories of my mother's care, the truth is, it became increasingly difficult for her to do. In the latter part of her life, for fourteen years, my mother battled dementia. It's a disease that affects the memory and other cognitive functions. Anyone who cares for a family member with dementia knows how hard it can be to watch the ways this disease wreaks havoc in the lives of our loved ones. This front-row seat to my mother's life with dementia was painful. It took away the strong, self-sufficient, and savvy woman that I'd known all my life. The way she showed up for people through the years had to be reciprocated. The deep ways she loved me were the ways I loved her even more deeply as I cared for her.

On May 4, 2021, five days before Mother's Day, my beautiful mommy passed away. When it came time to make the decision of when we'd have her services, there was no question. I would lay my mother to rest on Mother's Day. Who I am is because of her. She instilled every good thing in me, and I will miss her more than I can ever say. When I got married, on Mother's Day in 2001, I was three months pregnant with my first child. When I laid my mother to rest, on Mother's Day in 2021, I was three months pregnant with my last child. For these last twenty years, the years before that and for the years to come, I have been and will be surrounded by my mother's love, and so will my children.

I am the kind of mother I am because of the kind of mother I had. I give my children the world because it was given to me. RaaShaun is an amazing father, and he and I do well as a parenting team. We're also making financial investments now so that we'll be able to do for our children what my mother did for us and so much more. It makes me so proud that, as a unit, we can ensure that our children can live out their dreams without worrying about having the resources to do so. But more importantly, I want my children to know they can count on me specifically, as their mother. Whether it's creating the space to tell me something in confidence that they don't want to also tell Daddy or supporting them through a bad decision without judgment, I wanted to put myself in a position to help because I'm their mother.

Instilling integrity and kindness in all my kids is a priority. While I believe in doing everything I can for my children, I'm clear that I'm not raising any spoiled brats. My mother raised me with an appreciation for all that I was given, and I'm doing the same with our children. As a parent, I believe that we owe it to our children to give them everything they need to thrive, provided they *deserve* it. At the same time, I'm teaching our children that the world doesn't owe them anything and that entitlement won't be tolerated by me or by the world. If they want something, they have to work hard to get it, and they have to be fundamentally decent human beings. *How* I care for them is my responsibility and

> "As a parent, I believe that we owe it to our children to give them everything they need to thrive, provided they *deserve* it." —**GIA**

obligation. I must ensure that they become the best versions of themselves. But that doesn't translate into them expecting us to give them the things they want when they want them. I want to raise children who know just how blessed they are and show their gratitude not by flaunting things but by working hard to ensure that they pay these blessings forward.

Even though my mother is my blueprint, I've made it a commitment to show affection to my children. It's not that my mother did anything insufficiently; it's my choice to build upon what she did and make it even greater. For some, it's easy to criticize our parents for what they didn't do. For me, there's no reason to do that. I was so full of love that I hadn't even realized she wasn't

> "My mother is my blueprint." —**GIA**

demonstrative until I was a young adult. My mother had a different personality than me; perhaps she grew up not seeing love expressed in these ways. Whatever the reason, she had the beautiful ability to make me feel like nothing mattered more than me, instilling confidence and self-esteem. What a gift it is that she gave me everything I needed to be successful.

RaaShaun, I actually didn't tell my mother. Call it a mother's intuition—she knew and came to me to talk about it. But it wasn't to chastise me or tell me that she was disappointed. Instead, she told me that she wanted me to feel comfortable telling her anything I needed to about my sex life. If I had questions, she didn't want me asking anyone outside of her house who could give me the wrong information and didn't care about my overall health and spirit. And, on the chance that I got pregnant, she wanted me to confide in her and only her. Together, we'd discuss my options. "I don't want you going to one of those basement doctors," she said. What I understood was that, even if my mother didn't want me to have sex yet—and she didn't—she didn't want me believing that anybody knew better for me than her. So many young girls navigate their budding sexuality outside of the watchful eyes of their parents because they—and their parents—are afraid to be honest about what's going on with their bodies. My mother wasn't like that. Even though I didn't tell her I was having sex, my mother wanted me to know there wasn't anything I couldn't tell her and there was nothing that would ever separate me from her love.

Like any mother, I want my daughters to fall in love and marry before they're intimate with anyone. The number of sexually transmitted diseases and people who are out to just get what they want is enough to make their father want to lock them in the house until they're thirty-five. My approach is different. Making sure my girls are well informed about intimacy, the good and the bad, and knowing that they can always talk to me is paramount in everything that I do. I will always protect their hearts and equip them with what they need to make sound decisions about relationships. I can't protect them from heartbreak, even though I'd give anything to keep them from the pain. But I can make sure they have what they need to protect themselves.

I recognize how important it is to foster the same independence in my girls that my mother nurtured in me. What I model for them becomes the foundation for their own lives. I want them to know that they have capacities that exceed their wildest dreams. They come from a mother who entered a national pageant on her own when she was a child and from a grandmother who kept herself in a position to be able to help everyone she could. While women have made great strides in this country, there are some things that haven't

"I will always protect their hearts and equip them with what they need to make sound decisions about relationships. I can't protect them from heartbreak, even though I'd give anything to keep them from the pain. But I can make sure they have what they need to protect themselves." —**GIA**

changed or have even gotten worse. Raising strong girls to become powerful, confident women in a world that seeks to destroy them can be hard. But I'm teaching them that anything is possible and whatever they choose to do, I'll be right there. If they want to start a sanitation business, I'm going to help them have the top company in the country, with sights on widespread success. And if they want to be president of the United States, we're going all the way to the White House—and I'll move in to help with the kids.

As I look ahead to my years with my girls, I want to provide mothering that they will one day look back on with fondness, the same way I look back at my mother's parenting style. My confidence and all the ways I seek to be my highest self in the world are the fruits of her tree. I am one of the love offerings she gave this world, and I am committed to being the best I can be to honor

"Raising strong girls to become powerful, confident women in a world that seeks to destroy them can be hard. But I'm teaching them that anything is possible and whatever they choose to do, I'll be right there." —**GIA**

her. It is my responsibility as her daughter and I pray my daughters view me in the same way. If I am half the mother to them that my mother was to me, I know they will.

---

14. The Talk(s) (Envy)

As a black man raising black children in today's environment, I'm going to tell you the truth: I'm scared. Every day, it seems like we scroll through Twitter and Instagram and see another video of an unarmed black person being shot by police or white people calling the police on black people for absolutely no reason other than prejudice, conditioning, and unprovoked fear. This is the world we live in, and with the number of teens harming themselves and taking their own lives, we as parents can't afford not to take this seriously. As much as I want to protect them, I can't be with my two sons and four baby girls every minute of the day. So I have to do my best to prepare them for a world that is much more racist and ugly than I had ever thought.

I'm the son of a cop. I know the importance of law enforcement. All cops aren't bad. At the same time, I know that there are some who don't have their community's best interest at heart. There are some who bring their internal-

"As a black man raising black children in today's environment, I'm going to tell you the truth: I'm scared." —ENVY

ized racism and bias against people who look like me with them on the job every day, and I have to prepare my sons for encountering them, just like my dad had to prepare me. As black people, we know what it means to have "the talk" with your children about encountering the police. For years, it's been "if the police stop you, you do everything they tell you to do. Be respectful and polite. If they take you downtown, call us as soon as you can and don't sign or say anything until we get there." The talk, itself, hasn't changed. What has changed is all the footage we have of black people who have done everything right and still end up in jail, or worse, dead. I have to look at my kids and explain this injustice to them. I have to help them understand how we racism. As parents, we don't necessarily have all the answers, but these kids need them.

So how do we explain this to our sons? First, we've got to tell them that, as black men in American society, they live with a target on their backs. Society

> "As parents, we don't necessarily have all the answers, but these kids need them." —ENVY

will see them as a threat, and that's not their fault. They need to be aware that they are operating from a deficit. But we have to let them know that doesn't mean they can't make it and become whatever they choose to be. At the same

> "This idea of doing the right thing is *not* to prove hateful, racist people wrong. That's not their job. It's more than that; it's for ourselves." —ENVY

time, we have to stress to them that their behavior matters. They can't control how people view them, but as young black men, they can control what they do that can prove other people right or wrong. Doing the right thing, at all times, is what real men do. I teach that to my sons. This idea of doing the right thing is *not* to prove hateful, racist people wrong. That's not their job. It's more than that; it's for ourselves. Sharing stories of how I grew up, telling them about boys and men who aren't here because of some bad decisions they made, I'm showing my sons that it's up to them to decide how they'll move in this world. You can't pursue your dreams from a prison cell.

Another reality for us as parents is that we've raised our children in environments where they may not understand how racism is still alive and well. They

> "You can't pursue your dreams from a prison cell." —ENVY

see us having good jobs, living in nice neighborhoods, owning homes, and then they think that the playing field is level for all minorities. We have to teach them that that's not true. As we're helping them to be appreciative of their blessings, it's on us to explain to them that there are real forces in this world that keep people like them from being everything they hope to be. And when they ask us questions, we can't give them fake answers. Our kids know when we're not being up-front with them. Sometimes, we have to let them in on how Mommy and Daddy are feeling about the state of the world. I let my kids know I'm disappointed in how things are right now. We talk about injustice and what's happening in the world. They see me using my platform to address issues that are important to me and our community. Our kids have to see us working to change the conditions we see. That's how we show them that they have the power to make a difference.

There are going to be times when that sting of racism hits too close to home. One day, Madison came from school with a very sour look on her face. Noticing that she didn't do our normal daddy-daughter routine, I asked her what was wrong. With tears in her eyes, she told me how she sat in class while a

"Our kids have to see us working to change the conditions we see. That's how we show them that they have the power to make a difference." —ENVY

couple of kids behind her talked loudly about the number of black kids in the school and questioned if Madison "qualified" as black. She was fifteen years old and having her blackness called into question. As a father, I wanted to go into Papa Bear mode and protect my daughter. But as a Jamaica, Queens, native, I realized that my life had been lived around black and immigrant communities in a way that Madison's and the rest of my kids' lives have not.

At the time, Madison was one of only four black kids in her high school. Like Madison, I attended a predominately white high school, but all the black people knew each other. Then I left to attend Hampton University, a historically black university. Our experiences when it came to race were totally different. But none of that mattered when I saw my daughter crying. My first thought, and I expressed it to her, was, "Eff those kids!" I told Madison that they're ignorant and don't even deserve to be in the same space with her. Gia, always providing a more calm and reasonable approach, reminded Madison that we love her and explained that those kids probably don't even understand the full scope of what they were saying, but she can't allow them to affect her greatness with their ignorance.

None of us are ready to be hurt by our peers. We know it's coming, but it still hurts. And it hurts even more when the hurtful action is rooted in racism. Half of these kids don't really know what they're talking about and are just repeating things they've heard their parents say. Some of them think it's funny, and a few of them actually mean it. You don't know which one of these perpetrators your child is going to come across, but you have to be ready. Too many kids are internalizing the stupid things their classmates say and thinking less of themselves because of it. As parents, we not only have to develop our kids' self-esteem at home, but have to be their advocates at school as well. There's nothing wrong with following up with the teacher or administration to see how they're addressing these issues as they come up, or before they even become problems.

With each of our kids, we reinforce in them that not only are they beautiful, they are smart and can achieve any goal possible. What we give them is what they use to fight the pressures of the world. We have to make sure we've invested positive energy and light in them.

Once Logan had a teacher who gave him detention because, with her back turned, she assumed that he was the cause of a class disruption. When he

> "As parents, we not only have to develop our kids' self-esteem at home, but have to be their advocates at school as well." —**ENVY**

spoke up for himself and told her that it wasn't him, she ignored him and let the detention stand. We raised our kids to be respectful, and when they've done all they can do, it's time for us as parents to intervene. This is the same teacher who, on the very first day of school, singled him out to be the example for her punishment exercise and made him feel extremely uncomfortable.

Because Logan is a young black boy, I'm already aware of how society views him. With the racial makeup of his school, we can't afford for him to be labeled disruptive or used as an example for punishment. When we talked to his teacher, we made it clear that he has parents who care that he is respectful *and* respected. As a black man in America, I know what it feels like to be singled out and mistreated. It's hard to live in a world where, even in school, you're treated differently. It matters, when you're a child, to have adults advocating for you in this world.

Honestly, having the necessary conversation about police and racism isn't the only conversation we as parents have to have with our kids. Talking about sex and peer pressure takes my anxiety to another level. Gia has a very nurturing approach where she and the kids sit on our bed and talk about everything—and I do mean everything! When I found out she'd talked to Madison and Logan about anal sex, I almost had a heart attack! But the truth is, I'd rather our kids come to us with their sex questions than anyone else. Because I work in hip-hop, my kids are exposed to music and culture that have elements of sexual exhibition. And I know they've heard stories about their friends' conquests, whether true or not, as teenagers. In theory, I don't want any of my kids doing anything until they're in love, married, and out of my house. But as their father, it's not my responsibility to shut down conversations about sex just because I don't want them to have it.

Our kids have to trust us enough to know that they can come to us and not be afraid of our response. In these tough conversations, I tell my kids what I want for them and that if what I want doesn't happen, I hope they'll come to me so we can discuss what needs to happen *next*. I have to tell our crew that they may or may not have the love story like Mommy and Daddy and that's okay. They don't have to feel pressured to do anything they don't want to do or that doesn't come naturally to them. And that's why Madison and Logan know I'm in those DMs! Gia thinks I'm a bit too overprotective, but I know this world. I know how young men can be sneaky, how girls can be sneaky, and how nobody really has a clue about anything they're doing. Giving them the freedom to be on social media while also monitoring it helps me help them—and we all could use a little help from time to time!

Kids don't come with instructions. All of us parents are doing our best to create space where they can grow and be the best they can be. There are a lot of things that try to keep us from doing that. The world we live in isn't necessarily geared toward raising kids safely; that's why we have to protect them. The most important job you will ever have is being a parent, if it's a job you decide to undertake. What we do for our kids will determine the people they become. If we work to provide them with the right amount of freedom and discipline, with faith and good morals, they stand a fighting chance of becoming productive members of society. When we're honest about our hopes, dreams, and fears for them and the state of this world, we give them the tools they need to make wise and informed choices. We want to give our kids everything, but the truth is we can't. The best we can do is give them what they need. They need parents who will remember that, more than anything, we're there to help to guide them in the right direction and be a listening ear when they may have taken a wrong turn.

———

15. Five + Baby Makes Six

At the start of 2021, our firstborn was in college and we were pregnant! Sometimes, it's wild to look back at our lives as those fifteen- and sixteen-year-olds in love now that we're raising teenagers and small babies. But our family is a beautiful full-circle moment for us, and Madison, Logan, London, Jaxson, and Brooklyn (plus the one on the way) are the lights of our lives. But whether online or in person, people see our family pictures and tell us they can't believe we have this many kids. According to them, people don't have so many kids on purpose anymore. They think it had to be an accident, but it wasn't. While our original plan was just for two kids, we grew, changed, and chose to further beautify our lives with several more. We look at our children and think about how God had bigger and better plans than we could ever have imagined.

Madison (Gia)

Madison is our old soul, completely wise beyond her years. She's very particular and self-assured. As kids, it's very easy to succumb to peer pressure, and on some level, it's expected, but Madison is different. She doesn't feel the need to be anyone other than who she is. She's not going to say or act upon anything that isn't true to her. Being authentic matters to her, and she values her space. We saw it early in her selection of friends, and her choices always give us reassurance. Madison's not going to be around anyone who will negatively impact her energy. She's intentional about the kind of person she wants to be, and she's not going to let anyone deter her from those goals. She reasons things out in ways other teenagers typically don't. Once when she went on a date, the guy leaned in for a kiss and Madison stopped him. She told him they didn't know each other like that, and one date didn't entitle him to a kiss. It's that kind of self-awareness that has made it a little easier to watch her fly away from the nest. She's majoring in sustainable real estate development at NYU, and we can't wait to see all that she does in the world.

Madison and I are extremely close, always joking and kidding with each other. Our relationship reminds me so much of the relationship I had with my mother, and I'm grateful that I get to deposit the same pearls of wisdom into her that my mother offered to me. While away at school, she calls me several times a day just to chat, update me on certain things, and ask for advice. She told me that it reminds her of stories that I've shared about how I would speak to my mother ten times a day while I was in college. And she's grateful that that connection that I benefited from as a young girl is not lost on her in our relationship. And while it is true that Madison is my baby, she is a daddy's girl through and through. She and RaaShaun have an extraordinary relationship. They are true buddies, playing jokes on each other and conspiring to prank the rest of the family. The two of them get in the car and go on daddy-daughter drives, having conversations that only the two of them share. Madison has told us several times, "If I can't have what you and Daddy have, then I don't want it." Her father set the bar high for her in terms of what a man should be and should do for her. And she deserves to be treated like the jewel she is. After all RaaShaun and I have gone through in our relationship, it feels pretty remarkable for our daughter to want what we have.

Logan (Envy)

I know parents aren't supposed to have favorites, but you can't tell Logan that he's not his mom's favorite. Logan really thinks Gia loves him more than anyone or anything else on the planet. He talks to his mother about everything. And by everything, I mean absolutely everything. Logan is the definition of a mama's boy. They talk about nine to ten times a day. If Gia's out of the house, Logan's going to blow her phone up until she comes back. The boy can't do nothing without his mother. Once, he and I were in the drive-thru at Wendy's. I asked him what he wanted. This boy told me to call his mother! "Mom knows what I want." We were in the drive-thru, looking at the damn menu, and Logan wanted me to call Gia and tell him what to order. Don't get me wrong, I absolutely love their relationship. I get it. I think sons are supposed to be devoted to their mothers. But I told him he's got to start ordering his own food.

The kid is hilarious. How else can you describe anyone who says Logan Paul can beat Floyd Mayweather in a matchup?! Though it may not seem like it after saying something that crazy, Logan is actually very logical and analytical. He will not be manipulated. He wants to be heard and treated fairly. You can't just say anything to him and have him believe it. He looks at something from all sides and crafts his own argument. He's actually the only one in the house who can give Gia a run for her money in a debate. Watching the two of them go back and forth, exercising their brilliance, is like watching Venus and Serena play against each other. You don't have a favorite; you're just mesmerized by the skill on display. Logan's very good at using his words to convey what he means. We tell him all the time that, in addition to playing football, he should become an attorney. Speaking of sports, don't listen to Gia—he gets all his athleticism and ability from me.

London (Gia)

London absolutely amazes us. She is loving, helpful, and extremely bright. I know everyone says their children are smart, but London is truly gifted. Even at eight years old, her capacity to understand adult concepts is astonishing. The way that she processes information and articulates her thoughts makes her one of the most remarkable kids I know.

She is calm, rational, and kind. Although she's still growing into her own identity, she reminds me so much of myself, so I call her "Mini Mommy." She is a nurturer. The way she tends to her little brother and sister and shows care to our family and others makes me feel comfortable giving her responsibilities far beyond her age. She is meticulous and efficient, making sure that anything she does, she does well. At her young age, she is driven and motivated, asking to take part in more activities than the day will allow—wanting to learn IT ALL! Her brain is always at work, which makes her very curious. She seemingly makes herself invisible in a room so that she is able to be a "fly on the wall," soaking up all of the "adult business" that she can. It reminds me of stories that my mother would tell of finding me hiding under the living room sofa as a child to do the same.

London puts so much thought into the feelings of others, and because of that, London is extremely sensitive and doesn't want to disappoint anyone. I have to constantly remind her that she is not to live life based on the reactions of others. That is not her responsibility. Her life is her own. There's nothing she can do that will disappoint Mommy and Daddy. I don't want her growing up believing that perfection is the goal, because perfection does not exist. Even if these are parts of her personality, I want her to develop on her own and continue blooming into the flower that she is.

Jaxson (Envy)

What can I say about Jaxson? At seven, he's still forming his identity, but he loves fast cars like me, and we'll always have that in common. Jaxson is deeply affectionate. He owns his emotions and expresses them regardless of who is around. Just like Logan was at his age, he is not ashamed to run up to you after school, on the playground or on the sports field, to give you a big hug and kiss. He's not too busy trying to be cool; he's too busy trying to be himself. He respects his family and friends, but he also respects himself—letting you know when his feelings are hurt or when he needs to be alone. Those are the budding seeds of confidence necessary in a world that tries to condition you into what it wants you to be or mold you into societal norms.

He is appreciative, affectionate, and expressive. He never misses an opportunity to let us know exactly how much he loves us, telling us too many times a day to count. He'll give you a hug if he thinks you need it, and his eyes beam with sincerity. Teachers and other mothers tell us stories of how Jaxson is always armed with compliments or will pick a flower for them at lunch. He thrives on making other people feel loved and "seen," and that makes me so proud. He will outright ask you, "How can I make your day better?" He's always wanting to help—offering to do the dishes or clean the garage. He will choose toys from his toybox to offer a friend at school, simply to brighten their day. Often, I think about how wonderful it is to have two sons who are as sensitive and compassionate as Logan and Jaxson. We live in a world that doesn't want black boys and men to be those things. I want to protect that. It's a wonderful thing.

Brooklyn (Gia)

Brooklyn is my unicorn. She's going to be a thrill to raise, because she's so different from her older siblings. Brooklyn has been asserting her individualism since she was a baby. We're an affectionate family, cuddling, kissing, and hugging each other all the time. Even as a baby, Brooklyn would have an "enough of that" attitude. I'd be doing the kissy baby faces to her and she'd be staring back at me like I was crazy—"Didn't I already give you a kiss this morning? Get a grip." And I'm sitting there thinking, "You're a Casey, you better get with the program—you have about thirty-eight kisses left for the day." However, as she got a little older, she began to assimilate into the household's affectionate ways. Now she rubs her cheek up against ours, closes her little eyes, and her smile says it all. She begs to sleep in our room at night because she can't fall asleep without feeling our touch. And now she actually fights with her siblings over who gets to kiss us first.

When she was still little, and while all the other kids fell into the culture of the house, Brooklyn was determined to buck it. She told *us* that she wasn't going to wear diapers anymore because she was a big girl. We agreed, but when it came to wearing a diaper overnight, she wasn't having that either. We actually had to reason with her and compromise. We agreed on pull-ups as a middle ground. She's our fearless child. When a bird flew into our house, everyone ran away from it *except* Brooklyn, who tried to catch it and make it our pet.

She is our little firecracker. It amazes me that someone so little and sweet can be so tough and confident at the same time. At five years old, she makes her older siblings level up and gives off the energy that nothing moves in this house without her say-so. She is powerful, feisty, and self-assured—wanting to do everything herself, because as the youngest in the house for a long time, she never wanted to be seen as the underdog. No! She is the top dog because she is Brooklyn Jagger "Try Me If You Want To" Casey.

Baby Casey (Gia)

For years we wanted more children, and the journey to this baby was a difficult one. When we were blessed with this baby, we were thrilled! With all my other pregnancies, I had a feeling about what I was having. I would tell RaaShaun we were either having a boy or a girl, because that's what I was feeling in my gut, and it would prove correct. This time, though, I didn't have the same feeling. When RaaShaun asked me what I thought we were having, I told him the truth. I didn't know. I absolutely didn't know. Then I got the call that nobody wants to get. My mother had passed away, and this baby wasn't going to get the opportunity to meet her.

One night while lying in bed, I told RaaShaun we were having another girl. My mother's spirit came over me so clearly that I knew this baby would have her spirit too. In June 2021, my feelings were confirmed. At our gender reveal, held in MetLife Stadium, we learned that we're having a girl! Elated, I just looked up at the sky, smiled, and kept saying "Mommy!" She may have left me, but she isn't gone. Every day that I get to raise this beautiful baby girl, I will see and feel my mother. I cannot think of a greater gift.

***

We had Madison when we were young—twenty-two and twenty-three years old. We'd just graduated from college, were married, and were still finding ourselves and our way in the world. But even as we were in the midst of setting up our lives, we took parenting very seriously. Being Madison's parents was a real joy. We decided that we'd try again for a boy and, if we had a girl the second time around, we'd try a third time. A short time later, we had Logan. With a little girl and boy, we were content. It was in these years when hip-hop was beginning to dominate globally, and the DJ Envy brand was taking off. Having two was enough for us at that time.

GIA: Life got much easier for me when they got a little older. I know all mothers are supposed to say they loved the baby phase—and I did. But I really enjoyed when the kids were semi-self-sufficient. For some reason, I couldn't stand strapping kids into car seats. To think of it, car seats and strollers annoyed the heck out of me. They were big, bulky, and difficult to get into and out of cars, especially when you have more than one child and you're trying to prevent one child running out into the parking lot! I loved the fact that kids strapping themselves into their own car seats made them feel accomplished. I would celebrate them and their independence, knowing that I was also celebrating my freedom from dreaded car-seat duty. With the two babies, I was good. We were good. Financially, we were comfortable. It allowed us to afford the help that we needed. Ever since Madison was a baby, I had a full-time nanny, and my mother would help me out on the weekends. I had a husband who was pursuing his dreams and taking care of our family. I was incredibly blessed. We were doing well. We were the family we'd always said we wanted to be.

ENVY: After a few years, I would bring up having another baby, and Gia would look at me like I was crazy. We were settled and doing well. We'd gotten into a solid rhythm with our family, even though I was still working long days and crazy hours. And here I was, ready to mess that all up with diapers and midnight feedings. Gia wasn't having it. But I kept talking about it. Deep down, I knew that consistently talking about a third kid would make it more of a reality in our house. The more I talked about it with Gia, the more we began to see this baby as a part of our lives, and the more we wondered who this little one could be. But Gia still wasn't sold.

It wasn't until she talked to our neighbor that things shifted. Because we were still so young, our neighbor asked Gia if we were going to have any more kids. Gia told her that we'd been going back and forth about it, but she was really on the fence. Our neighbor told Gia the same thing happened with her and her husband when they were trying to decide if they were going to have a third child. "Think about it this way," the neighbor said. "Years down the road, when you look back on your life, if you don't go for it, you may experience regret, not having a third child. But, if you do go for it, no matter what, you will NEVER look back on your life and regret that baby." When she said that, Gia was sold.

GIA: I may have been sold, but I didn't tell RaaShaun right away. I kept it to myself. One day, we were driving back from a long trip, and out of nowhere, he looked at me and said, "let's just go ahead and have another baby." I asked him where that thought came from. He told me that it had been on his mind a lot and he just had "a feeling" that we should have baby number three. Although I was much more open to it after talking to our neighbor, I told RaaShaun we still needed to talk about it. "Gia, we've been talking about it for years. You always want to analyze everything, dissect everything . . . Let's just throw everything out the window and do it!" "Okay," I said. Shortly after that we went to the I Heart Music Festival in Las Vegas, and we conceived London there. While I was pregnant, we talked about having a fourth as soon as I could get pregnant again. London was going to be 12 years younger than Madison, and she needed to be paired with her own sibling playmate. From buying a stroller that could expand into a double to the way we arranged the playroom, we did everything as if we knew another baby was coming right behind London. And it happened just like that. I conceived Jaxson twelve months later at the I Heart Music Festival, again. Jaxson and London's birthdays are two days apart.

Things were great. We had our two pairs of children, and it was really wonderful. Then out of nowhere, when Jaxson was around a year old, RaaShaun had a crazy idea. "You know what, babe? I think we should have one more." What?! Was he playing? Was he crazy? No, he wasn't any of those things. RaaShaun was dead serious. He wanted another baby. And you know what? He didn't get any argument out of me. I loved being pregnant, and because we were already back in baby mode, I was thrilled at the idea of more children. We tried for several months but were unsuccessful. It took months, but I eventually got pregnant, and unfortunately, suffered a miscarriage.

ENVY: We were at the doctor's office for the nine-week checkup. We were all looking at the screen waiting for the heartbeat to pop up. The nurse's face said it all, and Gia asked what was wrong. The nurse said nothing as she walked out of the exam room to get the doctor. When the doctor came in, he told us that there was no baby. "What do you mean there's no baby?" That just didn't make sense. This wasn't our first doctor's visit, and a baby doesn't just disappear. Things weren't adding up. The doctor told us that the fetus, essentially, eliminated itself. He explained that Gia's body knew that it wasn't a viable pregnancy and didn't allow it to continue. While I'm sure there's a better and much more medical explanation for this, it's what the doctor told us. We were devastated. It's hard losing a baby, and there's nothing that can really prepare you for it. We just had to grieve and deal with it. If Gia didn't want to try again, I would support her. While it was hard for me, I had no idea what her body and her emotions were going through. If it didn't happen, it didn't happen. We still had four beautiful kids and a beautiful life. But Gia wanted to try again. Shortly after, our Brooklyn was conceived.

* * *

We have five very different children, all with their own unique quirks and personalities—and we cannot wait to meet our sixth and see what personality she has. There are commonalities in the ethics and morals we're instilling in them, but we're allowing them to be their own people. What we understand

> "What we understand about parenting is that it's not our job to make them into who *we* want them to be." —**ENVY**

about parenting is that it's not our job to make them into who *we* want them to be. Instead, it's to give them the supervised freedom to grow into themselves. We have a plan to purchase a rental property for each of our children upon college graduation. They will be able to manage it and receive a monthly income. With that security, they can go on to truly chase their dreams. They've watched us make careers out of our passions, and we want the same for them. We don't want them to be pigeonholed into jobs they don't want just to make ends meet. We recognize this is even more of an opportunity to be who they truly want to be.

As Gen Xers raising Gen Z and Alpha Generation kids, the differences between us and them are night and day. Add to that, these kids have been blessed to not know the same kinds of struggles we knew growing up. These generations do not see the world the same way we do. Their political views are different. The way they know and understand God isn't the same as the way we know and understand God. Some people get frustrated by this, and it's easy to do that. The Baby Boomers and our grandparents thought we were turning the world upside down too. They survived and so will we.

Our love for each other began in high school. Now we're raising high schoolers. When we look at our children, we get to see our love for each other reflected back to us and all the ways it can manifest in the world. We are our children's teachers, but they teach us as well. We've learned patience in ways we never knew. Wanting to discipline differently than what was culturally acceptable for us growing up, we got creative about punishment. We didn't run for the belt like previous generations. Children also teach us how to see the world through their eyes. We don't know everything; they don't either. But growing with them, watching them as they discover new things, shows us what's possible. The joy and the excitement they get when they learn something new or finally get something right on their own reminds us of all the wonder this world has to offer. And when we see how kind and loving children can be to other children who don't look like them, we're reminded of the good that can still be found in us all. Children save us from dull, uneventful realities. Even if we get frustrated with crayon streaks on the walls or toys that never seem to get put away like they're supposed to, our children are a gift.

We don't know all Madison, Logan, London, Jaxson, Brooklyn, and Baby Casey will become as they continue growing and evolving. We can only hope we're giving them everything they need. That's our deepest prayer. All any parent wants is to know that their children will be good, kind, creative, and productive citizens in this world. When we look at ours, we can see they're well on their way.

We understand that we have the resources to take care of our children in ways others can't. But it wasn't always this way, and we definitely weren't raised with the kinds of opportunities we're able to give. So much of raising children now has become about whether or not you have the money or wealth to do it. The question people get asked all the time now is "Can you afford to have children," not whether or not someone is ready to have kids. And we get it! Kids are expensive! As a parent, not having what you need to ensure they have what they need can make you feel like you're not doing it right. In black and brown communities, finances are listed as one of the greatest stressors among parents. We believe that, if we have more money, we can put our children into better neighborhoods with better schools. Those better schools will lead to better opportunities, including college admissions, scholarships, study abroad travels, and other experiences that will help to shape their lives. Unfortunately, our communities know what it means for our children not to have the same access to these opportunities that white children do. And parents ask us all the time how to make up the difference.

While the playing field remains uneven, there still are more programs and initiatives available to our kids than were available to us. It may take a bit of research and legwork on our end, but there are resources, such as mentoring programs and enrichment camps, out there to ensure our children can get what they need. As parents, we have to be willing to step up to give our children the best we can. And at the same time, we can't beat ourselves up when we fall short. We should never compare our efforts to what other parents can do for their kids. If you're a single mother working hard to make sure that your children have whatever they need, celebrate that and refuse to measure yourself against what a married couple is able to do for their kids.

They say that comparison is the thief of joy. That's especially true when it comes to parenting. Our main objectives should be to provide for our children to the best of our capability, while giving them love and room to grow into the best of who they can be. We can only hope that they will do just that. No matter how many books are written on the subject or classes offered, this job doesn't come with an instruction manual or orientation. Many of us are doing the best we can, but we should always remember that, at the end of the day, our children will reflect our efforts.

16. Do as I Say ... Not as I Did

We truly believe that one of the hallmarks of great parenting is honesty. Children want to know that their parents will tell them the truth. This goes beyond the run-of-the-mill answering of a million random questions your kids ask simply because, it seems, they like to hear themselves talk. In our home, we constantly find ourselves explaining to our children why we made a specific decision. For those who grew up in a "Because I Said So" home, that can seem confusing and counterproductive.

Some parents have decided that explaining themselves to their children is wrong because it will make the kids "too grown," instilling in them that they are entitled to an explanation. But we don't believe any of that. We believe that explaining some of our decisions to our children helps them understand just how we're caring for our lives. The magic of our family is cultivated in how we raise our children. We've planted seeds of care and honesty simply by having small conversations. We *could* just say no to a treat right before mealtime. But how much farther do we get with them when we explain that sweets spoil a meal and are reserved for after dinner? Parents *could* just place their kids on punishment after getting a bad report from school. But you teach them more when you explain to them just how their behavior impacts their classmates and goes against the family's code of behavior. Raising children requires a commitment to pouring into them every day. The work we do as parents is the beginning of who they become, and it's responsible for what they give to the world. Desiring honest children who are full of integrity, compassion, and empathy means being transparent about our wins, our losses, and the rationale behind it all.

Not only do we offer certain explanations and talk through discipline decisions with our kids, but we also believe in having age-appropriate conversations with them about our own mistakes and shortcomings. Raising Gen Z and Generation Alpha kids, as Gen X parents, presents its own unique challenges.

So many conversations and behaviors that were considered taboo for us are being normalized for them. For instance, take marijuana. When we were growing up, weed was considered a gateway drug that would lead to using narcotics such as crack and heroin. In many ways, marijuana was conflated with these harder drugs, and if you smoked it, you were on the fast track to a life of ruined dreams and unfilled potential. We knew kids who sold and smoked weed growing up, and they were heavily side-eyed by many.

But today, marijuana is legal in eighteen states, and cannabis is a billion-dollar industry. The presence of weed dispensaries and the various types of edibles sold in plain sight have normalized marijuana use for our kids in a way that will make their experiences with and perspectives of it much different than ours. And while we believe that the decriminalization of marijuana is a necessary step forward—and will result in giving thousands of black and brown people a second chance at life—smoking weed isn't something we even want our kids to think about until they can make fully informed and rational decisions about it. And to have a conversation about that, we've often revisited Gia's first time eating an edible.

Gia's Story

Growing up, I didn't drink or smoke marijuana. While kids did it in high school, it was never my scene. And though it definitely has its place in the industry and RaaShaun enjoys it in moderation, it just wasn't for me. I always wanted to be in control of my faculties and surroundings. Smoking and drinking was the best way to ensure I wasn't, so I opted out. And after RaaShaun gave me an edible, I completely understood why.

Well, I shouldn't say RaaShaun *gave* me one. He had to deejay at a club the previous night, and in celebration of the emerging cannabis industry, someone had given him a basket of edibles. Weed lollipops, gummies, a chocolate bar—there was even a marijuana-infused soda in there. Before bringing it home, RaaShaun took it to the station to share with Charlamagne and Angela. I don't always listen to the show in its entirety, but for some reason, this particular day, I was tuned in. Out of nowhere, RaaShaun just started laughing uncontrollably. Everything was funny. He couldn't finish his ad lines without laughing. At one point, he even fell out of his chair and stayed on the floor, amused at nothing. I had no idea what was going on with my husband, but I needed him to get it together before he came home.

That day was an unusually busy one at our house. Madison was off at summer camp. Logan was home, playing his video games. There were a group of men inside the house, working on our hardwood floors, and there was another group of men outside the house, installing our sound system by the pool. It was the first day for our new housekeeper, and after RaaShaun came home, some friends were coming over. But instead of coming in to make sure that everything was running smoothly, my husband decided to be mischievous.

"Eat this." RaaShaun extended a piece of chocolate candy, no larger than a dime. *So that's why he was a nutcase on air—he was high!* "Absolutely not," I said to him and went about my business. "Come on, live a little, Gia. You don't *always* have to be such a goody two-shoes . . ." At this point, RaaShaun was joking and making fun of me, so I playfully agreed. I popped the piece of chocolate into my mouth. It was so small. What harm could it really do? Ten minutes in, I realized all my worries were for naught. I felt perfectly fine, went about my work, and RaaShaun went outside to check on the sound system installation. Everything was fine.

If you ask me how I ended up on our bedroom floor "swimming" fifteen minutes later, I couldn't exactly tell you. All I remember was looking up at the ceiling, which had turned black, and then displayed some of the most beautifully vibrant colors I'd ever seen. Strangely, the colors made me feel euphoric and happy; I'd never experienced this level of happiness before. I felt it in my soul. Next thing I knew, I was in a field that had the most luscious green grass in the world. I know it sounds weird, but I actually felt the soft blades of grass growing beneath me as the warm sun beat upon my face. Then, I looked to my left and saw crisp, blue water and decided to take a swim. I dived into my own personal ocean.

Mid-stroke, paranoia began to settle in, but I couldn't stop swimming. This was around the time RaaShaun had to break into our bedroom because I'd locked the door and barricaded it with furniture. He saw me swimming on the floor. "Gia, what the fuck are you doing?" "Shhhh," I told him. "They'll hear you!" He was confused. "Who'll hear me?" I looked up and whispered in this terrified voice, "*the people!*" RaaShaun looked at me and, instantly, we both began laughing. It was clear I was quite high. But just as quickly, my laughter turned to total sorrow and I began crying uncontrollably. If you can't tell by now, I'm not a big a big "crier," so this freaked RaaShaun out. I started feeling deep feelings of resentment—RaaShaun had automatically become my enemy! Extremely concerned, RaaShaun drew nearer and asked what was wrong. I told him that I hated him and want a divorce. "You gave me this poison and you've ruined my life!" Completely unfazed, RaaShaun told me a divorce was fine, but I had to go downstairs and approve the floors. I was adamant that wasn't happening and he'd just have to do it himself.

When RaaShaun left our bedroom, I became terrified someone was going to enter and see me like this. That fear was only amplified by a knock on the door. "Who is it?!" I was frantic and terrified. "Gia, it's Adam. Is everything okay?" Adam owns the hardwood floor company and is a good friend of ours. He'd come to see how everything was progressing and was surprised to find me in my room and not overseeing the various projects going on in our house. "I'll be right there!" I don't know why I was yelling frantically but I was. And I don't even know why I put on a bathrobe and wrapped myself in a blanket when I was already fully clothed. But I did. By this time, Adam had gone back downstairs. He looked up at me when I emerged from my room as if he'd seen a ghost. "Gia, is everything okay?" I replied, "No, everything is NOT okay!" He was worried. My eyes narrowed and my frightened whisper returned. "I . . . can . . . not . . . talk to you right now." I rushed back in my room and locked the door.

Periodically, I'd peek out of my bedroom door, feeling paranoid—like the old lady in the attic. To protect myself from whoever I thought would see me, I needed to build a fortress. I began moving furniture back in front of the door to block anyone from being able to open it. I sat on our bed and cried uncontrollably for no reason. I couldn't even tell you why I was crying; my bathrobe was soaked with tears. RaaShaun actually had to go through my dressing room to get back into our bedroom when he came upstairs to check on me.

When I saw him, I felt nothing but an unexplainable level of rage. Never in my life had I hated something as much as I hated RaaShaun in that moment, and I had no problem telling him as much. After all, *he was trying to kill me*! Again, he was completely unfazed and told me it was time to pick up Madison, who was nine at the time, and her friend from summer camp. With seven-year-old Logan in tow, we headed out to get my oldest and her friend.

Before we left, our new housekeeper asked us to pick up some yellow cleaning gloves. For some reason, she was insistent about these particular ones and could not clean using anything else. I don't know if I said something, but it was understood that, before coming back home, we'd get those gloves. RaaShaun drove. Wrapped in a robe and blankets, I got in the car and reclined the seat all the way back so nobody could see me through the windows. When Madison and her friend got in the car, they didn't even know what to say. I was paranoid and out of my mind. I remember Madison crying and asking RaaShaun, "What did you do to Mommy?" He shrugged it off; "I didn't do nothing to her." Her poor friend. I was sure that she'd tell her mother, who was one of my friends, that she didn't want to do this carpool arrangement anymore.

If you ask me why my husband felt the need to stop at the Ethan Allen furniture store while I was high out of my mind, I would tell you that he likely did it for his own personal amusement. There he was, normally dressed and fully functioning, and there I was, looking like nobody loved me. RaaShaun was browsing normally—I was paranoid about every little thing. The saleswoman looked at me and asked RaaShaun if everything was okay. "Suuure! Everything's fine!" When RaaShaun looked away to continue shopping, the saleswoman pulled me to the side. "Are you here of your own free will?" I knew what she was asking me. I knew how I looked. I knew how it *all* looked. I nodded and told her that I was okay. I don't know if she believed me. I didn't even believe it myself, because I certainly wasn't okay. But at the very least, she needed to know that I hadn't been abducted!

Back in the car, I told RaaShaun that we couldn't forget to get the yellow gloves for our housekeeper. "What are you talking about? We got them already," RaaShaun lied. This only added to my paranoia, that I was so high out of my mind that I couldn't even remember stopping to get the gloves. I repeatedly ask RaaShaun if he was sure that we got the gloves. Each time, he told me that we already stopped and bought them. Panicked that I couldn't remember, I turned around and asked Madison if we indeed bought the gloves. "I'm not saying anything," was her reply. My poor baby was so scared and confused. All of this was hilarious to RaaShaun, and I was scared I'd scarred my kids for life. Logan was crying, and every time I told RaaShaun that I hated him, Logan said "I hate Daddy too, Mommy, for doing this to you."

Finally, we pulled up to my friend's house to drop off Madison's friend. When she came outside, I was still shrouded in my garb and looking ridiculous. RaaShaun exchanged pleasantries and told her that we'd see her tomorrow, but my friend's eyes were fixed on me. "Gia! Are you high??" My secret was out! The truth I'd spent the day hiding from the world was discovered by my friend in less than a minute. "How did you know?!" If I wasn't so paranoid, I probably would've been embarrassed and worried about what she thought her daughter might have seen or experienced while being with us. But my friend only had one question for me. "Got any more?!" We gave her everything that was left in the entire basket.

That was in 2015, and it wasn't until the next evening that I was fully back to myself. Our home was icy for a minute because I was so angry with RaaShaun, who now believes, as I do, that the chocolate was laced with something in addition to weed! We sat a traumatized Madison and Logan down and explained to them what happened. It was important to make this an even broader lesson about the choices they need to make while on their own. We used it as an opportunity to teach them to never give anyone the power to influence them to do something they don't want to do. Granted, RaaShaun is my husband, and I believe he always wants the best for me, but unfortunately, that can't be said for everyone who will cross our children's paths. We want them to know that it's okay to say "no," and saying it doesn't make you corny.

Today's kids are going to be confronted with many mixed messages about marijuana use. As their parents, you still get to have a say in how those messages are processed and countered. When your kids are old enough to fully comprehend what you're saying, I really encourage you to be honest about your missteps with any drug use. And if you don't have a story, I really hope you'll be honest with them about how you came to that decision and stayed strong in the face of everything else around you. Choose to be honest and watch those seeds harvest into children who will respect you and have the courage to make the right decisions when they're not around you.

Envy's Story

Our commitment to being honest with our kids doesn't stop with conversations about saying no to drugs. It means telling them about the reckless decisions we've made that could have jeopardized everything we've worked so hard for. I've had to come clean with my kids, particularly my sons, about my impulsive nature and how it doesn't always lead to the best decisions. I've done some dumb shit in my life, and I don't want them to make similar choices.

Around 2008, there was a rash of robberies and attacks on rappers, DJs, and anyone with a high-profile position in the industry. New York City was on fire, and it wasn't really safe for anyone. When doing parties, I always parked by a fire hydrant or in some emergency lane. I've learned that, if something goes down, I need to be able to get to my car fast. At the end of one night working at a club, my friends and I were walking to my car when two dudes approached me. Well dressed, they seemed to have just come from the party and I assumed they wanted an autograph. When they walked up on me and told me to give them my chain, I knew I was wrong about the autograph. My friends were on the other side of the car, and I got loud to grab their attention. "What did you say to me," I yelled. By this time, my friends realized what was going on and came to my aid. "What's up?!" It was the four of us against the two of them. One of them pulled out a gun and demanded the chain.

Now I know I could've given him my chain, which is the recommended action to ensure a peaceful ending. But I'm not built like that. If I couldn't have my chain, I damn sure wasn't about to just give it to him! As I tried to throw it on top of the building, the other guy hit my arm and the chain fell to the ground. Both of them were looking for it. I saw it, but I wasn't about to tell them that I saw it. When they found the chain, they grabbed it and the dude shot at us before they got into their car to speed away.

All my life, I've tried to understand why certain things happen. There is a reason for everything, and when it comes to me, I want to know what it is. In my mind, if this was a robbery and they got the chain, then there was no reason to shoot at us. But they did, and now I needed to know why. So I hopped in my car and chased after them. In what was nothing short of a scene out of a movie, my Range Rover chased down their X5 in Manhattan. Both of us were doing over 100 miles per hour. Any other time, the streets would have been filled with police. On this night, there wasn't one in sight. I wish I could tell you the rest of this story, but some things are better taken to the grave.

And I also wish I could say I never found myself in that kind of situation again. But a few years later, I found myself in a high-speed chase trying to catch two guys who tried to carjack me using fake police lights and sirens. In hindsight, as much as I say I live for my family, my decisions to go after these clowns didn't reflect that. In both instances, I made impulsive decisions and everything in my life could have changed in an instant. I could've gone to jail or, even worse, I could've been killed. Gia would have been left to raise our first two alone and the other four wouldn't even be here. I was blessed to get out of those situations with my life. I was lucky enough to escape those situations, and I want to ensure I'm passing down better decision-making skills to my kids. As fathers, we get to show our kids all of our flaws in ways that allow them to build their strengths and their character. We learned to change in certain areas so those wouldn't be stumbling blocks for them.

* * *

Our children are gifts that, as parents, we've been entrusted to nurture. We are always trying to strike a balance between the fun times that make growing up joyous and enough discipline that ensures we're not raising the next generation of serial killers and cult leaders. We are all trying our best. But our best efforts have to be rooted in honesty. We have to be committed to allowing our children to see our humanity even as we enjoy our roles as superheroes in their lives. We are our children's first loves and first protectors, even if, in our own lives, we haven't always gotten it right. If we are willing to tell them the truth about those times and what we learned from them, the love and protection can only grow stronger.

———

17. Ten Things Every Parent Should Know

1. You are not going to be perfect.

2. Honesty leads to respect and understanding.

3. Your children are always watching, listening, and learning.

4. You are your children's first and most significant mentors and examples.

5. The lessons that your children learn now will carry them through a lifetime.

6. The traumas that your children suffer now will follow them through a lifetime.

7. Your best is all your children will ever require of you.

8. Don't be so focused on raising your children that you forget to make memories with them.

9. Your children are your teachers too.

10. In your whole life, nobody will love you more than your children, nor will anyone love your children more than you.

━━━━━━━━

18. Envy Wins Father of the Year (Envy)

We'd moved into our first house in West Milford, New Jersey. The town will always be special to us because it's where we were able to afford our first home, but it was definitely secluded and off the beaten path. My commute to and from work was over three hours—not to mention, it's where some of the *Friday the 13th* movies were filmed. It was woodsy and spooky as hell.

Those days it was just the three of us: me, Gia, and Madison. Though I knew we'd have more children, I was proud of our little family. We were just getting started and we were happy. One day, the three of us were all sitting on the floor. Madison was crawling around; Gia and I were playing with her, talking and laughing. All of a sudden, the three of us see this shiny penny on the floor, under a chair. It was as if everything stopped for a split second, and it registered to each of us what that meant.

Madison looked at me.

I looked at Madison.

Madison looked at Gia.

Gia looked at Madison.

Gia and I looked at each other.

Having just turned one, Madison was in the stage where she put *everything* in her mouth. To keep that from happening, Gia and I dove to get the penny before Madison, but her little legs were moving and she got to it before we could. In one motion, she grabbed the penny and threw it in her mouth like it was an M&M. She didn't even try to chew it; she just swallowed it.

Frantically, I opened her mouth looking for the penny and couldn't find it. And, at this point, I start freaking out, believing I'd just killed Madison. I picked my baby girl up and started pacing the room, yelling for Gia to call 911. Of course, Gia's much calmer than I am. I'm crying at this point and my wife, though concerned, is the more levelheaded one trying to get clear about what needed to be our next steps. To her credit, Gia tried—unsuccessfully—to calm me down. "Listen, babe. It's a penny. It went in one end. It's going to come out the other end." But I wasn't trying to hear that. All I knew was that my baby had a dirty, nasty penny in her; it was going to tear up her insides, and I was convinced her life was over.

"911, what's your emergency?" Through tears, I told the operator what was going on. "My daughter just swallowed a penny!" I was crying and hyperventilating. Because the call was about a child and the operator could sense my anxiety, their voice rose a bit.

"Is she breathing?!"

"Yeah . . . she's breathing!"

"Is she acting normal?"

"Yeah . . . she's sitting here . . . but she's going to die! We've got to get this penny out!"

Once the operator realized Madison wasn't in any imminent danger and I was just a high-strung new father, their tone changed. "Sir, calm down," they told me. "There are babies who swallow nails and nothing has happened; it just went right through. So, don't worry. As long as she can breathe, there's no problem." Hearing that calmed me down a bit, but I was still nervous. Even though Madison was breathing fine and playing right now didn't mean something couldn't happen later. For the next thirty-six hours, I watched Madison like a hawk. I didn't sleep. I didn't move from her side. I watched her, making sure her belly went up and down as it normally would with no problems.

The operator had told me that the only way to know that the penny had passed through Madison was to thoroughly check her stool. Now, Gia has a thing for the two *P*s—poop and puke—meaning she doesn't go near either. And while she's the absolute best mom in the world and absolutely adored Madison, she made it clear she wasn't picking apart no shit to look for a penny! That didn't matter to me; I was Madison's father. I'd do it. Plus, finding it was the only way I would have any peace of mind that she was okay.

At the time, I was Fabolous's tour DJ, and we were heading out for another set of shows. Unfortunately, in those two days between when it happened and when I had to head back out on the road, I hadn't found the penny in any of Madison's poopy diapers. The custom for us, at the time, was that we'd be on the road for a week and come home for a week. When I got back from this particular run, there was a line of poopy Pampers waiting for me in our basement from the previous seven days. There were at least fifteen Pampers, and I had to go through each one of them until I found that damn penny!

Thank God I found it. We still have it—thoroughly cleaned and put out of a crawling baby's reach, of course.

———

REFLECTIONS

Madison Casey

My family is extremely close. We're always hugging and telling each other how much we love each other. And we tell each other everything. My understanding of life and the world is rooted in my family. I know that everyone may not always be kind to me, but I can always rely and count on my family. Everyone needs a space where there is no judgment. They are mine.

My parents are amazing. They're also absolutely ridiculous and hilarious. When I was in middle school, my dad picked me up in his convertible dressed like a baby! I mean bib, diaper, everything! I was totally embarrassed, and he thought it was the funniest thing ever. And my mom?! My beautiful and amazing mother is the perfectionist I love *and* hate working with. Only she can see crooked soda cans in the pantry when they are completely straight and not bothering anyone. Our crazy and fun arguments just prove that she would have made a powerhouse attorney.

More than anything, I am grateful for everything they've done for me and my siblings and all they've taught us. No amount of thank-yous would be sufficient. They support us in everything and only want us to be our best. My dad sacrifices so much sleep to ensure that we're able to live our dreams, and my mom is constantly pushing us to realize that no dream is too small. We are incredibly blessed.

When I went off to college, I decided to major in sustainable real estate development to follow in my father's footsteps. Concentrating in environmental science and justice, I want to help make the places people call home more safe and efficient. Because the opportunities we have been given aren't just for us; they're to help make life better for someone else. My parents taught me that.

Sean "Diddy" Combs

I love LOVE! I love BLACK LOVE! We live in a world that tries so hard to stop the power of us as black people to take care of ourselves, to love ourselves, and to provide for the next generation. That's why solid black couples and black families are so important. They show us what's possible, and they teach us what it means to keep pursuing black excellence in life, in business, and in love.

And when I think of couples who do that for us, DJ Envy and Gia Casey immediately come to mind. They've never shied away from talking about the good times and the hard times. For them, it's not just about having a beautiful family. It's about the work it takes to keep that family together. That's why I made sure their podcast, *The Casey Crew*, was the first podcast to premiere on REVOLT. They have so much wisdom to share, and I'm proud to witness how God is elevating them to be part of the Black Love movement and bring even more families closer together, making them stronger than they were before! LOVE.

Part Three Q&A

My husband seriously wants more children, but I don't. What should I do?

ENVY: *Communication* and *compromise* are two words that Gia and I use when we are at odds about something. But for something as major as having children, we have been fortunate to be on the same page. I would say that if you and your partner don't agree about whether or not to have more children, it will probably be the child you bring into the world who suffers the most from whatever decision you make. Parents need to keep that in mind. I've heard all types of stories about women who may not want more kids when their husbands do. Like, some have secretly done things to prevent pregnancy. I've heard of women who have been on birth control behind their spouse's back. I've even heard of men who have had vasectomies and have acted like they are trying to have children with women when they know they physically can't. The level of deception out here is real! But again, when you are in a relationship—especially a marriage—there needs to be transparency. I can't imagine not being honest with Gia about something as serious as having children. Ultimately, the two of you must come to an agreement based on whose point of view is more valid and carries more weight. Regardless of how strongly either of you feels, one of you will not have your way and will experience some disappointment. There will be tough talks ahead determining which one of you that will be.

GIA: In this situation, it is obvious that one of you will have to concede. The most difficult part is deciding which one that will be. So figuring that out may seem next to impossible. Whenever RaaShaun and I are at an impasse, my way of making the best decision is to determine who feels more passionately about their position and why. For instance, if he feels more passionately about having more children than you do about not having more children, the best decision may be to allow his passion to become a reality. In addition, a reasonable compromise may be that only one more child will subsequently come of your union. This is taking for granted that, as a couple, you are financially stable enough to take on the care of another life within your household, childbirth does not pose any health risks to you or the baby, and adding another child to your household is not detrimental to you and your existing family in any other way. On the other hand, if you feel more passionately about not having more children than he does about having more children, the best decision may be to decide to be happy with the family you have already created. He will have to revel in the joy that his already existing children bring. Regardless of who gets to have their way at the end, the two of you will have unveiled a new method of decision-making that is rooted in consideration of each other's deep-rooted feelings and respect.

I love all my kids unconditionally, but one of them is just so much easier to raise than the rest. How do you keep from having a favorite child?

GIA: Human beings are so multifaceted—even children. They evolve at such a fast pace that sometimes it's hard to keep up with their wonder. As parents, we must appreciate each of our children's individuality, because that is where their uniqueness lies. All five of my children are incredibly different, and I expect the sixth to be so as well. I often sit back and watch them carry on in a room so I can observe them. I am usually in awe and marvel at the people they have become—both big and small—and everything that comes along with that. Many of the things we do in life are intentional, deliberate, and within our control. For me, that can often include my way of thinking. By design, I have decided not to have a favorite child. I have taught and conditioned myself to see and celebrate the persistent beauty of each one. What you must be thoroughly conscious of is that favoritism creates insecurity and inadequacy in those who are not favored. It breeds resentment and can be the first falling tile in a domino effect of irreversible repercussions. I know adults who still have deep-seated and unresolved feelings directed at their parents because they felt favoritism in the place they called home. In your mind and especially while dealing with children, you may think that your words, actions, and devotion (or lack thereof) are undetectable and go over your children's heads. But they don't. Children notice it, but more importantly, they feel it. You can cause them to act out in ways that you would have never imagined. Worse yet, you can set them on a trajectory that can only harm them and those around them. As the adult, try to manage your emotions first, followed by your actions, and love all your children equally.

ENVY: When you have a basketball team of kids like Gia and I do, it's difficult not to have a favorite. Unlike Gia, I actually think it's okay to have one, but you have to be careful to not express or show your favoritism to any one of them. All your kids deserve the same love and treatment, but let's be honest, there is always that one kid who hugs you a little harder, who will kiss you a little more, or who will get you a soda and a sandwich from the refrigerator while you're watching TV. But the more experienced I become as a parent, the more I realize that your favorite may change from time to time. In September, it may be your daughter, and by October, it could be your son. Your oldest may be the most helpful one year and become the most misbehaved the next. It can be an ever-changing dynamic. It happens. In our family, we make it our business to spend time with all our kids equally. But it's also important to spend separate alone time with each of them as well, so they receive pointed and individual attention. It is all part of being a good and thoughtful parent. And as one, you must recognize that each kid is unique and comes with their own set of special qualities that contribute to your family. You must value and celebrate their individuality. Plus, you won't really know who your favorite is until you're old and gray and see who changes your diapers and comes to visit you the most . . .

I want to give my children all the things I didn't have growing up, but my family says I'm spoiling them. Is there a such thing as loving your kids too much, and how do I keep them from being spoiled?

ENVY: I see no problem with giving your kids the world, but it is important to make sure they don't turn out spoiled. In my mind, there is no such thing as loving your kids too much or giving them too much, but it's your job as a parent to make sure your kids understand the value of money, respect it, and embrace the work ethic that goes into obtaining it. They need to understand how hard Mom and Dad have to work to earn it. It is my ultimate financial goal to build generational wealth within my family, but that cannot be sustained if my children don't have the right tools to maintain what we have built for them. In order to do that, they must cultivate the right habits and belief system. It is my job as a parent to instill that in them. I admit that my children have a lot of things. But they have those things with the understanding that they had to earn them by being respectful, getting good grades, and doing what is expected of them inside and outside of our home. That is how we, as parents, lay the groundwork. If we don't instill the correlation between earning and receiving at a young age, we pull the rug out from beneath their feet before they ever have a chance to get their feet planted. As parents who are able to provide a comfortable lifestyle for our children, we never want them to expect things to come to them easily. So it is our job to make sure they have balance. Some ways to nurture that balance are to encourage them (if they are teenagers) to get a job or, if they're still too young to work, pay a small allowance for chores done around the house each week. Balance also comes from withholding their allowance if their behavior, their chores, or your expectations of them are not up to par. That will also help them to understand disappointment.

GIA: There is no such thing as loving your children too much, but there certainly is such a thing as spoiling them. As a mother who wants to give all her children their heart's desires, I refuse to raise spoiled children. When I think of the word *spoiled*, the first thing that comes to mind is *ruined*. It means "to diminish or destroy the value or quality of." It also refers to harming the character of a child by being too lenient or indulgent. I do not think there are many parents who would want to ruin their children for any reason or by any means. As parents, many of us desire the same things—to raise children who are well mannered, polite, and respectful. We do not want children who are entitled or feel as though we or the rest of the world owes them something. We do not want children who act out when they don't get what they want or who are unappreciative when they do. We do not want children who feel as though they can say and do what they want, when they want. Rather, we want children who are grateful and kind, have self-control, exercise restraint, resist the urge to talk back and acknowledge their blessings and who, put simply, listen . . . For many, that is not easy to achieve. You may have been raised in a strict household and have vowed not to raise your children with an iron fist, the way that you were. You may have been spoiled yourself and don't know any other way. You may be confused, have no sense of structure, discipline, or consequence, and parent depending on the way the wind blew you that day. If you are any of the above, in my opinion, you miss the mark. Parenting is a skill that thrives on the roots of the relationship you have nurtured with your child. In our home, we run a tight ship. Disrespect is not tolerated *at all*. We love them madly, but at the same time, they have been raised to understand our expectations of them and respect that they have no choice but to fall in line. We are loving and understanding parents who balance love, friendship, fun, and respect. People often misunderstand the term *spoiled* to only be associated with the showering of material things. A child can be spoiled in many ways exclusive of material things. A child who is allowed to speak disrespectfully to their parents, break the rules of the home, and regularly behave in a manner that is not becoming may also be spoiled. In my opinion, being spoiled is receiving anything—whether it be material items, privileges, or behavioral allowances—without deserving it.

How do you learn which discipline techniques work best for parenting your children without it feeling like trial and error?

GIA: The question that I pose to you is, what's wrong with trial and error? Children don't come with an instruction manual, and if they did, it would be obsolete, because all children are different—requiring different techniques as a tailored form of parenting. When it comes to raising children, nothing is absolute. A harsh tone may be enough to encourage one child to listen, while another may need a strict form of punishment. The type of punishment that will affect each child may differ as well. Some may respond to sitting in a corner for twenty minutes; others may respond to having a meaningful material item such as a toy, phone, tablet, or car taken away from them; while another may respond to privileges being restricted or removed. We don't necessarily know what will affect our children the most until we try and fail or try and succeed. So have at it.

ENVY: Experience really is the best teacher in this scenario. Being a parent is one of the hardest things you will have to do in life, so when it comes to disciplining your kids, you have to figure out what works best for you and for them. I think we looked at how we were raised and took things we liked that our parents did, and deleted the things we didn't like. Of course, we added our own special touches to raising our kids and figuring out the best way to discipline them. We were always firm, but we were also fair. These days, you may hear a lot of older people talking about "Back in our day, we used to whip our kids." I'm pretty sure I got my ass whipped once or twice. But disciplining your kids changes with the times. Baby boomers were raised differently than Gen X'ers, and Millennials were raised differently than Generation Z. Find out what works for your kids, because there may be a child or two who needs that belt, LOL! We are friends to our kids, and our kids understand that they can tell us anything, no matter how bad it is. It's something that has worked for us. I've heard people in my own generation be critical about this "friend role" that some parents play, because they believe it doesn't establish the right boundaries. That may be the case in their situations, but as for the Caseys, we're having real conversations, and talking things through with our kids has been the best form of discipline.

———

PART FOUR:

PRIORITIES AND GOAL-SETTING

We've come a long way from those inseparable teenagers we were twenty-seven years ago. We've created a family and are genuinely living our dream. And while it didn't happen overnight, it also requires us to be forward thinking in everything we do. The ability for any relationship to reach its ultimate potential and manifest the greatness that's possible relies solely on the work everyone is willing to do to set and achieve those relationship goals. When you're working together, nothing is beyond reach.

19. Own the Dirt (Envy)

There's this myth that everybody in hip-hop is wealthy. Don't get me wrong, people are getting money. But it's not as simple as people make it out to be. During the height of the mixtape craze, I could make anywhere from $20,000 to $30,000 every five weeks. Most of that depended on whether there was an exclusive song on the mixtape, and if so, I'd have to pay for those out of any money made. But whatever we cleared was still a lot of money for a kid fresh out of college. There were times when I was bringing in more than I ever would have in one of those more "stable careers" my parents wanted me to explore. Granted, it wasn't consistent work, and more times than not I was getting paid in cash, which meant that there was no paper trail to establish a "real" life, but my career was working out for me. I was able to take care of my wife and our baby girl, and have extra to really enjoy life.

It's not an understatement to say that being paid largely in cash is a problem when you're looking to do things like establish your credit and buy a house. When we graduated college, Gia got a job selling mattresses. She worked on commission, was an excellent salesperson, and made A LOT of money. Her paycheck was the most consistent one between the two of us. We didn't have to worry about "mom and pop" taking forever to send the "cash on delivery" payments back for the mixtapes they received. We knew that, every two weeks, a set amount of money was coming in and we could count on it. Not only that, Gia's job provided pay stubs and proof of income that were needed to do the things we wanted to do.

But the problem was that, as my career began to take off, Gia's documentation didn't reflect what we had coming into the house. Add to that, Gia deciding to stay home and care for the kids once she became pregnant with Madison. So it was on me to provide what our family needed, and what we needed was a house. When it was time to purchase our first home in 2002, I had no idea how it would be possible, considering I was being paid in cash for my "job" and just making regular bank deposits. At the time, Busta Rhymes and I were close friends, and knowing that he may have been in a similar situation at some point in his life, I reached out to him for advice. Immediately, he gave me the information for the banker who helped him buy his home. At the time, lenders offered a program called "no-doc loans." To get one, you didn't necessarily have to provide documentation of where the money came from; you just had to show that you had the money on hand and had the capability to continue getting it. These were legal loans that gave self-employed people the opportunity to use their income to own something, even if they didn't have the stability in earnings that other people did. That was me. I knew I could make my mortgage every month; I just needed someone to give me one.

When I met with Busta's banker, he told me that he could get me approved on a home valued at to $500,000 with an interest rate of 14 percent. Yep, you read that right: 14 percent. Not knowing any better and without consulting anyone, I jumped at it. I had the money and would keep getting the money, so what was the problem?! Too damn many problems. First, my interest rate screamed that I had no clue what the hell I was doing. I went into my house with a monthly mortgage payment that was what I should have been paying for a house more than twice its value, with a sensible interest rate. But when you don't know, you don't know. And I definitely didn't. I'll never forget the day we moved into that house. It was July Fourth weekend and 103 degrees inside the house. I know because that's what the thermostat read when I went to turn on the air conditioner. But something was wrong with the unit; it never clicked on. Frantic, Gia and I went from room to room trying to figure out why we couldn't feel anything as we wiped pools of sweat off our faces.

Always the one with jokes, my dad came in the house and asked us why we had the house so hot. We told him that we couldn't get the AC to work. He went over to the thermostat and then went outside. When he came back in the house, he said, "it's not working because you don't have one." Defiant, I corrected him and told him that the house listing said it was "AC Ready." My dad quipped, "Yeah, it's ready for you to put one in here" and went right about his business. To this day, the first thing I ask when we're looking at a house is whether it comes with an AC unit. Looking back, I didn't ask anyone's advice because I wanted to prove that I could do it on my own. So much had been said about my desired career path, and while I was doing well, I still wanted to show that I could take care of my family. It was an expensive lesson to learn that we can all ask for help and take some advice from people who have done what we're setting out to do.

Although those were two major hurdles in buying our first home, nothing compared to how exhausting my commute was from the city. We were living in West Milford, New Jersey, and it would take me more than an hour and a half to get home. I was falling asleep behind the wheel, and it was becoming too dangerous for me to ensure I got back home safely. After ten months of living there, Gia and I agreed that we needed to get something a little closer to the city. When we put our house on the market, it sold in less than a week and we received $100,000 more than what we'd paid ten months earlier. Gia and I said, "Oh shit—there may be something to making money through real estate," and thus began our family's whirlwind housing adventure. We would buy a home, live in it for a short time, renovate it, put it back on the market, and make a profit. We probably lived in four houses in three years, but we made a lot of money and were able to begin establishing a stream of income outside the industry. Of course, this was all before the housing crisis of 2008. When that hit, we couldn't move our house even if we wanted to.

I heard of and witnessed countless stories of rappers and other artists going broke. While you can make a lot of money in music, if you're not handling it properly, you're always one or two flops away from having nothing. And look, I get it. For many of us, we didn't grow up seeing this kind of money. Some of us grew up with modest means; others lived in poverty and music was the way out for the entire family. Either way, seeing tens of thousands and even hundreds of thousands of dollars pass through your hands in a given night is more than most of us ever thought was possible. And we want to celebrate that and enjoy a life of luxury that's often denied to black and brown people. But you can't pop bottles *every* night. You can't rent a Sprinter van and pay $3,000 dinner tabs every time you and your friends want to go out. You can't buy every car, piece of jewelry, or designer outfit you see. That adds up, and this industry is too inconsistent for that kind of lifestyle. Just because you dominated the charts this year doesn't mean you'll dominate for the next two. And as a radio personality, my behavior on air was always tied to my income. If I talked recklessly or did something that pissed an artist off, there was always the chance that they could ice me out, and my appearances at clubs and other events could stall. This would be the DJ's equivalent of flopping, and that was too much of a risk to take.

I wanted us to have income that wasn't contingent on the DJ Envy brand and would never be affected if something in the industry went left. The first opportunity came in the form of purchasing a car wash with a friend. It would be a place where those with classic, luxury, and exotic cars would come and experience top-notch service. It sounded like a good idea at the time. While my friend and I would own it, I got another one of my trusted friends, Lil Shaun, to manage it for us. Aside from a few hiccups—including a vacuum falling on someone's car—it seemed like all was going well. Then I began to learn that there were aspects of the business, entrusted to my co-owner, that were being ignored. Also, the numbers initially proposed that would make this such a good business venture weren't exactly the real figures. And then, as if it couldn't get any worse, Hurricane Sandy hit. With the shop located in one of the hardest-hit areas, customers would have to drive through dirt, mud, and construction right after getting their cars detailed, which defeated the entire purpose. We ended up cutting our losses and selling the business.

I learned a lot from that experience, especially about going into business with inexperienced friends, about making sure that you're always knowledgeable about every aspect of a business you own, and about what type of investment opportunities I wanted to pursue. A car wash could be a good investment; that one just wasn't the right opportunity. And I was becoming more and more interested in homeownership. I thought about the money Gia and I made when we sold our houses, and I wanted to take that to the next level. By this time, our family was pretty settled, and there was no way we were going to keep buying homes just to live in them and sell them. Those days were over. My vision was to have quality rental properties and affordable homes in our communities. Everyone heard stories of slumlords who took advantage of minorities because we couldn't afford access to better housing options, and I wanted to be a part of breaking that cycle. But I didn't know how to go about it.

One day, my cohost Angela Yee came into the studio and told us about homes that were for sale in Detroit. The loss of major industry jobs had gutted the city, leaving all these homes vacant. At the time, Dan Gilbert—owner of the Cleveland Cavaliers, cofounder of Quicken Loans, and a Detroit native—made a commitment to help revitalize his hometown. The city of Detroit was selling homes for $1,000 and buyers were, in turn, selling them for $10,000 to make a profit. When Angela told us about this, I saw it as an opportunity to get into real estate, and Gia and I made a purchase.

Again, we didn't know what the hell we were doing, and because we weren't in Detroit to oversee the property management, we were getting tickets for uncut grass and trash in the yard. To everyone else, our investments were nothing more than abandoned lots that we were paying for. The fun part came when we decided to remodel the homes and make them available for rent or purchase. Detroit homes had a lot of rooms—some had six bedrooms—but they were small. People were much more interested in open floor plans with larger bedrooms and kitchens. So we reconfigured a six-bedroom house into a four-bedroom home with upgraded appliances and amenities. And I loved the experience of remodeling these homes.

Every opportunity I got while on the radio, I sang the praises of moving into real estate. I had a lot to learn, but I still knew this was exactly what my black and brown communities needed. I was becoming the kind of landlord I wanted to see, offering my people quality homes at a reasonable price. Too often, newer homes in our neighborhoods are overpriced with basic features. I wanted to combat that with quality homes, premium features, and desirable neighborhoods. When it comes to homeownership, my philosophy is: "At least I own the dirt." Landownership is important. If something happens to the house and I need to rebuild it, I've got the land to do it. If the city wants to come through and build a highway, they've got to pay me for the land to do it. It's not so much the house that is of premium value; it's what the house is sitting on, and the more land we own, the more we can change the game.

The more I talked about real estate, the more people began to reach out to me to ask if we could invest in doing work together. I didn't respond to anybody. I'm not the type to do business with strangers. Plus, I was just getting into real estate myself; I didn't know enough to know whether or not I was being bamboozled. So I laid low, allowed the investments in Detroit to work, and looked for opportunities to do it closer to home. Cesar Piña, better known as "Flipping NJ," was one of the guys who reached out to me. At the time, I'd just gotten Fetty Wap for my album, and Fetty's manager and Cesar were good friends. He reached out to me and asked if I'd be willing to take a meeting with Cesar, and on the strength of having secured Fetty for me, I agreed.

The meeting was actually Cesar taking Gia and me on a tour of properties he owned in various parts of New Jersey. He owned everything from single-family homes to eight-family rental units. I'd never seen anything like it before, and I was inspired. His homes were well made, with quality upgrades that made you want to live there. This is exactly what I had in mind for black and brown communities. I knew Cesar and I could inspire black and Hispanic kids to want more for themselves from a more positive perspective than the way the drug dealers I saw when growing up inspired me with their fly cars and clothes. Through us, they could see how to make money and provide for their families legally, never having to look over their shoulders and worry about the feds or local competition. I told Cesar I was ready to work with him.

We did well together, and the first thing we wanted to do was share the information we learned with as many people as possible. There were already people doing real estate workshops—people who looked like us and some I even knew through the industry—and they were charging participants thousands of dollars for their seminars. We couldn't understand how people were even able to afford the cost of these workshops. And then we found out that the seminar leaders had partnered with banks, where lenders would advance participants a line of credit that would help cover the cost of the workshop. Before they even got started, these trusting people were already in debt and weren't receiving the most accurate information to help them purchase a property and be on the road to financial freedom.

Learning about this reminded me of my first housing purchase experience. When people know that you don't know what you need to, they'll take advantage of you. I didn't get into this for anyone to feel taken advantage of. Truthfully, we began to host seminars out of spite, because we knew these seminar leaders were exploiting people's desire for better opportunities. Where others were charging thousands of dollars for their seminars, we set our price point at $99. Initially, we hoped that we'd get a major sponsor that would offset the cost of securing the space and paying for speakers and presenters, but we didn't. We didn't make a profit, but we didn't care. Moving into real estate, "owning the dirt," had changed our lives, and we knew what it could do for others.

We expected two hundred participants for our first seminar. Seven hundred came. We began selling out as soon as we would advertise. Whenever we hosted a seminar in a city outside of New Jersey or New York, we made sure to have attorneys, lenders, real estate agents, and other investors from those areas who could speak to the specifics of home-buying in that state and would be willing to help guide interested buyers as they were going through the process. It was more work on our end, but it meant that those who attended our seminars got the specialized information they needed, and everyone left satisfied. People have been able to take what they've learned from our seminars and buy properties. That's the greatest feeling.

When Madison told us that she wanted to study real estate in college, I couldn't have been more proud. She's going to bypass all the mistakes and errors I made along the way and gain more knowledge than I ever could out here figuring this out on my own. And with her education and my on-the-ground training, we'll be unstoppable. That's what I've always wanted: a business that I could leave to my children that would ensure the financial security of their grandchildren. Too often, all we have to leave our loved ones is debt when we die, and that isn't always our fault. Racism and economic disparities make it hard for us to get ahead. But if we have the opportunity to do better, we should, and we should share that knowledge if and when we can.

"But if we have the opportunity to do better, we should, and we should share that knowledge if and when we can." —**ENVY**

I can't tell you how many times men come up to or DM me asking for advice to improve their financial situation. As men, we value ourselves based on our ability to take care of our families. And it can be embarrassing when our credit scores and savings accounts aren't where they need to be. But I always tell them that any financial situation can improve if you're willing to do the work. I went from no credit and having to accept terrible interest rates on everything to being in the best financial situation of my life. And it's not about the money I make. It's about paying my bills on time, working to clean up and protect my credit score, and making investments that make sense. And all of us can do that. During the COVID-19 global pandemic, I gave some brothers the suggestion to sell some of their sneakers on the StockX website, then put that money in their savings account or invest that money in the stock market. None of us were going anywhere, and we didn't know what the pandemic had in store. In essence, with these sneakers, we had money lying on the floor, and it could be used to put ourselves and our families in a better financial position.

I never wanted to be one of those cautionary tales in hip-hop. People weren't going to be asking, "What happened to Envy?" and whispering that they heard I blew all of my money on cars and fast living. While I grew up understanding the importance of hard work and being frugal, the tools of economic empowerment weren't necessarily taught to me. And, to be fair, the tools of today look much different than the tools of my parents' generation. Though I'm on the radio every day, my financial security doesn't look the same as someone who has been working for the same company, retiring after thirty years. There are still too many variables and unknowns in the careers of creators. But I've figured out how to make it work and created a beautiful life for my family. And when it's time, I'll pass this empire and its wealth of knowledge down to my kids.

———

20. We Got Us (Gia)

There's this moment that happens often in our home when I'm just *full*. We'll all be in the kitchen. Madison will be sitting on the counter, telling me about her day and her friends. RaaShaun would have just come in from picking up Logan from football practice, and Logan, in his muscle shirt, will head straight to the refrigerator. We'll have to watch where we're walking because at any moment, Jaxson will run in complaining that Brooklyn is right behind him copying everything he says. And I'll look over and see London sitting at the kitchen table, doing her homework and being the responsible one. I take all that in, look at my pregnant belly, feel blessed, and smile. It's in those moments where I look at my husband and can't help but become overwhelmed, thinking about the six little trajectories we've created that will go off and live entire lives.

In a world of oversharing, RaaShaun and I don't believe that we do. Some would beg to differ. They think that we're telling all of our business on the podcast, the radio show, or in our Instagram feeds. We're often asked how we maintain boundaries around our family to protect them from gossip and public scrutiny. Here's the thing: you can't. Whether you're in the limelight or are a more private person, people are always going to have something to say. So, from that aspect, I'm not bothered. We know who we are and we don't allow what others say to affect us.

RaaShaun and I see boundaries much differently than others. Often, when framing boundaries, it's always about keeping people out of your business or space. It's a protective measure, and don't get me wrong, it matters to have boundaries. But when we're constructing our boundaries, it's always about whether or not sharing this piece of information can help someone else. Would another person consider that oversharing? Of course. RaaShaun and I have been through so much, and a lot of it was trial and error. Why wouldn't we want to keep others from having to stumble toward better like we did?

There's a saying that there can't be a testimony without a test, and there's always a mess before the message. We've had the tests and the messes; we can let somebody else skip that part.

Often, I'll get emails and DMs telling me how much people love our Instagram photos from our vacation in matching colors and outfits. They wonder if I have to do anything to "trick" RaaShaun or the boys into doing it, and the truth is, I don't. We've raised our children to be proud of our family unit and, as a family, we dictate our own path. We always wanted to be the parents that grounded our family in what we came from, and we came from love.

"There's a saying that there can't be a testimony without a test, and there's always a mess before the message. We've had the tests and the messes; we can let somebody else skip that part." —**GIA**

Neither RaaShaun nor I came from a wealthy family, but we knew our parents loved us. They inspired and challenged us to be the best we could be. They gave us everything they could to ensure we could succeed. And when it was time to enjoy life through trips and vacations, they made sure we had those opportunities too. We wanted to do the same for our kids, and I think we're doing a great job.

We've always seen parenting as the capacity to change the world through our children, and we believe God has given us six different ways to do that. As a parent, it's your responsibility to protect that. What we've tried to show our kids is that you're always affecting other people. If your silent actions are rooted in ego and arrogance, you impact other people. And, if your outward actions are rooted in grace, you also impact other people. We teach our children that, no matter what you're doing, your actions will affect others, and it's always in your best interest for that effect to be positive.

"We've always seen parenting as the capacity to change the world through our children, and we believe God has given us six different ways to do that." —**GIA**

What the world sees as a cute little picture on social media, I have always seen as much more. It's one of the ways the Caseys can bring light into the world.

> "Who do you want to be? What do you want to be known for?" —**GIA**

I want our children to always bring light into every room they enter. That's our mission as a family. It sounds simplistic, but it's really about building a vision for your family. Who do you want to be? What do you want to be known for? How do you want to affect the people around you? These are just a few questions that you have to be willing to ask yourself when thinking about the role you want your family to play in the world. We wanted everything to be grounded in positivity. That also means that, as parents, we have to model that for our children. They watch us and do what we do. If there's anything we take seriously, it's knowing that our kids will follow in our footsteps.

If our family had a motto, it would be "We Got Us." From the beginning, we've instilled in our children that Mommy and Daddy will always have their backs. If their friends don't want to play with them, we've never had a problem getting down on the floor and joining in. If they've been stood up or not invited to a movie or a party, we will go to that movie as a family or throw our own Casey Crew party. In all the ways possible, we've shown the kids that they can always look to our unit for love and support. There are so many children who don't have loving and supportive families, and they grow up internalizing that. As a result, they seek validation in people and situations that don't care anything about them, fostering low self-esteem and a belief that they're not as valuable as others. We're not encouraging our children to isolate themselves, but we always want them to know that if the world turns its back on them, they always have us and each other. And while our children are grateful, they're much different from us. RaaShaun and I have been okay with having a few close friends and mainly spending time with each other. Our children, especially Madison and Logan, enjoy having friends. They believe in our "We Got Us" motto to its core, and they're also going to work to maintain their friendships and work to reconcile them, if it's necessary.

We're at this strong point as a family because, after a terrible experience, RaaShaun and I were willing to do the work to repair our relationship and keep our family whole because that was what was right for us. Those Instagram pictures aren't just for likes and shares. They are a testimony that, through faith in God and each other, all things are possible. There's enough pain in this world, and sometimes, we cause it to each other. If situations can be restored, we want to always show that's possible. Even if our children don't know the specifics of every dark time in our lives, they will understand that they're part of something bigger.

———

21. Family Mission Statements

What kind of family do you want to have? Most people never ask themselves this question. When we're younger, we often say things like we want two boys and a girl, an all-girl gang, or a set of twins. And the older you get, you learn very quickly that, unless you're relying heavily on science and spending thousands of dollars or adopting to create your family, you have absolutely no control over this. Beyond what the family will look like, few people ask themselves *who* their family will be.

Will others think of your family as hardworking, honest people? Will your children be pleasant and respectful enough to be invited into the homes of all their friends? Will your home be a place where others feel welcomed and safe? Answering "yes" to these questions doesn't just happen. Families have to make the active decision about the nature and character of their family. Throughout this book, we've called it our magic, which is, ultimately, the essence of your family. And you get to create it. We'll walk you through what it looks like to manifest your family's magic and create the family legacy you desire and deserve.

What is a mission statement?

When people see our Instagram pictures, it's a reflection of our commitment to who we want to be to each other, our community, and the world. We want to be a family that inspires joy, creates generational wealth and opportunities for our future generations, and shows other families what is possible. As a family, the characteristics and attributes that matter most to us are openness, honesty, integrity, joy, happiness, calm, and a peaceful presence. Everything we do must reinforce the family we want to be and how we show up.

As a group, take some time to think critically about the family you want to be. You can even make it a family fun night activity. There are even families who have created their own crests and "rules of engagement." As you're working on your family mission statement, you can do the same thing. Make this activity fun because, in the end, that's exactly what it's supposed to be.

As you're forming your mission statement, here are a few questions to ask:

1. What qualities best describe our family?

Nobody knows your family's magic better than you. Take a few minutes to think about all the things that make you smile and proud to be a part of your crew. These are the building blocks of your mission statement, and to a broader extent, your legacy.

2. What impression do we want to have on the world?

Expanding on your family's positive attributes, think about how you'd like people who come into contact with your family to describe you. Remember, magic is contagious. What you're developing inside the home will be experienced outside of it.

3. In what areas do we need to work together better as a family?

We all have growing edges and places where we can be more kind and loving to each other. As you discuss the answers to this question, make considerable effort to listen to everyone and work hard not to become easily offended. If the magic is the priority, the goal should always be to do what it takes to nurture and cultivate it.

4. What goals would we like to accomplish together?

Now, your kids may say they want to go to Disney every year or to the beach every weekend in the summer, so prepare yourself for that. This is their way of saying they want to spend quality time together. As you've been working on the magic of your family, you deserve the opportunity to create moments to celebrate and cherish it. But are you interested in getting healthier as a family, or do you want to read more and challenge yourselves? This is the time to set those goals.

LEFT TO RIGHT, FROM TOP: RaaShaun at ten months old (1978); Gia at seven months old, being held by by her mother, Norma (1979); Gia at three years old in Brooklyn, New York (1982); Gia and her brother, Roman, in elementary school while attending Mary Queen Of Heaven Catholic School in Brooklyn; Gia's softball stats card at ten years old (1989); Gia showing off her sunburn at a friend's house at thirteen years old (1992); Gia's father, Antonio Grante, during his younger years

TOP: RaaShaun deejaying a Sweet 16 at seventeen years old (1994); **BOTTOM, LEFT TO RIGHT:** Gia and RaaShaun at Gia's high school prom (June 1996); RaaShaun's college graduation picture (1999)

TOP: Gia and RaaShaun's wedding, at twenty-two and twenty-three years old, at Oheka Castle, Huntington, New York (May 13, 2001); **BOTTOM:** Gia and RaaShaun with their parents, Norma, Edward, and Janet, at their wedding

Gia and RaaShaun's wedding, at twenty-two and twenty-three years old, Oheka Castle

LEFT TO RIGHT, FROM TOP: Gia, RaaShaun, and Gia's mother, Norma, at their wedding at Oheka Castle in 2001; Gia and RaaShaun at twenty-two and twenty-three, nine days after their first child, Madison, was born (November 2001); RaaShaun and his parents, Edward and Janet, at his and Gia's wedding; RaaShaun holding Madison at her christening at nine months old, Abyssinian Baptist Church, Harlem, New York (2002); Madison and Logan at ages three and five at Disney World, Florida (June 2007); Gia's mother, Norma, holding both Madison (two years old) and Logan on the day that he was born (December 28, 2003)

TOP: Christmas family photo (2016); **BOTTOM, LEFT TO RIGHT:** Family photo in the Maldives to celebrate London's and Jaxson's second and third birthdays, while Gia was eight months pregnant with Brooklyn (June 2016); London and Jaxson in the Maldives

LEFT TO RIGHT, FROM TOP: Family photo in Turks and Caicos to celebrate Brooklyn's first birthday (August 2017); Gia with Brooklyn in Turks and Caicos; Gia and RaaShaun in Bora Bora, French Polynesia, celebrating Madison's Sweet 16 (November 2017); Gia with Madison, London, and Brooklyn in Turks and Caicos

TOP: New Year's family photo (2018); **BOTTOM:** Gia and RaaShaun at New Year's

LEFT TO RIGHT, FROM TOP: RaaShaun with London at five years old (March 2018); Gia and RaaShaun in Atlanta for Super Bowl Weekend (February 2019); family photo in Ocho Rios, Jamaica (July 2019); Easter photo of London, age five, and Brooklyn, age two (April 2019); RaaShaun and Madison enjoying some daddy-daughter time (November 2019); RaaShaun and Gia on their way to a charity event (April 2019)

Family photo in Ocho Rios, Jamaica (July 2019)

LEFT TO RIGHT, TOP: Family photo in Chichen Itza, Mexico, celebrating RaaShaun's birthday (September 2019); family picnic in Central Park, New York City (July 2019); **BOTTOM, BOTH:** The family at a Disney cruise stop in the Bahamas to celebrate London's and Jaxson's fifth and sixth birthdays (June 2019)

CLOCKWISE FROM TOP LEFT: RaaShaun holding London (age five) and Brooklyn (age two) on Easter Sunday morning (April 2019); Gia, London, and Brooklyn in Riviera Maya, Mexico, to celebrate RaaShaun's birthday (September 2019); Gia and RaaShaun at the Palace of Versailles in France (October 2019); Gia and RaaaShaun at the NAACP Image Awards (February 2020); Gia and RaaShaun in Cognac, France (October 2019)

TOP: The family playing Monopoly, our favorite family game (February 2021); **BOTTOM:** "The Babies" on their way to do some holiday shopping (December 2020)

Family photo (February 2021)

TOP LEFT: Madison, London, and Brooklyn in Puerto Vallarta, Mexico, celebrating RaaShaun's birthday (September 2021); **TOP RIGHT AND CENTER ROW:** Family photos in Puerto Vallarta (Logan stayed at home for football camp), while Gia was seven months pregnant with baby number six (September 2021); Logan in football gear (2021); **BOTTOM:** Gia holding baby Peyton Blair moments after her birth on November 28, 2021. (Please note: This picture was taken after the written portion of the book was already completed.)

Your mission statement may look something like this:

> We are the Casey family. Our family is built on love, honesty, fun, and faith. We will always support each other. We will show and tell each other how much we love each other every day. When there is a problem, we will listen to each other, respect each other, and work together to find a solution. We will spend quality time together and always represent our family with pride when we are outside of the home.

Allow your children to have as much input in the family mission statement as possible. If you want to display it in your home, might we suggest a big print in the family room and smaller versions along with a family photo in everyone's room.

Living Out the Mission Statement

Now that you've created your family mission statement, it's time to discuss how you will live this mission in the home and out in the world.

Home

No matter who you are or what role you have in the family, it's everybody's responsibility to ensure peace and joy in the home are maintained. Whether it's the kids doing chores or making sure your attitude from the workday doesn't spoil everyone else's mood, take time as a family to talk through what behaviors and activities are needed to make the home thrive.

Maybe it will include creating a schedule with time for chores, work, quiet time, and family fun. Establishing a family rhythm now will be even more beneficial as more of the world begins to open back up post-COVID and life goes back to the "new" normal. And remember those family goals? Here's a great time for you to come together to create strategies to accomplish those goals and the ways you'll celebrate them. It may not be Disney every year, but you should definitely think of opportunities to annually celebrate accomplished goals and achieved dreams. Plus, it helps to teach your children the value of hard work.

Work

As a family, we represent each other. As such, our responsibility as their parents is to be mothers and daughters, fathers and sons they can be proud of. How often do you think of representing your children well at work? When catty, messy conversations that seem harmless are happening, do you steer clear of them because you also want your kids to emulate those positive behaviors? Are you constantly setting professional goals for yourselves that will also inspire your children to set goals and achieve them?

Who you are at work and in professional settings matters. Understand that we're not saying it's not important to develop identities outside of your roles as a spouse or parent. It absolutely is. People deserve full identities. At the same time, it matters to recognize your actions and behaviors don't just reflect you. If our children are our teachers too, then we are always learning from them and should always be willing to "show our work."

School

All of our kids' teachers have remarked on how well-behaved, well-mannered, and polite they are—supportive of their classmates and an overall delight to teach. At home, we've modeled for them the correct behaviors and drilled into them positive attributes. We're grateful that our kids get it. They represent us and our family at school. Have you ever explained to your children why it's important to be on their best behavior at school? We know that most of us weren't raised to explain ourselves to children, but it's okay to explain certain things, especially the rationale for proper behavior, to them.

Behaviors reflect the family mission. Wanting to create a strong family legacy requires the kids do their part, and that includes going to school, getting their work done, and behaving while there. They have to understand that when they're not on their best behavior in school, they're in contradiction of the family mission, and there have to be consequences. What those consequences are can be solely up to you, or a collaborative effort with the kids. As you create effective parenting and discipline strategies, always drive home the point that the mission is to make the family as strong as possible.

Community

We've taught our kids that, whenever they go to someone's home, they are to shake the parent or guardian's hand, look them in the eyes, and express their gratitude and appreciation for the invitation. We don't allow them to sleep over at everyone's home, and of course, the older kids have more freedom than the younger ones. Still, their behavior matters, as they represent our family. We've gotten calls from other parents who want to affirm the work we're doing as parents to raise respectful children. If you're a parent who sees the hard work of another parent paying off, take a moment to send that word of encouragement. We're all out here trying our best, and kind words go a long way.

Some families create a "code of conduct" for behavior outside of the home. This is different for many of us who grew up with our code of conduct being "don't touch nothing and don't ask for nothing," and that was it. But creating a code of conduct really helps to give everyone a sense of ownership in how the family is to be viewed by others. When everyone has "buy-in," we're all more than likely going to ensure success. Plus, nobody wants badass kids at the playdate, and nobody wants to be *that* parent who's the topic of all the side conversations and group chats about how "If they can't control them when they're out . . . you know those kids are giving them hell at home."

The World

So much is happening in the world today. Online trolls make it hard to enjoy social media. Laws and policies are being passed making life harder for women, as well as black, brown, and other marginalized communities. People's own political views have made it difficult to be in community with each other. Looking at the world, it's easy to say, "That's not my problem." But creating a safer, more just world is all our problem. As a family, we want to put out as much joy and kindness in the world as possible, and we believe that joy and kindness can help change it. We're not responding to or acting like trolls online. We make a commitment to causes that promote justice and equality. We care about our place in the world and are committed to being light in this world.

All families have the capacity to be this impactful. Teaching children that they matter to this world first starts with parents believing that they themselves matter. And you don't have to be an activist, community organizer, or movement leader to make a difference. If your family works to change the street you live on, that's enough. If you believe that in order to change the world, you've got to be the best person you can be first, that's enough too. We all have a vested interest and stake in making the world a better place for the people we love and those coming behind us.

* * *

Clear visions matter. The kind of family you want is in direct relationship to the amount of effort you're putting into *creating* it. As a collective unit, you pray that the seeds you've planted will bloom into something you can really be proud of, and we genuinely believe they can. You may not have started out with a strong family unit. You may not have seen healthy, lasting families in your own family or neighborhood. You may even doubt whether you can have this kind of family yourself. But that doesn't mean you can't. You absolutely can have this family of your dreams. It will take commitment, understanding, and discipline. It will also be fun and worth every minute of the effort.

22. All Is Fair in Love and the Fifty-Yard Dash

If there were two words to describe us as a couple, they'd be "passionate" and "competitive." To know us is to have seen a simple conversation evolve into a footrace. Like that time we were in Las Vegas for Logan's basketball tournament and a crowd left the arena just to watch us race. (Who won depends entirely on who you ask.) If you follow us on Instagram, you've seen the arm-wrestling competitions and a few of the sprint contests. While they're all in good fun, we don't play when it comes to besting each other!

GIA: Ask RaaShaun about the time we were doing a fifty-yard dash and I fell into a hole. He didn't even stop to see if I was okay!

ENVY: Technically, that's not true. I stopped to see if she was okay . . . *after* I made sure I won. But ask Gia about the time we were wrestling and she almost killed me with her sleeper hold!

GIA: To be fair, I thought he was joking.

ENVY: My entire body went limp. I wasn't playing!

GIA: He sure wasn't. He was mad at me for days!

Since we were young, we've been involved in sports. As adults, we still lead active lives. We've got to if we want to keep up with all of our kids! But being active, for us, isn't just about maintaining physical fitness and being healthy. It's a way to stay connected and remember the joy we've always had in our relationship. In the good times and bad, we've always been able to race each other and gloat! There's an intimacy to it, even if that seems counterintuitive.

GIA: Well, it's hard to gloat when RaaShaun blames all his losses on a baseball injury from the eighth grade.

ENVY: I know Gia ain't talking. Ask her about the bee that nobody but her saw at softball practice. Go ahead. Ask her.

GIA: Oh my goodness—how do you explain someone perfectly catching ball after ball with the exception of one?! Why would I lie about a bee?!

ENVY: I don't know why you lied about it, but that black eye and nearly broken nose from the baseball hitting you in the face didn't lie.

GIA: The bee distracted me! What part of that don't you understand?!

Surviving as a couple means having things that you can enjoy as a couple. What do you like to do together? What are some things that, when you may be feeling disconnected, can remind you of better days and happier times? For us, it's sports and leaning into our competitive natures. For other couples, it will be different. But whatever it is, finding the fun string that ties the relationship together is important. There's enough in this world that tries to keep us down individually and as a collective. Any time you can lean into joy and good times is lifesaving.

There will be days when we won't be able to run as fast as we used to, and it will take more than a Gatorade to recover from pushing ourselves to the limits just to beat each other. When those days come, we'll have the memories. We'll have the stories and the laughs. Most of all, we'll have each other.

———

23. 12 Days (Gia)

For the past fifteen years, RaaShaun and I have been observing our own tradition called "The 12 Days of Christmas." It's a time when he goes back to the things that made me fall in love with him the most. Ever the romantic, RaaShaun spends those days writing beautiful love letters and poems and surprising me with gifts. Each year it gets better, and I'm reminded of how special our love truly is.

Admittedly I was skeptical about putting our "12 Days" on social media. I was concerned that people would focus more on the gifts and their cost than the effort and intention behind them. RaaShaun told me not to worry. One, he loved me and wanted the world to know it. But more than that, he believed that the people who have truly been supporting us would understand and get it. And they did. I've gotten so many emails and DMs from couples who have said that we've inspired them to begin their own special "12 Days" during the holiday season. One husband even emailed us to say that he wrote a letter to his wife every day for twelve days and the romance in their relationship returned. Other families have included their children in their "12 Days" to help remind them that it's not just about the gifts but the love their family has for each other.

Reading these messages and emails always warms my heart because it means that we're all working together to create healthy relationships and families. No matter what we do, we want to inspire people to believe in what is possible for their families and to do what it takes to reach those possibilities. Our "12 Days" is one of the ways to do it. Too often, we can get so busy and bogged down with the holiday season itself that we forget the most important aspect: our families. We're running around looking for the perfect gift and we forget our presence in each other's lives is what matters most. And there are others who observe this time outside of the holiday season just so they can focus on their families without the distraction of anything else. Whenever you observe it, I know that your family will only grow stronger and closer once you do.

So, here's my challenge to you: Create a "12 Days" for your significant other and your family. Make it work for who you all are and don't worry about anyone else. If you want to give gifts, set a budget and happy shopping! If you want to leave your family with lasting words of affirmation, write letters and send cards. If game nights and cooking together are your thing, set aside twelve consecutive nights for fun in the kitchen and family room. It's about being together and showing love in a more intentional way than you do throughout the year.

Everybody wants to feel special. We may already know that we're loved and respected, but every once in a while, we also want to know our loved ones will go the extra mile to surprise us with their love and care, and "12 Days" gives you an opportunity to do just that. I can't wait to read your messages and emails and hear from you about the elaborate plans you made and how happy they made the ones you love.

———

24. Three Steps to Creating a Vision for Your Marriage and Family

Proverbs 29:18 says, "Where there is no vision, the people perish." We understand that to mean that if we don't have a proper understanding of who we are and where we're going as a family, we are already lost. "Perishing" doesn't have to mean an actual death, but so many of us experience loss when we don't take the time to create a direction for our lives. Healthy marriages and healthy family dynamics don't just happen. As we told you earlier, it takes **understanding**, **commitment**, and **discipline** to create the magic that will hold your life and love together. Here are three steps to creating the vision that will ground the relationships that mean the most to you.

1. Decide what kind of spouse and parent you want to be.

Do you want to be patient and understanding with the love of your life? Do you want to be the kind of parent who fosters creativity and freedom in your children? You can become that and so much more! Even if you've never seen or experienced that kind of relationship or parenting, it's still possible. You just have to make the decision that it can be yours.

2. Set your intentions to manifest the relationship you want.

Nothing just happens . . . or at least it doesn't have to. While factors can be out of our control, it's always up to us how we respond to them. Contrary to popular belief, you don't have to argue in your marriage. Despite how you grew up, you don't have to physically discipline your children. You get to create the conditions under which your family will thrive and flourish. And the benefit to setting these intentions is that, in making them real, you also have the ability to get the tools you need to accomplish your family goals.

3. Always make the choice to return to your decision and pursue the goal.

Tough times are inevitable, and they can make or break any relationship. It's in these moments when we often make the mistake of doing or saying something that will hurt our partners or our children—and some things we just can't take back. It's during these times we need to step back, take a deep breath, and remember who we believed we could be. The commitment to the decision to be the best partner and parent we can be should always be at the *forefront* of our minds. We are not perfect, but we can always be better.

———

REFLECTIONS

Charlamagne tha God

There was a time, not only in hip-hop culture but also within the entire entertainment industry, when having a family wasn't necessarily the sexiest thing to showcase. It was all about the player lifestyle and playboy image, which was nothing more than childish nonsense that ultimately led to nothing but regrets and emptiness. But, as 1st Corinthians 13:11 so eloquently states, "When I was a child, I spoke as a child, I understood as a child, I thought as a child; but when I became a man, I put away childish things." The good brother RaaShaun "DJ Envy" Casey is a prime example of a man who has learned to put those childish things away.

What he has with his wife, Gia Casey, is truly special. Which is why I'm so happy that they're sharing their strategies and secrets (and stumbles) in this book. For too long, many of us brothers were encouraged to give the appearance of being single. We were told many things. *Don't wear your wedding ring. Always make it seem that you're available to women. At all costs, make it seem like you're a player.* That mindset has ruined a lot of relationships.

Thankfully, I'm seeing the culture start to shift. With people like Beyoncé and Hov, LeBron and Savannah, Remy Ma and Papoose, Gia and Envy, all these beautiful black and beige couples are putting their families front and center. It helps create new goals. Instead of just promoting money, cars, and jewelry on Instagram, I love to see people taking pride in their families. Because there's no doubt the black family unit shines brighter than any diamond!

I've got a lot of jobs these days, but nothing I do makes me feel more important than being a husband and father. And having spent every morning with Envy for the past decade, I know he feels the same way. Our job on the air might be to talk about culture, but our bond offline is talking about fatherhood.

Personally, I did not have the best role models growing up when it came to building a happy and lasting marriage. I witnessed a lot of dysfunction that took me years to unlearn. Therapy and introspection helped me break what were really generational curses when it came to marriage and family.

If you come from a similarly dysfunctional background, or if you're just looking to strengthen a relationship that might not have gotten as much maintenance as it deserves, then I'd really encourage you to pay attention to what Envy and Gia are sharing in this book. They have built something really special. And with the right amount of discipline, respect, and love, you can build something similar too.

Financial legacies are great, but you can't take the money or material things with you. Family legacy, however, is the game changer that lasts forever. Black Love is the real currency.

50 Cent

I see the Caseys as the royal family of hip-hop. People don't often look at relationships from the right perspective, which I truly believe is friendship. Envy and Gia have that. They've been together for so long because they are friends first. And because they grew together, it's clear they've learned how to become compatible with each other. And honestly, I'm a little envious of that, because a foundation of friendship would alleviate a lot of confusion.

I think this is why Envy is so successful in business and the other ventures in his life. He has focus because his family is grounding him. When you look at the people around artists, the ones who are most able to help them reach their levels of success are grounded themselves. They're married, their priority is family, and they're just different. Their focus is solely on doing good business because, at the end of the day, they're taking their asses home to the people who matter most.

There are so many ways to build what you believe to be your future. Too many times we're just playing it by ear, or we're not even conscious of what we're trying to build. And when we do that, we end up with what picked *us* instead of what *we* picked. Gia and Envy picked each other and were able to build a beautiful family and successful businesses. They built a life that inspires so many. It makes you wonder what we all can build if we start with the right foundation.

———

Part Four Q&A

It feels like my spouse spends money as soon as he gets it, and we can never seem to save. His financial irresponsibility is causing a strain in our marriage, and I'm almost ready to give up. What should I do?

ENVY: In our household, we discuss everything that we buy. We have a household income, and my wife and I are equals. If I want to buy a pair of jeans, I usually call Gia, and no, I don't need her permission! It's just that we have that type of relationship. Gia will do the same thing with me when she goes to the store to purchase something; she usually tells me first. We have the same goals in our relationship. We want to grow and create generational wealth for our children. In order for us to be on the same page at all times, everything regarding our money has to be put on the table. There is no *my money* and *her money*. It's *our money*. Financial irresponsibility will absolutely strain anyone's marriage. Disagreements about money are the second leading cause of divorce. Marriage is about sharing everything, and that includes your money. Again, this is what works for us. If your spouse has some serious issues with managing the marital money, I would start by communicating your concerns, and trying to set up allowances for each of you. There should always be an agreement about money, and your partner should stick to that agreement.

GIA: This is the case for you: You are married to a spendthrift. His relationship with money is one that demonstrates that money is solely for enjoyment. And while, in many cases, it is, money is also for security and stability. His frame of mind is often coupled with the idea that more money can always be gotten. People like this typically don't plan for unexpected circumstances and are hardest hit when they appear. A person who desires to be financially responsible is challenged to temper both uses of money for the greater good. It is clear that in your case, a decision has to be made. You must both make concessions in your financial wants in order to get on the same page. Making these concessions will show each other that each of you is willing to give a little for the purpose of compromise. No one should feel as though their financial rights have been stripped from them in order to make another person happy. I have seen this play out in many unfortunate ways. This is where stealing from the marriage can occur, lying and making purchases that you are dishonest about, and—most prevalent of all—hiding money. Once this behavior begins, it's all downhill. Remember, feelings like this begin with a seed of resentment where a person feels as though they are forced into these tactics because their partner wouldn't budge. This breeds justification for the bad behavior. In contrast, we must give a little to get a little. Show understanding of each of your individual financial needs. Both of you should put your most important financial goals on the table and respectfully negotiate them. Budgets should be set for certain forms of spending as well as for saving. In situations like this, respect and compromise are the keys. If your partner refuses either or both, the nature of the relationship needs to be reevaluated. This may be a deal breaker for you. We cannot spend our lives spinning our wheels and having the same arguments repeatedly. Relationships are a two-way street, and both have to determine whether the relationship is more important than the use of the money that enters it.

My husband is a great provider, but he's just not as present in the home and with our kids as much as I'd like him to be. How do I explain the problem to him?

GIA: Before you are able to explain the problem to him, you must uncover the problem. Begin by asking yourself, *What is it that is keeping him away from home, and while he is here, what is it that is keeping him from interacting?* Some people will buy beautiful flowers so that they can enjoy them and admire them, but do not want to do the work to ensure that they thrive. This person might leave it to their housekeeper, let them die, or just buy fake plants instead. Many people love having a beautiful family but put their own interests and personal time above the needs and well-being of that family. Another potential problem may be that he is extremely tired when he gets home from work and is physically spent, making spending time with the family in a qualifying way difficult. You both may be working parents, or you may be a homemaker. Either way, it is the mindset of many men that regardless of your roles outside of the home, the responsibility of family within the home falls on the woman, as an inherent gender role. Some men (and women, as well) get bored with family life over a period of time. The initial sensation of falling in love and subsequently creating a family begins to wear off, and they look for other things to thrill and excite them. Some people refer to this as a midlife crisis. It is a drastic life swing, because it is riddled with disappointment—a person's own disappointment with themselves in their life choices as well as the disappointment of their family, who are let down as a result.

What is pulling him away from the home may be one of these reasons or none of these reasons. The bottom line is that you must figure it out. If you are lucky, it may only require a conversation. If you're not, it will require you putting together all of the context clues and paying attention to all of the red flags. Use your intuition to help you determine where the problem lies. If answers don't come easily, demand them. Make it very clear that without those answers, you will be put in a position to draw your own conclusions and make choices that put you and your family's needs and well-being first, in the same manner that he has been doing. Remember that leaving that interaction without clarification is not an option. You are not powerless when it comes to the way that your day-to-day life is lived. As much as I don't like to use the word *ultimatum*, one may have to be delivered if a resolution is not reached. Don't expect anything to happen overnight, but as one-half of a marriage, you are entitled to only do half of the work to make it last.

ENVY: I've been the main provider for my family, and with everything I have going on, sometimes I just have not been as present in the home as I would like to be. Gia has been amazing when it comes to understanding this. I recognize that, appreciate it, and try to do my best to be present for her and the kids, even when it means I have to get up extra early to take an earlier flight or skip an event to stay home with the family. I'm always of the mindset that we have to do our part. If you're telling your partner what you want and need and they are ignoring that request, then that's a bigger problem than him or her not being present in the home. The first act is to make sure your partner is aware of how much it's bothering you. But every situation is different, and it takes understanding of each situation. For me there is nothing that I love more than spending time with my family, so it's not like Gia has to ever get me to *want* to be there. She knows me well enough to figure out ways to make me look forward to being home. Are there things you can do to make your spouse want to be there? Is your spouse not there because financially, he just can't be? Depending on the reason he isn't spending as much time in the home with you and your kids, there may need to be either some adjustments made or a bit more understanding.

My family is considered the black sheep of our extended family, and it's causing me not to want to be around them. I want my children to have a relationship with their grandparents, aunts, uncles, and cousins, but I can't take the disrespect and mean things they say. Am I wrong for keeping them away?

ENVY: Defining family is difficult in situations once you start your own. There's family and then there's extended family. I know what's best for my family, and we've been fortunate enough to have great relationships with both Gia's and mine, resulting in one big, happy family. I know this isn't always the case. Sometimes families just don't get along. It's great to want your kids to have a relationship with their grandparents, aunts, uncles, and cousins. And listen, every kid needs to see a little dysfunction. You don't want to shield your kids so much that when they get out into the real world, they have never seen crazy before. In this respect, the unhealthy can be healthy at times. Everything in moderation. We all got that one crazy family member. It's more common than not. As the parent, you can gauge when things have gone too far. If the disrespect is something you feel your kids just aren't ready to see, then by all means, it's your job as a parent to guard them from it. Unfortunately, some kids are exposed to it right in their immediate family. There's no wrong or right to this; it's a matter of knowing what works for your family.

GIA: In a word, no. Your children's happiness, innocence, and safety will always be your number-one priority. Becoming the black sheep may have been a process that began long before the children ever became a part of the scenario. If the children's grandparents, aunts, uncles, and cousins have a problem with the adults in your immediate family, that should be dealt with on that plane, alone. Children should never become casualties of adult warfare. If there are adults involved who are making children feel ashamed or unworthy, those adults should immediately be removed from their lives. If not, there can be long-lasting effects, such as insecurity, low self-esteem, or self-loathing.

I want my family to have a stronger relationship with God. How would you suggest we go about creating it?

GIA: Engage in regular practices such as praying with your partner/spouse and children before meals, before you go to bed at night, and/or first thing in the morning when you wake up together. For many people, especially those who are new to praying, discomfort and embarrassment can be felt while praying aloud. That may take practice until you find your stride. But your children need to hear you praying aloud, so the humble act of praising God becomes normalized and no longer seems weird. Many people have told me they do not *know how* to pray. To those people, I say, "Just have a conversation with Him. Speak from your heart. Acknowledge and thank Him for all that is good in your life. Thank Him for all that is bad as well, as those bad experiences come with life lessons that will benefit you one day, even if that benefit is nowhere in sight. Express to him your shortcomings and ways in which you would like to be better. Ask him for the strength and guidance to do so. Ask for the ability to resist and reject the selfish temptations of the world. Ask for peace and clarity in your decision-making, not only to benefit you, but to benefit others as well. Ask him for a hedge of protection to shield you from all negative influences and entities that may want to impose their will upon you. Ask of your wants and needs and to live a life *deserving* of having those wants and needs met. Ask for ways in which you can serve him so that others will also experience the happiness that you stand to experience by welcoming Him into your life."

This is just a suggestion. This is what I do—every day. You can use it as a beginning if prayer is not in your wheelhouse. Otherwise, prayer is extremely personal. You have the ability to develop your own unique relationship with God. God is not a force to be scared of. He is a force to embrace, to find comfort in. I am most at ease while I am engaged in prayer. God is my companion and most highly respected friend. He is always there, and I feel as though when I speak to Him, He's truly listening. I tell Him the absolute truth, even when I am not proudest of myself. He is all-knowing, so it does not serve you to try to deceive Him. Forge a relationship with Him, admit your wrongs, ask for forgiveness, do better, and be blessed!

ENVY: Practice what you preach. As the patriarch of the family, I know I set the tone when it comes to something as personal as spirituality. I want my family to have a stronger relationship with God, but I understand that my kids' minds may not be ready to grasp the concept of God and religion in the way I've come to understand it. Kids like stability and routine. If they see you praying every night, or five times a day, they will fall in line. When they are old enough to have their own experiences with God, your kids will have a better understanding of their spirituality. But until then, it's all about leading by example. I can't expect my kids to go to church if I'm not going myself. I can't expect them to pray unless I'm praying. My kids, and I suppose all kids, are curious and ask a lot of questions about God. At a certain age, they start to look for answers. They know I don't have all the answers, but I try to teach them the concept of faith and how I apply it in my lifestyle, so they can have a better understanding.

Conclusion:
We Created This

Without question, we live an exceptional life. We have a beautiful home where our family is safe and happy. Our children are healthy and thriving. Our businesses are doing well, and our philanthropic efforts are helping to change the lives of so many. And our relationship, which grounds it all, is stronger than it's ever been. We are truly blessed.

But we are not blessed and our life is not exceptional because of tangible or material things. Over the course of nearly three decades together, we can look back and say that we are incredibly blessed because we did what we needed to do to make this life a reality. Brick by brick, moment by moment, seed by seed, we created it.

As black people, the odds have always been stacked against us. Even as we've been honest about our own failures and shortcomings, we know they exist in a much larger reality of our collective experiences. Many of us didn't grow up seeing healthy relationships modeled in front of us for many reasons. Maybe you lived in a single-parent household and only saw one parent doing it all by themselves. Or maybe both of your parents were there, and the way they interacted with each other and with you wasn't healthy or didn't create the most loving example. It's possible that you were bullied throughout childhood, never quite fit in, and that's impacted all of your relationships. Maybe your inability to deal with your own past traumas and pains has caused you to perpetuate that hurt and harm the people you love and who love you.

We get it. Life hasn't been easy, and things can get really complicated very quickly. The next thing you know you've been walking around in a loveless relationship and with strained connections to your children for years. We hear it all the time from podcast listeners, people who slide into our DMs, and people who stop us on the street. They acknowledge where they've messed up and fear it's about to cost them everything they really want and the people they love.

It doesn't help that we live in a society where it's so easy to throw people away after they make a mistake. As soon as you say something people don't like, they're quick to take to their social media platforms to harass you and tell the world why you are no longer worthy of dignity. Now, many of us are mature enough to weed through comments and read between the lines and determine the difference between trolling and genuine calls for accountability. But what happens when the climate of the dominant culture takes over our personal relationships? What happens when the only response to pain and disappointment in relationships is "canceling" each other?

We want to stress here that we're never advocating for people to remain in abusive relationships, and as you've read, we've been pretty honest about the times our relationship was unhealthy and toxic. We know that there are couples who will recognize that the best thing they can do for themselves, each other, and their families is to end the relationship. And while we grieve that reality with them, we hope they've been able to find truth in these pages that has helped them tell the truth to themselves about their part in the relationship. We hope they've found something that will help them do what they need to do to be better for themselves, their children, and the new love that has entered or will eventually come into their lives. Even after the pain of divorce and abandonment, all is not lost; you can still create a beautiful life.

And then there are the rest of us, who, after the dust has settled, determine that there is still something worth preserving. We are not better than those who decided to walk away. Our circumstances were just different. And sometimes the noise of society, our family, and the people we think have our best interests at heart can be so loud that we think ending things is the right thing for us to do. But we have to be willing to listen to the voice inside of us and the God who is guiding us to ensure that we do what we know to be right. It takes work, but even after the pain of betrayal, you can still enjoy a happy and fulfilling life together.

From the beginning of this book, we knew that we were going on a journey with each and every one reading this to discover and nurture the magic in their relationships and families. We knew that magic would root your relationships to endure and be stronger than ever before. Relationships, like nature, go through seasons. Some are much more glorious than others. But the one thing that will always distinguish a healthy relationship from all the others is its roots. Strong roots make your relationship strong. With them, you can get through the tough times.

In addition to our own transparency and vulnerability, we've provided you with exercises to get at the heart of what really matters: your relationship's roots. Without strong roots, there's nothing enabling that tree to grow strong and feed the fruit. And trust us, the fruit matters too. Because who doesn't want to enjoy the result of all their hard work? It also requires defining what fruit is for you and being honest about it. And here's the thing: If you really want a lasting relationship and a loving family, your fruit can't be defined or consumed by worldly or tangible things.

So many people fixate on the luxury car or the big house. And while those things are enjoyable, consider reframing them as affirmations, like:

> *"The fruits of our relationship include safe, reliable shelter and transportation for our family."*

Instead of money and vacations, consider affirming:

> *"The fruits of our relationship include opportunities to laugh together, experience joy, and make memories as a family."*

See the difference? Shifting the language and reframing the "end goal" allows you to transition from placing value in tangible things to caring more about who you can be together as a couple and as a family.

But we still want you to go deeper. Ask yourself what really matters. When you look at the person you've committed to spending the rest of your life with, what do you want with them? For us, we defined our fruit as:

Joy

God consistently at the center of everything we do

A committed, loving, trusting, and honest relationship where each person grants the other grace

A commitment to constant evolution, becoming better human beings

What we had to say to each other was that if we stripped our relationship down to its core, if we have nothing else, we always want to have these things.

We encourage you to take stock in what fruit you've selected to be the product of your relationship, recognizing that the fruit tells you everything about the roots. You can't have meaningful fruit with shallow roots. You can't have a relationship filled with grace if you keep harboring resentment and unforgiveness. You can't enjoy fruits of honesty and transparency when you're continuously lying and being shady. You can't have ripe fruit of strong family bonds when you're all on your phones doing your own thing every time you're together. Good fruit takes substantial roots.

GIA: Looking back, I don't think many couples have the foresight to think about what marriage truly encompasses. We think about it beyond the wedding in terms of: We'll be living together, we'll have children, and we'll figure it out. Broad strokes. But marriage and real partnership is so much more than "figuring it out." It's about intentional actions and behaviors. I guess that's why many churches and pastors require marriage counseling a few months to a year before the wedding. RaaShaun and I found a loophole. For whatever reason, we were opposed to premarital counseling and had someone say we'd been in counseling with them so we wouldn't have to go through it with the pastor who married us. We were young, and neither one of us had a strong relationship with God at the time. Plus, we'd been with each other for seven years already, since high school—what didn't we know about each other? All of this factored into us making a decision that wasn't necessarily the best one. We most definitely would have benefited from counseling. So don't be like us. Take advantage of premarital counseling and use it as a real opportunity to nurture good relationship roots so you will be ready for whatever comes your way.

I'm not saying that to be trite or cliché. Things will happen, but doing the work to create strong roots in your relationship is the most important commitment you can make to it. That commitment will hold you accountable to yourself when you feel like walking away. That commitment is making the daily decision to be happy and decide the person you are with and the life you have created are *enough*. There will always be "something else" out there. To deny that is to be dishonest. But to focus on the something else to the point where you're thinking about what could be or to even decide to go find out, that's what rots the fruit.

ENVY: *Trust me.* I know. Your journey may look different from mine, but repairing my marriage and becoming a better man taught me so much. It taught me about true love, God, and how amazing grace really is. It taught me that I have been incredibly blessed to go through life with someone as dope as Gia. At the end of the day, we both just want to be better—daily. We want to be our highest selves for God, for ourselves, for each other, for our children, and for the world. And yes, we are choosing each other every day. We choose each other through the corny stuff. Like when Gia instigates a play fight on the bed or when I fart and immediately leave her in the room or the car with it. We choose each other through the hard stuff. Like when she took me back after being a complete dumbass or when I had to have a real conversation with her about the way she communicates and how it can hurt me. We choose each other through it all. And in choosing each other, we're saying, "I love the soul of you. You're the shit and you're worth the work."

The goal of a healthy relationship should always be goodness, self-actualization, righteousness, and grace. We should always remember that we are on the same team. There have been times when all of us have forgotten that, no matter our role in the relationship or how "good" we thought we were. For those moments and times, we owe our lovers apologies and a commitment to being better than we have been and a willingness to let them hold us accountable to what we say. After all, who wants to enjoy good fruit alone? Is that even possible? In the Casey household, we say no.

So we come back to the place where we started: two crazy kids who were in love even if we didn't really know what love was. Now those crazy kids have children of their own, and our life sometimes feels like a whirlwind. If you gleaned anything from us, you know that it's possible to create the life and love you want. There will be long nights, tears, and hard conversations. But there will also always be deep smiles, laughs from the pit of your stomach, and eternal butterflies. You can grow, you can evolve, and you can be happy. You can look back over your life with pride at the strong roots and good fruit you've cultivated through the years. You will have created a legacy. They will be your greatest testimony.

As you've journeyed through this book with us, perhaps it's time for one final assignment. It's time to celebrate yourself for the commitment you've made to healthy and strong roots and the magic that keeps your love alive and your family together. It's time to enjoy the fruits of your labor and truly cherish this life with the ones who matter most!

———

Acknowledgments

We would like to thank God, the architect of our love story. Without Him, nothing in our lives would be possible, and we choose to live each day in deep gratitude for what He has given us.

To our parents: Antonio and Norma Grante and Edward and Janet Casey. Thank you for modeling hard work, consistency, and love. You are models we strive to live up to, and we pray that we make you proud. Thank you for every piece of wisdom, discipline, sacrifice, and joy you have given us. You are our greatest teachers.

To our children: Madison, Logan, London, Jaxson, Brooklyn, and Baby Casey. We live for you and love you more than anything in this world. You already make us proud, and we can't wait to see all that you do in this world. Know that, in everything, we will be right by your side.

To our family: Roman Grante, Aaron Grante, Kaitlin Grante, Michael Grossett, Jason Grossett, Teniel Grossett, Kasey Grossett, George Fox, Vivian Fox, Jemal Fox, Lleone Murdock, Carolyn Foye, Brian Foye, Vernon Foye, Eddie Montpleasie, Carmen Montpleasie, and Geran Montpleasie. We've grown up together, and you all have had a front-row seat watching this love grow and evolve. Thank you for how you've loved and supported us individually and collectively.

To our closest friends: Carl Blair (June), Ingrid Crossman, Shaun Evans (Lil Shaun), Danny Francis, Kharisma Gonzalez, Brian Grimsley, Dahlia Haynes, Wilfrance Lominy, Rasheed and Sasha McWilliams, Natina Nimene, Reggie Ramsey, Ernesto Shaw (DJ Clue), Danielle Thomas, Renan Thybulle (DJ Mono), and Mercedes Walker (Benz). Thank you for knowing the real us, loving us, and always having our backs. Life is amazing with you all riding with us!

To Candice Marie Benbow, Tess Callero, Samantha Weiner, and everyone at Abrams Books: Thank you so much for believing in us and helping to bring our story to the masses in this way. We are grateful for the opportunity and truly enjoyed the journey.